Building Wealth:
The New Asset-Based Approach to
Solving Social and Economic Problems

The Democracy Collaborative at the University of Maryland

April 2005

THE ASPEN INSTITUTE

The principal author
of this report is Steve Dubb
under the direction of
Gar Alperovitz, with supporting
contributions from Ted Howard,
Jessica Gordon Nembhard, Aziza Agia,
and Katharine Nelson.

For more information contact:

Ted Howard
Executive Director
The Democracy Collaborative
1228 Tawes Hall
The University of Maryland
College Park, MD 20742
Tel: 301-405-9266
Fax: 301-314-2533
thoward@civilsociety.umd.edu
www.democracycollaborative.org

The Aspen Institute
One Dupont Circle, NW
Suite 700
Washington, DC 20036

Published in the United States of America in 2005
by The Aspen Institute

Printed in the United States of America

ISBN: 0-89843-434-3

05-013

1474NSPP/05-BK

The Aspen Institute is an international nonprofit organization founded in 1950. Its mission is to foster enlightened leadership, the appreciation of timeless ideas and values, and open-minded dialogue on contemporary issues. Through seminars, policy programs, conferences and leadership development initiatives, the institute and its international partners seek to promote the pursuit of common ground and deeper understanding in a nonpartisan and nonideological setting. The Institute is headquartered in Washington, DC, and has campuses in Aspen, Colorado, and on the Wye River on Maryland's Eastern Shore. Its international network includes partner Aspen Institutes in Berlin, Rome, Lyon, Tokyo, and leadership programs in Africa. To learn more about the Institute or to sign up for one of its seminars, visit www.aspeninstitute.org.

Nonprofit Sector and Philanthropy Program

The Aspen Institute's Nonprofit Sector and Philanthropy Program (NSPP) seeks to improve the operation of the nonprofit sector and philanthropy through research and dialogue focused on public policy, management, and other important issues affecting the nonprofit sector. It includes the:

Nonprofit Sector Research Fund (NSRF): The Fund is a grantmaking entity that awards support to university-based and other researchers studying nonprofit activities. It also produces a variety of publications, including grant guidelines; an annual report; working papers based on Fund-supported research; Nonprofit Research News, a newsletter reporting on the Nonprofit Sector Research Fund's activities and research; and Snapshots, brief, easy-to-use bulletins summarizing key findings and practical studies supported by the Fund. The Fund also publishes an electronic newsletter, Aspen Philanthropy Letter (APL), which reports on new ideas and other developments that may affect the field of philanthropy in the years to come.

Kellogg-Kauffman Seminar Series for Mid-Continent Foundation CEOs: The Kellogg-Kauffman Seminar brings together a small group of mid-continent foundation executives to discuss issues of mutual interest. **The State of America's Nonprofit Sector Project:** The State of America's Nonprofit Sector Project, a collaborative initiative with Lester Salamon of Johns Hopkins University, will report every several years on the major developments affecting the overall nonprofit sector and each of its major fields of activity (i.e., health, education, social services, arts, etc.).

Fast-Growth, High-Impact Nonprofits: In partnership with Duke University's Center for the Advancement of Social Entrepreneurship (CASE), the Fast-Growth, High-Impact Nonprofits Research Project will examine the strategy, organization, and leadership that fuel the success of today's leading nonprofits.

Community Giving Resource: Developed by the Neighborhood Funders Group in partnership with the Nonprofit Sector and Philanthropy Program, the Community Giving Resource provides objective, accessible information to small family foundations and individual donors committed to strengthening low-income communities.

Nonprofit Sector Strategy Group: The Strategy Group was a leadership forum that met from 1997-2001. The initiative convened top nonprofit, government, and business leaders to address the most pressing issues facing the nonprofit sector in America.

For more information about the Nonprofit Sector and Philanthropy Program's activities, visit www.aspeninstitute.org or www.nonprofitresearch.org.

The Aspen Institute
Winnifred Levy
Communications Manager
Nonprofit Sector and Philanthropy Program
One Dupont Circle, NW
Suite 700
Washington, DC 20036
Phone: (202) 736-5814   Fax: (202) 293-0525

The Nonprofit Sector Research Fund is currently supported by:

The Ford Foundation	Charles Stewart Mott Foundation
Bill and Melinda Gates Foundation	The David and Lucile Packard Foundation
William Randolph Hearst Foundation	Skoll Foundation
W.K. Kellogg Foundation	Surdna Foundation

Preface

Across the United States new forms of community wealth-building institutions have expanded dramatically in recent decades. Community development corporations have grown from a mere handful in the late 1960s to around 4,000 at present. Today more than eight million workers participate in employee-owned firms. Cooperatively-owned businesses involve more than 100 million members nationwide. Non-profit organizations have increasingly turned to income-generating enterprises to support their public service missions. And a host of local municipal programs and enterprises that anchor jobs and contribute to the tax base have gained the support of Republican and Democratic mayors alike. As of 2004 the total assets of the various sectors exceeded $1.5 trillion.

These seemingly diverse institutional strategies share important principles and values. First, they change the nature of asset and wealth ownership in a way that benefits the community. Second, they offer new ways to provide and anchor local jobs, as well as to help finance community services. In so doing, they provide critical resources to solve social and economic problems by making communities more stable and economically viable, providing greater security, furthering equality, and strengthening democratic practice and participation. Taken together the various efforts suggest the possibility of a new, more democratic vision of community building as we enter the first decades of the 21st century.

Few Americans are aware of the steady and continuing build-up of new and alternative forms of economic enterprise. The range of practical activity - and the implications for the future - has rarely been appreciated even by practitioners and experts working on such matters. Specialists in one sector (community development corporations, for instance) often have little knowledge of other sectors (such as employee-ownership or municipal enterprise). This "silo" effect prevents the transfer of experience and knowledge between sectors and works against collaboration. It also has made it difficult for participants in the growing movement to understand the principles they share in common.

The primary aim of Building Wealth is to help illuminate and bring attention to the vast range of efforts currently under way. We hope that this report may facilitate conversation, connection, and collaboration among those working within the field, and encourage the support and participation of new constituencies which previously have not been involved in democratic, wealth-building programs. We would be pleased if this study were to suggest new ways for policymakers, political leaders, practitioners, and communities to work together to solve the many new and difficult challenges facing America's communities.

Acknowledgements

This report reflects the contributions of more than one hundred individuals, without whom this work would not have been possible. These practitioners, experts, and scholars participated in interviews, helped identify essential articles, suggested key people to interview, and provided assistance in tracking down important data sources. A list of interview subjects and their affiliations is attached in an appendix, as is a list of others who provided critical data collection assistance.

A number of people read and commented on considerable segments or entire drafts of the manuscript at different stages of the writing process. These reviewers included Barbara Berglund, Jason Busto, Alex Campbell, Hubert Dubb, Joe Guinan, Allan Kotin, Brendan Leary, John Pratt, Julia Sass Rubin, Heerad Sabeti, Michael Swack, Mary Rice Thurman, and Thad Williamson. Thanks also to Winnifred Levy of The Aspen Institute, who edited the final draft of the report.

In addition, many sectoral practitioners reviewed specific chapters and provided valuable comments. Larry Brown and Leslie Parrish reviewed the section on individual development accounts. Ed Barker, Samantha Beinhacker, Beth Bubis, Christopher Gunn, Janelle Kerlin, and Michael Shuman reviewed the section on social enterprise. Barbara Abell, Dale Robinson Anglin, Kevin Kelly, Dominic Moulden, Christopher Walker, and Robert Zdenek reviewed the section on community development corporations. Jeannine Jacokes, Mark Pinsky, Margaret Lund, and Michael Swack reviewed the section on community development financial institutions. J. Michael Keeling, Loren Rodgers, Corey Rosen, and Adria Scharf reviewed the section on employee stock ownership plan companies. Stephanie Lessans Geller both reviewed the section on community land trusts. Frank Adams, Richard Dines, and Walden Swanson reviewed the section on cooperatives. Beverly Bunch, Ron Lunt, and Beverly Nykwest reviewed the section on municipal enterprises. Joel Solomon and Julia Sass Rubin reviewed the section on pension and investment policies. Jim Crawley reviewed the section on international developments. Michael Torrens reviewed both the introduction and conclusion.

Steve Dubb would also like to thank Barbara Berglund for her love, friendship, and support.

Finally, we would like to acknowledge the partnership with our colleagues at the Aspen Institute, especially Alan Abramson and Rachel Mosher-Williams, and the administrative support provided this project by Szilvia Rohoska and Tamara de Silva of The Democracy Collaborative.

Table of Contents

The Democracy Collaborative was initiated by the University of Maryland to advance a new understanding and practice of democracy for the 21st century. The Collaborative works to leverage the resources of higher education to promote sustained and widespread civic engagement. One of its major research and action programs focuses on asset-based approaches to building community wealth.

For general information: www.democracycollaborative.org.

For specific information on democratic, community economic development: www.community-wealth.org.

BUILDING WEALTH:
THE NEW ASSET-BASED
APPROACH TO SOLVING SOCIAL
AND ECONOMIC PROBLEMS

*The Democracy Collaborative
at the University of Maryland*

Executive Summary and Introduction

Building Wealth: The New Asset-Based Approach to Solving Social and Economic Problems

When government and non-governmental groups use "asset-based approaches" to advance social purposes, they use strategies and institutions to improve the ability of communities and ordinary people to acquire and accumulate wealth. Asset-based strategies often supply surprisingly effective responses to social and economic need by directly providing income or savings, by facilitating the development of locally based jobs and enterprises, by building up and stabilizing local assets and wealth, and by enabling local governments to apply existing resources more efficiently to better serve more citizens. Many asset-based approaches move beyond strictly economic activity to include cultural, educational, and other efforts that cross and blur conventional lines that mark the different sectors.

This study examines the development of a wide range of innovative, asset-based social and economic strategies that are being employed with great public benefit across the United States. This is the first across-the-board attempt to survey the development of these approaches—and their strategic interaction—in a comprehensive fashion.

Several factors account for the expanding use of asset-building strategies. Among the most important is increasing political resistance to raising taxes, which has pushed governments to seek alternative revenues and has led governments and others to promote indirect service provision. In addition, the rise of a global economy that is subject to economic fluctuation puts a premium on investment strategies that keep capital anchored more firmly at home.

Asset-based approaches include an impressive range of activities. Three principal modes of asset building can be identified. First and most well known are individual asset accumulation programs that help low-income individuals develop savings so they can gain greater access to wealth-generating resources such as home ownership, educational advancement, or self-employment through proprietor-owned business or microenterprise. In a second kind of asset building, small, local "publics" employ a variety of for-profit and non-profit forms to build assets in neighborhoods, workplaces, and communities throughout the United States. In a third asset-building form, government acts in an entrepreneurial fashion to help create jobs and spur locally based capital formation. In all the approaches, individuals and various public groups gain direct or indirect benefits by building asset ownership.

Figure 1: Asset Approaches by Type

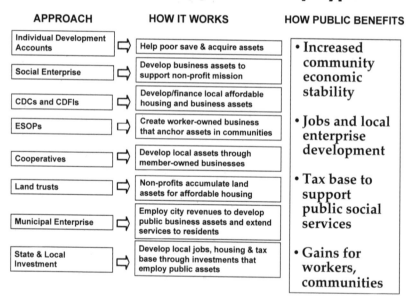

APPROACH	HOW IT WORKS	HOW PUBLIC BENEFITS
Individual Development Accounts	Help poor save & acquire assets	• Increased community economic stability
Social Enterprise	Develop business assets to support non-profit mission	
CDCs and CDFIs	Develop/finance local affordable housing and business assets	
ESOPs	Create worker-owned business that anchor assets in communities	• Jobs and local enterprise development
Cooperatives	Develop local assets through member-owned businesses	
Land trusts	Non-profits accumulate land assets for affordable housing	• Tax base to support public social services
Municipal Enterprise	Employ city revenues to develop public business assets and extend services to residents	
State & Local Investment	Develop local jobs, housing & tax base through investments that employ public assets	• Gains for workers, communities

Individual Asset-Based Programs

A critical wealth-building principle can be usefully illustrated by considering one of its most straightforward and well-known applications: **the individual development account** (IDA). While traditional strategies to alleviate poverty hinge on social services and/or income support, the IDA approach focuses instead on changing structural aspects of poverty: it helps low-income people build wealth by matching their savings with government or philanthropic funds. The matching funds are typically restricted to helping low-income people develop wealth through education (human capital), home ownership, and small business development.

IDAs and similar efforts to promote individual assets offer promising possibilities for creating at least a modicum of savings among the poor, but these efforts remain in their infancy.

Community-Based Approaches That Build Wealth

A much more fully developed approach is that of economic organizations that promote social purposes by accumulating community assets. Many of these efforts blend the small business' commitment to local community with elements of the public corporation's broader dispersion of ownership. Most also provide critical tools for anchoring otherwise footloose capital in communities.

The kinds of businesses involved range from community development corporations, community development financial institutions, and "social enterprises," to community land trusts, employee-owned enterprises, and cooperatives. All form part of a growing category of institutions that promote local asset accumulation by pooling locally based capital in ways that create new jobs, anchor existing jobs in communities, generate taxes to support social services, promote democratic practice, and benefit the public in other ways. Over the past thirty years, many have matured to the point where they now have considerable experience, expertise, support groups, and political backing. They also involve what are sometimes termed "cross-sectoral" organizational forms that advance social purposes and build locally based assets. The range and expanding number of enterprises are suggested by the data listed in Figure 2.

Figure 2: Community Asset-Based Approaches Key Features & Statistics

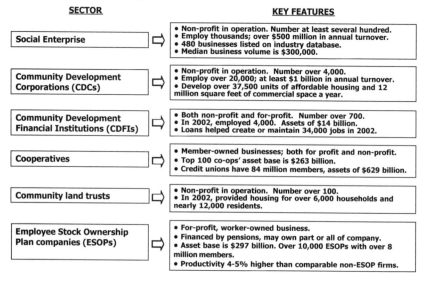

SECTOR	KEY FEATURES
Social Enterprise	• Non-profit in operation. Number at least several hundred. • Employ thousands; over $500 million in annual turnover. • 480 businesses listed on industry database. • Median business volume is $300,000.
Community Development Corporations (CDCs)	• Non-profit in operation. Number over 4,000. • Employ over 20,000; at least $1 billion in annual turnover. • Develop over 37,500 units of affordable housing and 12 million square feet of commercial space a year.
Community Development Financial Institutions (CDFIs)	• Both non-profit and for-profit. Number over 700. • In 2002, employed 4,000. Assets of $14 billion. • Loans helped create or maintain 34,000 jobs in 2002.
Cooperatives	• Member-owned businesses; both for profit and non-profit. • Top 100 co-ops' asset base is $263 billion. • Credit unions have 84 million members, assets of $629 billion.
Community land trusts	• Non-profit in operation. Number over 100. • In 2002, provided housing for over 6,000 households and nearly 12,000 residents.
Employee Stock Ownership Plan companies (ESOPs)	• For-profit, worker-owned business. • Financed by pensions, may own part or all of company. • Asset base is $297 billion. Over 10,000 ESOPs with over 8 million members. • Productivity 4-5% higher than comparable non-ESOP firms.

Non-profit "social enterprises," the newest of the emerging efforts, are non-profit organizations that develop businesses both to make money and to further their mission. Responding creatively to fiscal constraints, many non-profits (especially in the social services) have found that by developing their own subsidiary businesses they can generate more revenue internally and also complement job and life skills training programs by directly providing entry-level jobs for the clients they serve. In San Francisco, a group of over a dozen non-profit owned, social-enterprise businesses have provided employment for more than 2,200 people drawn from high-risk populations with high percentages of people who have been homeless, had criminal histories, and/or had experienced mental health problems. Two years after their hire, 77 percent were still employed either by one of the city's social enterprises or another employer, with the average wage earned roughly equal to the city's living wage of $10.25 an hour.

While the rise of social enterprise is a relatively recent development, the idea of the **community development corporation** (CDC) can be traced to the 1960s. Forged initially in a crucible of urban riots and rural neglect, CDCs were devised as a revitalization strategy that would employ non-profit, community-based firms to develop locally controlled assets. Roughly 4,000 CDCs produce more than 37,500 units of affordable housing and 12 million square feet of commercial and industrial space each year. CDCs also own more than 280 businesses, with equity stakes in another 250 businesses, and they own supermarket-anchored shopping centers in over a dozen U.S. cities. From 1993 to 1997 alone, the number of CDCs increased by more than 50 percent. Growth has continued since then: Local Initiatives Support Corporation (LISC) and The Enterprise Foundation, two leading support organizations for CDCs, have seen their loan and grant activity to fund CDC projects more than double over the last decade.

Community development financial institutions (CDFIs) have developed more recently than CDCs. CDFI is a general term that refers to a range of community-based financial institutions including community development banks, credit unions, loan funds, venture capital funds, and microenterprise loan funds. CDFIs aim to fill capital needs that are not served by conventional sources of finance, a problem that historically has been particularly severe in minority communities where bank industry "redlining" has made raising local capital difficult. The number of CDFIs in the United States doubled from roughly 300 to 700 between 1994 and 2001—assets under management tripled during this period. From 2001 to 2003 assets under management increased an additional 84 percent—to $14 billion. In 2002 the CDFI industry employed over 4,000 people nationwide, providing financing for the renovation or new construction of more than 30,000 affordable homes and for local micro-enterprises that create or maintain 34,000 jobs.

Community land trusts (CLTs) provide another promising asset-based strategy. CLTs enable non-profit community-based organizations to take land off the market and place it in a trust, thereby preserving housing affordability. Typically, a majority of the equity gain accrues to the trust (only a minority accrues to the resident), allowing the trust to offer housing to a subsequent low-income owner at an affordable price. From 1991 to 2002 the number of U.S. households leasing land from land trusts tripled to over 6,000; the number of residents in land trust households now exceeds 11,000. Although the sector remains small, community land trusts are increasingly seen as an important way to preserve affordable housing in gentrifying neighborhoods.

The growth of **employee ownership** has different roots than some of the other asset-based approaches. While all of the community asset accumulation approaches described thus far are dominated by non-profits, employee ownership is a for-profit form of business that provides an important tool for local asset accumulation. In these enterprises workers own either all or part of the company. The most common involves financing by workers' pension contributions in the form of an **employee stock ownership plan** (ESOP). As a business, the ESOP's primary responsibility is to make a profit. Yet the ownership structure of the ESOP itself promotes critical social purposes. In particular, the ESOP mechanism has enabled several hundred, if not thousands, of family business owners to sell their companies to their employees, thereby both expanding employee assets and helping preserve the long-term economic (and tax) base of their communities. Three decades ago, there were only about 200 ESOP companies in the United States. Aided by favorable tax legislation, U.S. employee ownership has grown rapidly. Estimates of the number of ESOPs vary, but today there are somewhere between 9,000 and 11,000 ESOPs with over eight million employee-owners.

Not all community asset-based strategies have emerged in recent decades. The **cooperative** principle is older than capitalism. Cooperatives, which have existed in the United States for over a century, have begun to show renewed vitality in recent years. More than 100 million Americans are currently members of a co-op or co-op credit union. Some are small; some large and more like corporations. Like ESOPs, the distribution of asset ownership across a broad membership base provides significant benefits. Co-ops also offer other benefits. For instance, a 2003 U.S. Department of Agriculture study found that the member-owned structure of cooperatives in the state of Minnesota meant that profit income was also realized locally, resulting in a tax base $600 million greater than if the businesses had been privately owned. The top 100 U.S. co-ops alone had sales of $117 billion in 2003.

Governments Acting Entrepreneurially to Build Wealth

In addition to supporting many of the efforts so far mentioned, municipal, county, and state governments also increasingly play a direct role in building wealth. One little noticed but fast developing approach involves **municipal-owned enterprises,** which—under both

Republican and Democratic mayors—provide jobs and services, while at the same time generating revenue for cash-starved local governments. Municipally owned enterprises are not an entirely new phenomenon. However, municipalities have been rapidly expanding the scope of their business ventures. From 2001 to 2003, for example, the number of public utilities offering telecommunications services increased 54 percent, greatly improving residents' access to broadband services. Municipalities have also become progressively more adept at earning revenue from real estate investment and using property ownership to shape development. One common strategy has been to focus and own high-density development around transit stations. Although the élan of enterprising government has something to do with this expansion, more important has been the need to compensate for shortfalls in tax revenue and/or private investment. A decade ago, few cities would have considered owning large hotels. Today city-owned hotels—in which cities partner with private hotel chains to develop hotels to support convention centers—have become much more prevalent, with new ones opening in the past ten years in Austin, Houston, Chicago, Omaha, Overland Park (KS), Sacramento (CA), Marietta (GA), and Myrtle Beach (SC).

Related to all of this is a dramatic change in how state and local governments deal with **capital investment** to achieve public goals, and how they steer investment capital to promote local asset building. Both through the creation of venture funds and by investing pension funds in private equity firms where they can exercise more control over their investments, municipalities and states are increasingly becoming active community investors. In the process they have been creatively employing public assets as a way to meet community development goals while economizing on direct expenditures. A 1996 survey by Susan Clarke and Gary Gaile found that 56.3 percent of cities surveyed using equity investments as part of their economic development strategy. A September 2002 survey found that state pension funds had $69.4 billion worth of holdings in real estate and that 31 states had invested a total of $51.8 billion (an average of 4.7 percent of fund assets) in private equity. Such holdings have in turn increased their capacity to use pension funds to promote job and economic development goals. In some states, like California, these goals are made explicit, as pension trustees have pledged to invest $5 billion in the state's underserved communities. It is not simply "liberal" states; the conservative state of Alabama has long been a leader in this field.

Directions for the Future of Wealth-Building Strategies and Research

We have also included material in this report drawn from a preliminary review of related developments abroad, particularly those which offer lessons for possible U.S. application. International asset-based strategies range from the Mondragón system of worker cooperatives in Spain to town and village enterprises in China. A resource guide is also provided to aid readers in further study of these issues.

There clearly remains much room for further work. A new political-economic paradigm is rapidly emerging with important implications for policy development. In part due to the "silo effect," the range of practical activity—and the rate of growth—has rarely been appreciated even by experts. As awareness grows, we can anticipate greater collaboration and coordination of increasingly sophisticated asset-based strategies.

The promise of the new strategies is particularly great in connection with community rebuilding efforts. A decade ago, Robert Putnam of Harvard University wrote, "I believe that the weight of the available evidence confirms that Americans today are significantly less engaged in their communities than was true a generation ago."[1] Yet even as individual rates of civic participation appeared to decline, promising new community-based institutions have been emerging, especially in deprived and disadvantaged areas—including the wealth building initiatives examined here.

To date the various strategies often have worked in relative isolation from each other. In our research we have found that while practitioners are aware of growth within their own sector, they often fail to see the broader patterns that are emerging, leading many to view their own sector's growth as an isolated event. One important goal of this report is to help stimulate interest in the broader patterns by mapping the growth of key sectors; identifying points they share in common; highlighting innovative practices, challenges, and opportunities; surveying the international context; and recommending common policies that might contribute to further development.

Individual Development Accounts

> Asset-based policy for the poor began as a practical
> idea. It is about ownership and controlling one's life. In
> fundamental respects these are American themes.
>
> Michael Sherraden [2]

In one widely discussed asset-based strategy, government agencies or philanthropic groups match the private savings of low-income individuals. Typically, matched funds must be spent on specific wealth-building activities, such as home ownership or renovation, business start-up or expansion, or education. At present, over 20,000 low-income Americans have individual development accounts. Current efforts in Congress promise to expand these programs.

Asset-based policies have a long and distinguished pedigree going back to the Homestead Act of 1862 and the GI Bill of 1944. The Homestead Act gave nearly free title to settlers who could demonstrate they had farmed and "improved" land for a five-year period, while the GI Bill has provided financial assistance for veterans seeking a college education for over sixty years. The Homestead Act transformed post-Civil War America: 1.5 million families achieved land ownership. The GI Bill played a major role in building the middle-class social base of post-World War II United States. [3]

Although current IDA efforts are limited, advocates of Individual Development Accounts (IDAs) believe that asset-building programs operating on IDA-like principles over time could grow to have a similar effect in promoting home ownership and college education for low-income families. Basic statistics regarding the reach of IDAs today are provided in the following chart:

Individual Development Accounts: [4]	
Participants	At least 20,000
Programs	500
States operating IDA programs as of June 2004	34
Average "matched" withdrawal over 2-year demonstration period	$2,586
Participants who saved at least $100 in demonstration project	56%
Average accumulation per demonstration program participant	$1,543
Typical savings "match rate" per dollar saved by program participant	2:1

IDAs rely on a central feature of the asset-based approach—namely a focus on long-term wealth building. While traditional poverty alleviation programs provide important social services and income support, the asset-building approach assumes that in the long run, low-income individuals must be given the tools they need to develop their own income-generating capacity. Michael Sherraden, a professor at Washington University in St. Louis, is credited with pioneering the IDA concept. According to Sherraden, the IDA is a special savings account with the following core elements:[5]

- Accounts start as early as birth.
- Savings for the poor are matched up to a specified limit.
- Multiple sources of matching deposits are an option.
- Account funds may be used for homes, education, and business capital.
- A financial education component is offered.

IDA advocates note that the Homestead Act and the GI Bill are hardly the only examples of individual asset-based policies. Essentially, any policy that encourages individuals to invest in business or home ownership, save money for retirement, or pursue an education would be included in this category. Sherraden has noted, too, that "asset-based tax benefits are the most rapidly growing" part of domestic policy. Some reasons for this growth are clear. The current political climate, shaped by large federal budget deficits, makes it difficult to gain Congressional approval of many kinds of direct expenditures. Greater bipartisan political support may be more easily mustered for targeted tax cuts with an expected return, since they partially pay for themselves through investment-related returns. The global economy also makes support for investments, particularly in education, more important.[6]

Asset-based policies have historically tended to reinforce existing income and asset distributions. According to a study by the Corporation for Enterprise Development, federal benefits—mostly in the form of tax credits and deductions—totaled $335 billion in 2004. Among these were $110 billion in home ownership incentives (including mortgage interest and property tax deductions), over $100 billion in retirement savings tax incentives, and more than $120 billion in reduced long-term capital gains tax rates and life insurance tax deductions. More than a third of the resulting tax-deduction benefits went to the top 1 percent of taxpayers, 84 percent to the top 20 percent, and 96.3 percent to the top 40 percent. In absolute dollars, the average tax benefit for a household in the top 1 percent of taxpayers was $38,107.10; the average tax benefit for a person in a household in the bottom 20 percent of taxpayers was $4.24. IDAs provide a way to begin to even the scales.[7]

Mechanisms that enable the poor to accumulate savings and build up assets can often have a substantial effect. When low-income individuals have savings, they can choose to purchase a home, pursue higher education, or start a small business—choices that might otherwise be impossible.[8] In 1998 Congress approved the Assets for Independence Act, legislation that involved a 5-year, $125 million IDA pilot program (since extended), known as the American Dream Demonstration. The program has helped over 2,300 low-income people to accumulate, on average, a modest, but not insignificant, $1,543 in two years. IDA advocates also were successful in 1996 in getting IDAs included in the welfare reform law (Temporary Aid for Needy Families) as a state policy option.[9]

As of June 2004, 34 states provided at least some financial support for IDA programs.[10] In some states, donors to IDA programs receive tax credits while other states allocate matching funds directly to support the programs. States that support IDA programs are shown in Figure 3.[11]

Figure 3: Independent Development Accounts State-Funded Programs, 2004

Shaded areas indicate states with IDA programs

Source: Center for Social Development June 2004

Although most states provide some support for IDA programs, funding has been very modest. As a result, foundation backing for IDAs has been crucial. The Joyce, Ford, Annie E. Casey, Charles Stewart Mott, and Citigroup foundations have all provided financial support. According to the Corporation for Enterprise Development, which hosts the IDA network of program administrators, total private support of IDAs exceeded $50 million between 1993 and 2003, a significant addition to the $184 million in state and federal dollars spent on IDAs during that period.[12]

As of 2004, over 20,000 people had joined an IDA program and had started their own individual development accounts. These accounts are administered through about 500 community-based organizations, with funding provided by a broad range of public and private sources.[13]

An important potential drawback of the IDA approach is that its focus on promoting individual saving does not encourage the kind of broader asset formation that can have an impact on communities as a whole. Individual families may benefit while concentrated poverty in the surrounding communities remains.[14] Community and individual efforts can, however, be combined—for instance, by directing the IDA savings to pay for shares in a cooperative.[15] In New Hampshire, a community land trust called the Concord Area Trust for Community Housing is working with Neighborhood Reinvestment on an IDA program to help families save for homeownership.[16] The Childspace Workers Cooperative of Philadelphia also combines individual and collective asset-building strategies: it builds community assets through its business, while administering an IDA program to support individuals' savings efforts.[17] The First Nations Development Institute of Fredericksburg, Virginia, has found IDAs to be helpful in supporting homeownership, small business development, and financial education efforts in eleven indigenous communities.[18]

The biggest challenge for IDAs remains one of scale. Presently, account management functions fall under the purview of community organizations, something that Sherraden points out cannot work "if IDAs are eventually to reach millions of people." The 1998 Assets for Independence Act provided IDAs a token amount, $25 million. According to the New America Foundation, a rough estimate of the potential reach of a full-scale approach based on the present two-year, matched savings, IDA pilot program would be somewhere between 40 and 50 million people and would cost upwards of $30 billion.[19]

To date the impact of IDAs has been limited. However, IDAs have demonstrated the ability of low-income individuals to save, hinting at the potentially much greater effects that asset policies, if expanded, could have. The amount expended so far on Individual Development Accounts is modest, but backing for IDAs is growing, with both Democrats and Republicans voicing their support. In the Fiscal-Year 2005 budget, the Bush Administration proposed the creation of a 100 percent tax credit for up to $500 per individual account. If approved, this legislation could result in an additional 300,000 IDA accounts by 2010.[20]

A second bill, introduced in Congress in July 2004 with bipartisan sponsorship, is called the America Savings for Personal Investment, Retirement, and Education or "ASPIRE" Act. The ASPIRE legislation, patterned after legislation scheduled to take effect in Great Britain in 2005, would create a "baby bond" of $500 when every child is born, with children from low-income families receiving an initial allocation of $1,000. Additional matching funds would be available for children of low-income families whose parents make further contributions.[21] Although neither proposal was approved in 2004, reintroduction of similar legislation in the next congressional cycle can be expected. Given the bipartisan support IDAs have had to date, further expansion of IDA programs—and related efforts to develop a broader wealth-building system as ASPIRE Act supporters contemplate—appears likely.

Social Enterprise: The Rise of Non-Profit Entrepreneurship

If we're going to get our clients to be self-sufficient, it's only going to happen if we, as an organization, are prepared to role-model that and take responsibility for being self-sufficient ourselves.

Michael Burns, President, Pioneer Human Services[22]

Social enterprise organizations are non-profits that operate businesses both to raise revenue and to further their social missions. The recent development of the notion of "social enterprise" makes sector measurement difficult, but trade associations report rapid growth. Data from the National Center for Charitable Statistics indicates that as of 2001, 50,000 non-profits in environmental, employment, youth development, and human services fields generated a total of $48 billion in commercial revenue, a rough estimate of the potential reach of the sector. Practitioners need to ensure that social enterprise development does not inadvertently lead to mission displacement.

Although it was not so long ago that non-profits were known primarily as "charities," the image of the non-profit agency that relies solely on grants and fundraising for its support has always been a bit of a myth. Nearly everyone knows the names of some of the large non-profit organizations that have long had business operations: Goodwill Industries, Salvation Army, the Girl Scouts, and the YMCA are a few prominent examples. And this list excludes the largest sectors of non-profit enterprise—hospitals and universities. Indeed, it is in large measure because of their enterprise activity that non-profit organizations employ nearly 11.6 million American workers—9.3 percent of the total labor force.[23]

The idea of a "social enterprise" is of more recent vintage, only gaining popular currency in the 1990s. The term typically implies something more than simply a non-profit agency that receives fee income. Rather, "social enterprise" most often refers to a non-profit organization that goes into business to provide services to the general public, both to raise revenue and to advance specific mission-related benefits.[24]

Non-profit organizations increasingly find it beneficial to build their capacity to generate internal revenues to improve long-term sustainability. When they build up business assets that are directly under their control, they can also convert program clients into active enterprise participants.[25] When they are well managed, non-profit enterprises can also help break down non-profit paternalism by bringing staff and service recipients into more mutually supporting relationships.

Non-profits can set up businesses in myriad ways—often as for-profit or non-profit subsidiaries of the parent organization. The division is used for legal reasons, but also facilitates effective oversight and management by keeping the business unit(s) organizationally distinct from the non-profit's direct service functions. The resulting "social enterprises"—sometimes referred to as "social-purpose businesses"—employ market mechanisms to meet such key organizational goals as providing job opportunities to "clients" in the businesses they operate. In addition to direct employment benefits, the income social-purpose businesses generate can often enable non-profits to be more innovative in their service approach. For instance, San Francisco-based REDF (formerly the Roberts Enterprise Development Fund) found that the income earned by social-purpose business ventures freed the non-profit organizations from certain government constraints. This led to much more favorable results, as enterprising non-profits were able to "employ individuals for longer periods of time and … provide transitional and permanent employment to individuals outside the economic mainstream." Basic statistics regarding social enterprises appear below.[26]

Social Enterprise: Basic Statistics[27]	
Overall non-profit income from fees, 1977	46%
Overall non-profit income from fees, 1997	47%
Social service non-profit income from fees, 1977	13%
Social service non-profit income from fees, 1997	28%
Human services non-profit estimated commercial revenue, 2001	$41.6 billion
Enterprises listed on industry directory, June 2004	480
Founding of U.S. trade association, Social Enterprise Alliance	Nov. 1998
Median venture income, based on 2002 industry survey	$300,000
Median venture staff size, based on 2002 industry survey	5

In 1977, well before the term "social enterprise" was coined, fee income already provided 46 percent of total non-profit revenue. Twenty years later, that share had risen to 47 percent, hardly a dramatic increase. The apparent stability in aggregate fee income figures, however, masks major changes. While fee income has remained a fairly constant percentage—actually falling slightly—for health, education, arts, and cultural organizations, this is not the case for civic organizations and social services where reliance on fee income has grown markedly. For civic organizations, reliance on fee income increased from 19% of total income in 1977 to 34% by 1997; for social services, reliance on fee income more than doubled from 13 percent of total income in 1977 to 28 percent by 1997.[29]

What is the size of the "social-enterprise" or "social-purpose business" sector? No one knows for sure, but there is abundant evidence that it is growing. The Yale School of Management-The Goldman Sachs Foundation's Partnership on Non-Profit Ventures (Yale-Goldman Sachs Partnership) has run an annual award competition for the best social-enterprise business plans since 2002. It has had more than 1,500 organizations participate in the competition over the past three years and has had more than 8,000 people register on its web site. The Social Enterprise Alliance, a leading trade association of nonprofit organizations with business enterprises, has also experienced rising participation rates. From March 2003 to November 2004, participation in its Non-Profit Enterprise listserv expanded from 400 to over 1,300. Attendance at its 2004 conference was 50 percent higher than the year before, with over 600 attendees, including over 400 non-profit business practitioners.[30]

The National Center for Charitable Statistics (NCCS) in the Center on Nonprofits and Philanthropy (CNP) at the Urban Institute maintains databases based on the IRS Form 990 that most nonprofit organizations with gross receipts over $25,000 must file annually with the federal government. Unfortunately, "commercial revenue" can mean many things. "Commercial revenue" may refer to fees paid by clients, a practice which raises revenue but can also sometimes reduce access to the services non-profits provide; it can also mean social-purpose businesses that contribute to the social mission of the non-profit, as well as to the bottom line. The IRS does not distinguish between the two. Nonetheless, the figures on the chart below, generated by CNP researcher Janelle Kerlin—although preliminary and subject to revision—are suggestive of the potential reach of social enterprise.[31]

Estimated Commercial Revenue of Selected 501(c)(3) Nonprofits in 1999

NTEE major group (A-Z)	Number of Organizations		Program Service Revenue		Net Income from Sales of Goods		Net Income from Special Events & Activities	
Environmental Quality, Protection, and Beautification	4,394	9.50%	$793,123,933	2.00%	$44,414,500	4.40%	$43,210,951	6.80%
Employment, Job Related	3,280	7.10%	$3,315,127,175	8.50%	$296,136,777	29.50%	$13,768,627	2.20%
Youth Development	6,027	13.00%	$989,276,438	2.50%	$346,702,806	34.60%	$247,307,459	39.00%
Human Services - Multipurpose and Other	32,770	70.50%	$33,881,487,756	86.90%	$315,980,933	31.50%	$329,605,760	52.00%
Total	46,471	100.00%	$38,979,015,302	100.00%	$1,003,235,016	100.00%	$633,892,797	100.00%

Total Commercial Revenue 1999: $40,616,143,115

Estimated Commercial Revenue of Selected 501(c)(3) Nonprofits in 2001

NTEE major group (A-Z)	Number of Organizations		Program Service Revenue		Net Income from Sales of Goods		Net Income from Special Events & Activities	
Environmental Quality, Protection, and Beautification	5,104	10.20%	$991,104,779	2.10%	$49,466,641	4.40%	$49,824,610	7.10%
Employment, Job Related	3,394	6.80%	$3,931,850,920	8.40%	$332,294,721	29.70%	$15,519,527	2.20%
Youth Development	6,648	13.20%	$1,131,646,540	2.40%	$402,090,144	36.00%	$251,746,442	35.90%
Human Services - Multipurpose and Other	35,042	69.80%	$40,875,154,507	87.10%	$334,605,484	29.90%	$383,951,979	54.80%
Total	50,188	100.00%	$46,929,756,746	100.00%	$1,118,456,990	100.00%	$701,042,558	100.00%

Total Commercial Revenue 2001: $48,749,256,294

For this study we selected four segments of the non-profit world where we would expect to see a high incidence of social enterprises: human service organizations, youth development, environmental quality, and employment services. As can be seen in the charts, in two years, from 1999 to 2001, non-profit revenue in these sectors increased 20 percent from $40.6 to $48.8 billion while the number of non-profits earning commercial revenue increased 8 percent from just under 46,500 to over 50,000. The average revenue per non-profit also increased during the same period by 11 percent from an average of $874,000 in 1999 to $971,000 in 2001, an increase 4.5 percent greater than the rate of inflation during the same period.[32]

Where are social enterprises to be found? Community Wealth Ventures and Social Enterprise Alliance jointly host a database of social enterprises. As of July 2004, the database listed 679 ventures in 40 states plus the District of Colombia. About 200 of these are strategic alliances, international ventures, or are listed as "other," but some interesting patterns emerge from the remaining 480 or so enterprises. The majority of the enterprises are in five categories: retail, light manufacturing, education and training, restaurant/cafés, and consulting. A more thorough breakdown is below:

Non-Profit Ventures by Type
Community Wealth Venture/Social Enterprise Alliance Database, July 2004[33]

Retail	84	Agricultural	12
Light Manufacturing	53	Construction	10
Education & Training	48	Information Technology	10
Restaurant-Café	47	Wholesale	9
Consulting	38	Landscaping	9
Thrift Store	30	Recycling	7
Staffing Service	29	Heavy Manufacturing	6
Janitorial	19	Home Heath Care	5
Property Mgmt.	15	Housing Rehabilitation	3
Clerical	13	Packaging/Distribution	3

As the above table makes clear, social enterprises span many industries. What we find, in fact, is a rapid expansion of enterprise development at the local level. In a survey of 72 non-profit organizations conducted by Community Wealth Ventures, the median start date of the ventures surveyed was 1996, even though the median date of the founding of the parent organizations was 1980. The size of the ventures ranged greatly; the median gross revenue was $300,000, but the mean was over $7 million (because of six very large ventures that were included in the survey).[34]

A second database of social ventures is provided the Yale-Goldman Sachs Partnership. This database provides a good indicator of interest in future social enterprise development, as approximately 64 percent of the business plans submitted are for businesses that have not yet started operations at the time of entry into the competition. As can be seen in Figure 4, roughly two-thirds of all entrants fit into eight broad categories: arts, community development, education, employment/jobs, health, housing, human services, and youth development.[35]

Figure 4: Yale-Goldman Sachs Non-Profit Venture Proposals by Sector, 2002-03 to 2004-05

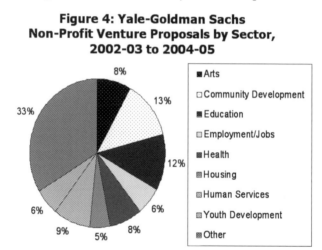

One prominent venture that illustrates the key principles involved is Greyston Bakery in Yonkers, New York. Founded in 1982 by a Buddhist teacher to employ his students, the organization's mission later expanded to provide jobs for neighboring inner city residents. After landing a supply contract with Ben & Jerry's (the bakery's first contract involved producing brownies for Ben & Jerry's chocolate fudge brownie ice cream), the bakery grew rapidly. It now supplies many additional products to Ben & Jerry's, has become a supplier of Haagen-Dazs, sells cakes to many upscale New York restaurants, and generates $4.3 million in revenues a year. In the process, it also provides employment and training for 55 hard-to-employ workers.

According to Bakery CEO Julius Walls, the market discipline helps make the work experience more transferable to the "real world" than a simple job-training program. As Walls says, "Because we are subject to the discipline of market competition, bakery employees develop skills that are genuinely valuable and marketable." In addition, Greyston has added many other businesses and services, including a day care center that provides services for 42 children, a housing development operation that to date has developed and now manages 168 units of housing for low income individuals and people with HIV/AIDS, four community gardens that are used by 150 adults and 290 children, a technology education center, and other counseling and support services. In 2002, 73 percent of Greyston's $12.3 million in income was generated internally through its businesses. In 2003, Greyston moved its bakery from a 9,000 square foot facility to a brand new 23,000 square foot facility, which it hopes will allow it to expand both production and profits that it can funnel back into non-profit service expansion.[36]

Manchester Bidwell Corporation of Pittsburgh—and its two subsidiary companies, the Bidwell Training Center and the Manchester Craftsman's Guild—provides an example of an explicitly "cross-sectoral" model of social enterprise, in which community development and arts promotion missions are integrated in a mutually reinforcing and sustaining way. This dual mission is achieved through a variety of programs that include teaching arts in the schools, providing vocational training for adults, developing real estate (the organization leases 30,000 square feet of commercial space to the University of Pittsburgh Medical Center), training students in horticulture at the organization's 40,000 square-foot greenhouse, and running the record label MCG Jazz. The MCG Jazz record label has not yet turned a profit, but the business is growing. In 2001, MCG Jazz released *A Nancy Wilson Christmas*, which was the fifth best-selling jazz record of 2001, according to Billboard magazine. As of 2004, business income provided 10 to 15 percent of Manchester Bidwell's $7.5 million budget; the group aims to increase that percentage to 40 percent within five years.[37]

While Manchester Bidwell combines art and community development, San Francisco's Golden Gate Community Inc. (GGCI) combines environmental sustainability and community development. GGCI's mission is to improve the lives of at-risk youth and young adults by providing employment, housing, and support services. GGCI is aided by REDF, a San Francisco-based organization that has supported social enterprises that have provided jobs to more than 2,000 people. GGCI operates three such social enterprises: a print shop (Ashbury Images), a restaurant serving organic and locally grown produce (Grow Café), and a bicycle repair shop (Pedal Revolution). Additionally, GGCI operates a safe house for homeless mothers and a Youth Development Initiative program that focuses on support services and leadership development. According to an REDF survey of GGCI employees conducted between 1998 and 2001, two-thirds of the enterprise's hires suffer from some form of mental health illness, half are at risk of homelessness, 22 percent are homeless, and 29 percent had a criminal record. Of the 18 employees the survey followed, all were employed two years after their initial hire; in many cases, employees had progressed to a second job outside the non-profit businesses.[38]

GGCI's businesses provide a major part of its revenues. In 2002, 64 percent of organization gross revenues ($1.9 million of $2.95 million) came from business income. Particularly successful has been the print shop, where revenues have increased from $600,000 in 1998 to $1.5 million in 2003. While increasing sales volume, salaries have also climbed from $7.50 to $10 an hour—still low, given the high cost of living in the San Francisco Bay Area, but a considerable improvement. Profits from the store contribute to funding the non-profit's service programs, such as the safe house. A 2004 study by REDF that examined wage levels at GGCI and other area social enterprises found that two years after an employee's initial hire, 77 percent still held a job, with their wage rising from $7.54 an hour when hired to an average of $8.81 an hour when still employed by a social enterprise and rising further to $10.16 when obtaining a job with another employer.[39]

No overview of social enterprises would be complete without a brief mention of Pioneer Human Services of Seattle. Founded in 1962 to assist people at the margins of the community—those suffering from addiction, the homeless, ex-convicts, and others—the organization has grown to generate $55 million in total revenue and employs over 700 people in eight different businesses, including a precision light metal fabricator that supplies Boeing. All told, 99.6 percent of its budget comes from the sale of products and fees for services. This income allows Pioneer to provide many services, which, in addition to jobs and training, include a residential recovery program, low-cost housing, family and youth counseling services, and two drug treatment centers that can help up to 200 people at a time. Pioneer is in the enviable position of being able to do all of this without fundraising.[40]

The potential of social enterprise to build locally based assets that promote social purposes is clear. Indeed, in places such as Pittsburgh, Seattle,

San Francisco, and Yonkers, it is already happening. By retaining and rein-vesting earnings in businesses that serve the needs of low-income com-munities, social enterprises not only meet pressing social needs, but also anchor assets in those communities, thereby expanding the income-gen-erating capacity of the communities they serve.[41] Some of what can be found under the rubric of social enterprise, however, is problematic. Burton Weisbrod of Northwestern University, for instance, cites the exam-ple of a multi-million dollar sponsorship of a 1997 Chicago Field Museum dinosaur exhibit by McDonald's and Disney as the kind of development that erodes public confidence in non-profits. In this case, the corporate sponsorship was so prominent—including the right of Disney and McDonald's to display dinosaur replicas to market their products to chil-dren—that it threatened to overshadow the museum's educational work.

Angela Eikenberry and Jodie Drapal Kluver, in a 2004 article in *Public Administration Review*, contend that too intense a pursuit of enterprise income can lead to a reduced focus on organizationally beneficial but unprofitable community outreach activities (such as volunteer recruit-ment), a lower quality of service delivery, and unsavory marketing deals, such as a 1996 decision by the American Cancer Society to endorse a par-ticular brand of Nicotine gum and patches in exchange for monetary support. Pablo Eisenberg of Georgetown University warns that non-prof-it groups that focus too much on being business-like may end up keeping themselves from fulfilling their service or advocacy missions.[42]

User fees are another growing area of non-profit income that has lit-tle to do with the formation of social enterprises, but can certainly be a source of mission displacement. Indeed, in the hospital industry, where nearly all non-profit income is generated through fees or government contracts, the gap between non-profit and for-profit entities has nar-rowed considerably. Dennis Young, Case Western University, and Lester Salamon, Director of Civil Society Studies at the Institute of Policy Studies at Johns Hopkins University, see the growth of commercialism as being broader than any one practice; rather, there is a cultural shift, as market culture "now pervades the very manner in which non-profits conduct their day-to-day affairs."[43] Still others believe that government programs distort mission goals even more than commercial initiatives.

On the other hand, some hold that the threat of mission displacement by traditional fundraising may be as great or greater. As Weisbrod com-ments, "When there are strings attached to donations, those revenues are essentially akin to sales." Regarding the distorting effects this can have on a non-profit's mission, social enterprise participants Michael Shuman and Merrian Fuller write: "If Mohandas Gandhi were a typical leader organizing in a nonprofit environment like ours, he would probably be wearing a three-piece suit and working in a plush office with his law degree prominently displayed. He would have little time to lead protests, since every other week would be spent meeting with donors—and those power lunches would hardly go well with fasting."[44]

One well-known figure, Jed Emerson, a co-founder of REDF, sees the development of hybrid enterprises as a way to simultaneously minimize mission displacement and maximize efficiency. According to Emerson and co-author Sheila Bonini, the goal ought to be "to create a blended value consisting of maximizing the performance of economic, social and environmental components." Hybrid organizational forms such as social enterprises, Emerson argues, can in some cases be more effective at meeting dual social and economic goals than either traditional charities or for-profit businesses, as one often places too little emphasis on efficiency while the other frequently neglects social objectives. Julia Lopez of the Rockefeller Foundation puts the case this way: "Clearly, pure market, pure charity or pure government strategies don't work—it will take a blend of both strategies and organizational forms to succeed."[45]

Certainly, many unanswered questions remain, including such basic issues as the size of the sector and even how the sector should be defined. While community impact data is available for some individual social-purpose businesses, most lack such indicators. And a basic census of the sector, although needed, is unlikely as long as the definition of the sector itself remains in flux. Still, a few things seem clear. Social enterprise, despite the ambiguities of its boundaries, is clearly in a growth phase. We know there are many social enterprises that succeed at meeting both economic and social goals. And the potential for further expansion is evident.

Support groups and foundations have played an important role in developing the social enterprise sector in some cities, such as in Pittsburgh and San Francisco. Greater support would likely fuel further expansion. Conferences and electronic mailing lists, such as those organized by the Social Enterprise Alliance and the Yale-Goldman Sachs Partnership, have also encouraged sectoral growth. Although the social-enterprise field faces many uncertainties and dangers, it also shows great promise and potential.

Community Development Corporations: Rebuilding America One Neighborhood at a Time

CDCs succeed in so many diverse places with so many
diverse sources of support and investment because
they embrace American values that transcend ideolo-
gy: self-help, entrepreneurship, community building,
local control, and public/private partnership.[46]

Paul Grogan and Tony Proscio

*Community development corporations are non-profit organizations
that have proved particularly adept at the development of both residential
and commercial property, ranging from affordable housing to shopping
centers and businesses. First formed in the 1960s, they have expanded
rapidly in size and numbers since. Success has brought its own challenges,
however. In particular, CDCs struggle to maintain an appropriate balance
between serving as a community organizer and representative as well as an
effective developer working through traditional financial channels.*

No sector of the expanding asset-based economy is more celebrated
for its success than community development corporations (CDCs). In
part because of the visibility of their success, they are also frequently
criticized for their shortcomings. Community development corporations are typically neighborhood-based, 501(c)(3) non-profit corporations—with a board composed of at least one-third community residents—that promote the improvement of the physical and social infra-
structures in neighborhoods with populations significantly below the
area median income. In some cases, CDCs extend far beyond the[47]
bounds of a single community to cover an entire region. From hum-
ble beginnings, the CDC movement today has grown to an estimated
4,000 CDCs spread throughout all 50 states and in nearly every major
city. Basic industry statistics are below:

27

Community Development Corporations: Basic Statistics[48]

Community development corporations, 1997	3,600
Median CDC age as of 1997	15 years
Median CDC staff size, 1997	6
Median CDC staff in LISC & Enterprise partner CDCs in 23 cities, 1999	11.5
CDCs having completed non-residential projects as of 1997	31%
Average housing production per year, 1994-1997	37,500
Average commercial/industrial space developed per year, 1994-97	12 million sq. ft.
LISC & Enterprise loan and grant disbursements to CDCs, 1997	$72.8 million
LISC & Enterprise loan and grant disbursements to CDCs, 2003	$157.3 million
Estimated CDC employment based on 1998 survey	20,000
Estimated CDC annual turnover based on 1998 survey	$1 billion

From a simple production standpoint, the results of CDC actions are significant. According to the most recent industry survey, during the four years from 1994 through 1997, CDCs developed 150,000 units of affordable housing and 48 million square feet of commercial and industrial space, and the number of CDCs increased by over 60 percent from 2,200 to 3,600. Of the roughly 1,200 CDCs that responded to the survey, 108 indicated that they had full or partial ownership in businesses, 280 businesses were owned directly, and CDCs had equity stakes in an additional 254 businesses.[49]

CDCs have strongly influenced many of the communities in which they work. Paul Grogan and Tony Proscio contend that in many cities CDCs have helped stem the tide of a decades-long period of urban decline—a development also touted in an October 2003 *Business Week* article titled "An Inner-City Renaissance." According to Grogan and Proscio, "In some cities, including Boston, New York, and Chicago large sections of the city would today still be in ruins without them. CDCs have become a force in America—a vast new decentralized apparatus of urban neighborhood problem solving."

A 2002 Urban Institute study of 23 cities where CDC activity had been supported by the National Community Development Initiative (now Living Cities) found that CDCs noticeably improved multiple neighborhoods in eight cities, improved one neighborhood in each of another eleven cities, and had more limited "block-by-block" impacts in the remaining four cities. An econometric study found that REACH CDC's efforts in Portland, Oregon led to a 60 percent increase in property values over and above those that would have otherwise occurred and that in Denver, HOPE Housing Inc.'s work led to a similar 50 percent increase in values. Based on these findings, Christopher Walker of the Urban Institute concludes: "Over the past 30 years, the most promising alternative model to direct government administration of community development programs has been that of community development corporations."[50]

As general production numbers since the last industry survey are limited, we examined the activities of Local Initiatives Support Corporation (LISC) and The Enterprise Foundation (Enterprise)—the nation's two largest community development "intermediaries." LISC and Enterprise work to raise money from foundations, banks, and corporate sources and have used those funds to provide training, education, grant support, and financing for community development corporations for over 20 years. As Walker's study makes clear, national organizations such as LISC and Enterprise have made a tremendous difference in supporting the burgeoning community development industry. From 1997 to 2001 growth was rapid, with financing levels more than doubling on a national scale. It should be noted that typically loans are highly leveraged—so the actual volume of CDC projects with LISC or Enterprise participation is more than ten times the amount shown in Figure 5. After a dip in the 2002 recession, grant and lending activity recovered in 2003 to match 2001's record levels.[51]

Figure 5: LISC & Enterprise CDC lending activity 1994-2003

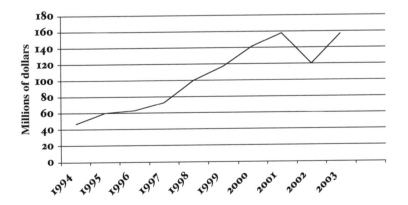

The increase in private funding has helped garner support for new public funding. In December 2000, years of lobbying by CDCs, CDFIs, and CDC intermediaries such as LISC and Enterprise paid off with passage of the New Market Tax Credits bill. Patterned in part after the housing tax credit that CDCs have used since 1986, the New Markets Tax Credit provides a way to sell tax credits to build equity for community development projects. The value of the New Markets Tax Credit, however, is less than half that of an equivalent Low Income Housing Tax Credit—which means while New Market Tax Credits can help attract investors to fund slightly below-market projects, the credits alone can't make an unprofitable deal attractive to private investors. To date, $6 billion in such credits have been "awarded," but much less had actually been allocated. Indeed, one "round one" (2002) awardee interviewed by the authors was still waiting to receive the credits as of July 2004.[52]

Although CDC achievements to date have been impressive, they face many challenges. After praising the success of CDCs in turning around the South Bronx, for instance, Grogan and Proscio also indicated what was *not* done: "Poverty levels in the South Bronx at the end of the 1990s were little changed … What changed the South Bronx from Fort Apache to a functioning community was not a sudden influx of wealth, but a careful restoration of order." It is also worth noting that rising property values, although a sign of the success of CDCs in improving neighborhoods, can lead to gentrification which displaces some of the very community residents on whose behalf the CDC is ostensibly acting. Moreover, CDC success may at times have the perverse effect of letting government off the hook. As James DeFilippis notes, in some cities CDCs have taken on social service roles that "formerly virtually defined municipal government functions. This role has been embraced not only by CDCs themselves, but by the state, as it willingly walks away from the provision of these services, and looks to the community-based sector to fill in the holes that it has left behind."[53]

Randy Stoecker of Case Western University argues that CDCs may be very good housing developers, but they may also discourage advocacy work that could build political coalitions to obtain the resources that could make deeper subsidies available. Especially in the 1980s, funders often insisted that CDCs, and in particular smaller CDCs that were trying to establish themselves, concentrate their efforts on showing "measurable results." As a result, many CDCs focused on tangible issues, such as creating affordable housing, while broader community development work often suffered. And in some cities CDC housing production has been offset by the decline of existing affordable housing, as use restrictions that help maintain affordability in many older buildings have expired.[54]

In general, according to a 2004 national study by the National Low Income Housing Coalition, while housing for those making greater than 30 percent of area median income improved, housing availability for the very poor worsened considerably. Nationwide, for those making less than 30 percent of area median income at the time of the 2000 census, there were only 43 affordable rental units available for every 100 families who needed them. Public housing stock that serves that population has been cut. Current affordable housing construction programs—such as the Low Income Housing Tax Credit—are most often designed for people earning 50-80 percent of area median income. This, in turn, hinders CDC efforts to make housing projects for poorer individuals work financially. Resources are limited, and far greater subsidies are required to build housing for the very poor than for the moderately poor.

Many CDCs are cognizant of these problems. One response is to take a more "holistic" approach to community development. LISC, once a leading proponent of a housing focus, now advocates a broad community-building agenda that includes such things as "anti-crime projects, graffiti removal, policy advocacy, retail promotion, and so on."[55] The National Congress for Community Economic Development (NCCED), the leading CDC trade association, has long taken a more comprehensive view of CDC strategy.[56] At its October 2004 annual conference, for instance, more than half of the sessions featured topics other than housing. Some CDCs are moving more decisively to actively engage broader community organizing strategies. Andy Mott, former Executive Director of the Center for Community Change, contends that some CDCs are finding that activism can "add to their organizations' power to gain the cooperation, resources, and policy changes they need to have a substantial impact on housing in their communities."[57]

The New Community Corporation in Newark, New Jersey is an exemplary case of a more "comprehensive approach" to CDC community development. Founded in 1968, in the wake of 1967 riots that left many dead and over 1,000 injured, New Community is now the nation's largest community development corporation. Over a period of 36 years, New Community has grown to amass its present net worth of well over $200 million in real estate and other business assets. New Community's real estate holdings include a shopping center and over 2,000 units of housing. Additional enterprises include a restaurant; a dress-making-and-upholstery shop, which also makes New Community's uniforms; a credit union; a Dunkin' Donuts franchise; and a staffing company that trains and places workers in Newark-area businesses. All told New Community houses over 7,500 people, while its enterprises employ 1,600 neighborhood residents and generate over $50 million in economic activity each year.[58]

Business proceeds have helped New Community leverage grant funding to develop a wide range of social service programs which include: job-training education programs; health care; day care; after-school programs; a Hispanic Development Center that serves Newark's growing Latino community (30 percent of the city's population as of 2000); a nursing home; a medical day-care center for seniors; a visiting nurse service; a school of practical nursing that trains Licensed Practitioner Nurses; and a mental health service agency. Health care services have grown particularly rapidly. New Community Health Care employs 700 professionals and has an annual operating budget of $12 million; in 2001, it served 4,335 clients. New Community has opened two charter schools—one in 1999 and the other in 2001—that teach a combined total of 1,000 elementary school children. New Community also runs a Youth Automotive Training Center, which provides trainees who complete its courses with guaranteed jobs offering $20,000-plus starting salaries.[59]

The successes of New Community and other CDCs in Newark have led some observers to declare that Newark is experiencing a renaissance. The city's population has stabilized, crime fell by half between 1995 and 2000, and a number of corporations are relocating there. Still, between 1990 and 2000 the city's poverty rate increased from 26.3 percent to 28.4 percent and median household income fell by 7.5 percent from $29,088 to $26,913 (in constant dollars). Arguably, some of the gains may be too recent to be reflected in the 2000 census figures. Nevertheless, the observation made by Grogan and Proscio regarding the South Bronx would seem equally applicable to Newark. Improvement of the physical and even social infrastructure alone does not reduce poverty rates—at a minimum, one can expect a long lag period before seeing any effect on poverty rates.[60]

Despite continuing poverty, New Community's work may well be establishing preconditions for a Newark Renaissance that does reach the neighborhoods. In the words of Director of Real Estate Development Raymond Codey, the CDC has long considered itself to be a "marathon runner." Prospective board members are required to commit to stay on for 20 years. This long-term perspective appears to be paying off. By slowly building an asset base over decades, New Community now enjoys a luxury that many other CDCs lack—namely, it is able to take chances and sometimes fail. Still, failure has its costs. In 2002, New Community sought to change Newark's political landscape in the mayoral election by backing challenger Cory Booker, who campaigned on a platform promoting a greater focus on neighborhood issues. As New Community's Director of Resource Development Dale Robinson Anglin acknowledges, in part because it was on the losing side and in part due to other unrelated federal funding reductions, New Community's government revenues fell from $15.5 million in 2002 to $5.4 million in 2004. A weaker CDC would likely have been sunk by such cutbacks. Because of the business and real estate assets it had amassed, however, New Community has been able to sell some assets, stay afloat, and still remain the nation's largest community development corporation.[61]

New Community illustrates the potential—as well as some of the risks—of taking a comprehensive approach. Its scale may also seem daunting for many CDCs, which might have one-tenth or even one-hundredth of its staff and asset base. Even in complicated areas of operation, such as retail development, however, New Community has found plenty of imitators. Indeed, the shopping center New Community manages is just a small part of a growing trend of CDC-developed (and, in most cases, managed) shopping centers. A partial list of CDC retail projects over the past 25 years is below:[62]

Partial List of CDC Shopping Center Development, 1979-2004

CDC	City	Year
Bedford-Stuyvesant Restoration Corp.	Brooklyn, NY	1979
Dineh Cooperatives	Chinle, AZ	1981
Vermont-Slauson Economic Development Corp.	Los Angeles, CA	1981
Marshall Heights CDC	Washington, DC	1983
Tacolcy Economic Development Corp.	Miami, FL	1985
CDC of Kansas City	Kansas City, MO	1986
New Community Corporation	Newark, NJ	1990
Dorchester Bay Economic Development Corp.	Boston, MA	1995
Northwest Corridor CDC	Charlotte, NC	1996
Virginia Park Community Investment Associates	Detroit, MI	1997
Renaissance Cooperative	Houston, TX	1997
Anacostia Economic Development Corp.	Washington, DC	1997
Asociación de Puertorriqueños en Marcha Inc.	Philadelphia, PA	1998
The Fund for Community Redevelopment and Revitalization	Chicago, IL	1999
Hartford Memorial Baptist Church Foundation	Detroit, MI	1999
Abyssinian Development Corp.	New York, NY (Harlem)	1999
Triumph CDC	Philadelphia, PA	1999
West Side CDC	Chattanooga, TN	1999
Northwest Side CDC	Milwaukee, WI	2000
East Bay Asian Local CDC	Oakland, CA	2000
Vermont-Slauson Economic Development Corp. (second project)	Los Angeles, CA	2003
Santee-Lynches	Sumpter, SC	2003
Bethel New Life	Chicago, IL	2004
United Durham, Inc. CDC	Durham, NC	2004
Mid Bronx Desperadoes CDC	Bronx, NY	2004

Shopping centers provide CDCs with considerable lease income and can serve as a centerpiece for community revitalization efforts. As Loretta Tate, former President of the Washington D.C.-based, Marshall Heights CDC (an early CDC-developed shopping center) explains, "Lloyd Smith [our executive director] had a vision to be self-sufficient. He looked at projects that would generate revenue. With two loans and help from the previous owner, we bought 40 percent of the East River Shopping Center." Success with the shopping center led the then-fledgling CDC to more success. As Tate put it, "LISC bought into our philosophy of grocery stores being anchors and has invested heavily in our organization since then."[63]

As the list above makes clear, CDC retail-development activity has accelerated in recent years. Between 1995 and 2004, CDCs participated in a dozen-and-a-half successful shopping center development ventures. The boom was in part due to LISC's increased financial support of retail development, partially realized through LISC's creation of an equity fund called The Retail Initiative in 1993. While many of the projects on the table above were financed by other means, LISC's support was important both in providing financing for some projects as well as in encouraging others to emulate its example.[64] In 2004, LISC chose to begin phasing out the program, in part because of its high expense—the program had spent $20 million by 2002—but by then the program had largely succeeded in making its point; namely, inner city retail markets are underserved and private investors who choose to invest in these neighborhoods will earn a profit. The message seems to be getting through. Increasingly, private investors are launching inner city shopping center developments on their own. For instance, Shaw Supermarket partnered with a local CDC and The Retail Initiative to open a supermarket in New Haven, Connecticut in 1998, and followed up by opening an inner city store in Dorchester, Massachusetts in 2002. According to Barbara Abell, a consultant for the National Congress for Community Economic Development and author of two books on the subject, because of accumulated CDC knowledge and greater private support for projects, the withdrawal of LISC's retail program at this point is unlikely to have a significant adverse effect on future supermarket center development by CDCs.[65]

While some large CDCs might be able to imitate New Community and develop shopping centers, most of the smaller CDCs cannot. According to the 1997 NCCED survey, the mean size of a CDC staff was 24 and the median only six. The mean was so much larger only because of a small number of much larger CDCs such as New Community. Some CDC critics suggest that smaller CDCs ought to merge to acquire the scale and financial self-sufficiency necessary to adopt a comprehensive approach. Stoecker, for instance, contends that "pursuing economic development is a more difficult task for many CDCs. The really large ones ... have played a significant role in developing their local economies. In many other cases, however, CDCs are simply pass-through organizations for government programs." The advisability of mergers can only be determined on a case-by-case basis. However, there are often strong arguments for CDCs to join together to have greater efficiency and scale even if this runs the risk of increasing separation from the community. Another option is for CDCs to develop network organizations, as they have done in Cleveland and some other cities, to share service and administrative costs. For member CDCs, such groups can help free up the time and money necessary to engage in more complicated development work.[66]

It is also important to note that while it may not be possible for a small CDC to develop a shopping center, it is possible for a small CDC to undertake a comprehensive approach to community development. A good example is Manna CDC, in the Shaw neighborhood of Washington, D.C., which was founded in 1997 and has a staff of six. Entering the conference room at Manna CDC's offices, it is hard not to notice the large campaign organizing strategy chart on the wall. There's a reason for that. Manna CDC is the rare CDC that seeks to directly integrate community organizing with its development work. As Dominic Moulden, Manna CDC's Executive Director, explains, "I have a background in organizing, but I have done real estate. I believe there is a way to do both organizing and development. With our staff, we have a tenant organizer, a community organizer with a public policy/education focus, a popular education specialist, a housing/real estate development person, a community economic development person, and me."[67]

A word of caution is in order: Manna CDC was started by an established and much larger parent organization, Manna, Inc., a Washington D.C. citywide community development corporation. This meant that the fledgling neighborhood-based CDC had a parent organization with considerable community economic development experience to back it up and gave the new CDC a level of security to try new approaches that few start-up CDCs enjoy. At the same time, Manna CDC is not so unique. First, many CDCs are started by established non-profit organizations. Additionally, it is important to note that LISC and Enterprise can and often do provide support for stand-alone organizations similar in size to Manna CDC. According to an October 1999 Urban Institute survey, the median CDC staff size was only 11.5. However, the typical organization of that size was able to diversify their activities sufficiently to run three or four separate programs.[68]

According to Moulden, organizing is central to Manna CDC's work because "the way people learn is by organizing themselves ... we're doing something unique that the whole country needs. All this fits together; you have to be creative enough to put it together." Maintaining support for organizing is not easy, however; as Moulden says, "It is hard to get funders or even residents to believe in the value of organizing until there is a crisis—and then it is often too late."[69]

How does Manna CDC put organizing and development together? It starts with community planning. To develop its initial strategic plan, staff went door-to-door to have a dialogue with the community. As Moulden explains, "It was what we called the Listening Project. We went out and listened to people. We're always trying to dialogue. We do initiate some things, but we try to be responsive." The responses centered on three things: "Jobs were the community's first priority, housing second, then opportunities for young people."[70]

In the area of job creation, the CDC partnered with the ICA Group, a worker ownership consulting firm based in Boston, to set up Enterprise Staffing Solutions, a worker-run temp agency that has provided jobs for as many as 30 people at a time; in 2004, it had $600,000 in gross wage receipts in the first half of the year. A second business, aimed more at youth, is a small bike repair shop called Chain Reaction, which employs 4 or 5 people. The CDC also operates a MaggieMoo's ice cream store franchise, and started a fourth business, Cultural Tourism DC, which provides bus and walking tours of the U Street area of Washington, D.C., an historically significant African-American cultural center.[71]

Manna CDC also has sought to develop ten units of limited equity cooperative housing, but has been stalled by private developers who have pushed for market-rate housing in the area. In addition, the CDC is helping groups of tenants buy their own buildings—one for about $1.5 million—by taking advantage of a Washington, D.C. law that gives tenants the first right to purchase the property if the landlord chooses to sell. As Moulden says, "For us, we're making an impact. Where can you go and find a small team of people that is organizing 1,000 units of subsidized housing in a gentrifying area?"[72]

Manna CDC and New Community illustrate two approaches. Another is Mid-Bronx Desperadoes, a CDC established in 1974 in the South Bronx at a time when "arson for profit" had become common and local unemployment was as high as 85 percent. Through its efforts, the CDC has amassed over $300 million in real estate assets, including 1,600 units of affordable housing and a 26 percent ownership stake as the managing partner of a 134,000 square foot shopping center, including a 48,000 square foot Pathmark supermarket, which opened in July 2004. The center is projected to create 400 jobs, of which 85 percent must be local hires. Proceeds from apartment management and project development fees provide the CDC with 60 percent of its core $1.5 million budget—an amount the CDC expects to be supplemented later on by commercial lease revenues—and help support many services, including a job training program that placed over 500 people in jobs in 2004.[73]

CDCs also operate in a number of rural areas. As of December 2004, LISC's "Rural LISC" program was working with 74 rural CDCs in 37 states. As with their urban counterparts, many rural CDCs have adopted a comprehensive approach that involves advocacy as well as business ownership and housing development. For instance, Quitman County Development Organization, a CDC founded by civil rights activists in a majority African-American area of rural Mississippi, has not only developed and rehabilitated housing, but owns a credit union that over 20 years has grown to amass 3,500 members, has made $12 million in loans, and has assets of $5 million. Coastal Enterprises, based in Wiscasset, Maine, has developed a broad approach to development in rural Maine that includes business loan and equity financing, affordable housing, research, advocacy, and public policy development. Since 1977, it has provided over $400 million in financing for 1,200 local businesses, helping to create or sustain jobs for more than 11,000 people.[74]

It is unlikely that the tensions between organizing and development or those between housing and more comprehensive approaches will ever be fully resolved. But some shift toward organizing and more comprehensive approaches does appear to be taking place. One area where advocacy has made a difference for CDCs is the creation of housing trust funds. As of 2002, more than 275 housing trust funds in cities, counties, and states across the United States provided $750 million a year in support of affordable housing, with 34 of 50 states having a statewide fund. Half of these state funds and more than two-thirds of municipal and county funds have been created since 1990. These funds have, in combination with federal monies and foundation support, helped CDCs expand their affordable housing production. Most often housing trust funds are created by the legislature, but they have also won approval at the ballot box in some places, including Burlington, Vermont; St. Louis; Seattle; San Francisco; and the state of Ohio.[75]

Andy Mott confirms that much of the renewed organizing activity of CDCs takes place through housing advocacy political coalitions. In 2001, after a three-year campaign, CDCs participating in such a coalition in Los Angeles helped secure approval of a $100 million per year trust fund. In New York, a similar effort was nearly derailed by political fall-out from the attacks of September 11, but the coalition in December 2002 secured a commitment from Republican Mayor Michael Bloomberg of an additional $500 million for affordable housing, resulting in a total city commitment of $3 billion over five years to create 65,000 units. One advantage that coalitions offer CDCs is that "they feel less visible and vulnerable to retaliation when they are one among many working on an issue." While the risk is never zero, the rewards can be great. Mott estimates that the Center for Community Change in 14 years spent $2.5 million on campaigns that resulted in $600 million in annual allocations of trust fund dollars.[76]

Still, the heart of CDC asset-based work is likely to remain at the level it began: block-by-block, project-by-project, and deal-by-deal. There are disadvantages to this extreme localism, but this is also the core source of CDCs' political and economic wealth-building strength. As a report authored by Michael Porter of the Harvard Business School—not normally considered a CDC fan—noted, "In some inner cities, CDCs function as the neighborhood's strongest institution … CDCs are often critical players because of their ability to attract subsidies, their patience and determination in assembling and preparing sites, and their political knowledge and connections."[77]

Community Development Finance: Democratizing Capital

The community development financial system must be equally facile in both the mainstream marketplace of wealth and the more populous world of economically disadvantaged people and communities.

Mark Pinsky,
National Community Capital Association[78]

Community development financial institutions (CDFIs) include a variety of non-profit and for-profit financial institutions—including community development banks, credit unions, loan funds, venture capital funds, and micro-enterprise loan funds—which provide credit, technical assistance, and other financing services that help low-income individuals, community development corporations, and other community-based entities pursue and implement effective wealth-building strategies.

How can poor communities obtain the capital they need when neither traditional banks nor the government will provide sufficient resources? Finding a solution to this question has proven anything but easy. Historically, mutual aid societies played a role in pooling capital for a wide variety of needs including insurance, medical care, and home loans. During the Great Depression, African-Americans formed the first community development credit unions. The modern community development financial institution (CDFI) industry is varied and follows in the tradition set by mutual societies and other community efforts, including CDC business loan programs originating in the late 1960s. In addition to community development credit unions, the sector also includes community development banks, loan funds, specialized micro-enterprise (typically loans of $25,000 or less) loan funds, and venture capital funds. Today, CDFIs are found in every state in the nation. Basic sector statistics can be found on the table below: [79]

Community Development Financial Institutions: Basic Statistics[80]

Estimated number of CDFIs (excluding micro-enterprise groups), 1995	300
Number of government-certified CDFIs, Sept. 2004	718
Estimated employment of CDFIs responding to industry survey, 2002	4,000
Estimated housing units financed by CDFIs, 2002	34,500
Assets under CDFI management, 1999	$5.4 billion
Assets under CDFI management, 2003	$14 billion
Assets under management of community development loan funds, 1985	$27 million
Assets under management of community development loan funds, 2003	$3.6 billion
Total federal government CDFI Fund awards (grants), 1995-2003	$650.25 million
Micro-enterprise loan funds and support groups, 1992	108
Micro-enterprise loan funds and support groups, 2002	650

The modern CDFI industry began to take shape in the 1970s with the founding of community development banks such as the South Shore Bank (now "Shorebank") in Chicago in 1973 and of larger community development credit unions, such as the Santa Cruz Community Credit Union in 1977. These early CDFIs aimed both to counter banks' redlining practices and to respond to economic restructuring as the decline of blue-collar industries and the related shift to a more suburban economy led to disinvestment in many communities.[81]

Such problems were compounded by changes in the financial industry. The rise of money market funds, for instance, reduced the amount of deposits that banks held and resulted in the closure of many banks' less profitable inner city branches. For ShoreBank's founders the challenge was obvious. By building a community bank, however, they believed that they could show the error of the big banks' ways and "prove that a strong, independent banking presence in the neighborhood could help get a community back on its feet again."[82]

By the 1980s, in addition to community development banks and credit unions, three other forms of community development financial institutions began to establish more solid foundations: community development loan funds, community development venture capital funds, and microenterprise loan funds. Today community development loan funds are the largest of these three segments, amassing $3.6 billion in assets by 2003. Mark Pinsky of National Community Capital reports that as recently as 1985 loan fund assets only totaled $27 million—less than 1 percent of the current amount.[83]

Community development venture capital funds make equity investments according to socially oriented community development criteria; they are a recent innovation. The first such venture fund dates back to a community development corporation in London, Kentucky that began making equity investments in local enterprises in 1972. As recently as the early 1990s there were only a half dozen of these funds nationwide. As of 2002, however, the community development venture capital sector had grown to 79 funds with $485 million in capital under management.[84]

Microenterprise loan funds (and support organizations) make small loans to individual and family-owned businesses too small to qualify for Small Business Administration loans; the number of these groups increased from 108 in 1992 to 650 in 2002. A survey of 308 micro-enterprise loan funds found that in fiscal year 2000 these groups made loans to 9,800 micro-enterprises, and they provided educational and technical assistance to an additional 90,145 businesses. Sixty-two percent served a majority of female clients, and 45 percent indicated that a majority of their clients were people of color. For 70 percent of the loan funds, at least half of their clients earned less than 80 percent of the area median income. Micro-enterprise has seen the most growth in the following industries: specialty foods; jewelry; arts, crafts, and gifts; clothing and textiles; furniture; computer technology; daycare; and environmental products and services.[85]

Ironically, federal cutbacks in housing and other urban development programs in the 1980s played an important role in spurring the development of CDFIs. From 1981 to 1989, the federal government's spending on housing fell by over 70 percent in real terms. As Kirsten Moy, a long-time participant in the CDFI industry, and co-author Alan Okagaki in a 2001 *Capital Xchange* journal article note, "As direct federal funding was reduced, the task of financing affordable housing development fell increasingly on local communities and states. Many communities responded, in part, by organizing CDFIs specializing in affordable housing."

In addition to local public and bank funding, another important source of early finance for CDFIs came from religious investors. The Sisters of St. Francis were an early funder of The Reinvestment Fund, based in Philadelphia. Other funds with religious roots include the Boston Community Loan Fund (founded by Old South Church, a

United Church of Christ congregation) and the New Mexico Community Loan Fund (founded by the New Mexico Council of Churches and the Diocese of Las Cruces).[86]

Later on, once the fledging CDFI industry began to grow, sector leaders found the lack of equity to be a stumbling block and lobbied for federal support. For community financial institutions building equity is critical, since loan loss reserves must be backed by equity capital funds. Most CDFI boards have set a minimum capital-to-loans ratio that they need to maintain based on the risk of the overall loan portfolio. Added equity capital thus allows CDFIs to lend out money for more projects and accept greater risk. In 1994, as a result of a strong early track record, CDFI lobbying efforts, and President Bill Clinton's backing, legislation creating the CDFI Fund was signed into law.[87]

The spread of CDFIs has been rapid ever since. In its first eight Federal funding rounds (FY1996 through FY2003), the CDFI Fund made a total of $650.25 million in awards to 1,582 community development organizations and financial institutions. Billions of dollars in private-sector commitments to community development finance has been leveraged by this small federal contribution of less than $100 million a year, combined with official encouragement given to CDFIs through Clinton-era revisions of the Community Reinvestment Act (CRA) regulations that made bank loans and investments in CDFIs count as CRA-qualifying activity. Encouraged by growing federal support, the number of CDFIs nationwide doubled between 1994 and 2001, while the volume of assets under CDFI management tripled. As shown in Figure 6, all CDFI industry segments experienced greater than 100 percent growth in the four-year period between 1999 and 2003.[88]

Figure 6: Community Development Financial Institutions, 1999-2003

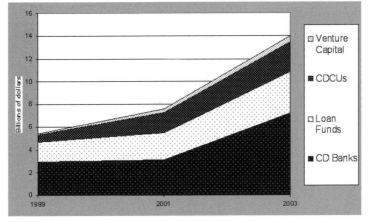

Source: Social Investment Forum

The effect of CDFI financing on job creation and affordable housing production has been significant. A CDFI survey covering only slightly more than a quarter of the industry conducted in 2000 found that the survey participants alone had provided $2.9 billion in financing, which was used to create or retain 137,000 jobs and 121,000 affordable housing units. And all of this was achieved while maintaining loan loss rates on a par with those of commercial banks.[89]

Since 2001, the momentum provided by the federal support, combined with an increasingly strong track record, has led to the continued expansion of CDFIs, even as federal allocations to the CDFI Fund were cut from a high of $118 million in 2001 to $61 million in 2004.[90] In only two years the CDFI sector nearly doubled in size again, with assets under CDFI management rising by 84 percent to $14 billion. According to the CDFI Data Project industry survey, in 2002 the CDFI industry employed over 4,000 people nationwide, provided financing for new or renovated affordable housing for over 34,500 housing units, and helped local micro-enterprises create or maintain over 34,000 jobs. Still, the effects of the CDFI Fund cuts are real. As one CDFI director explained, what the allocation cuts do is constrain "the ability of new CDFIs to get started and for current CDFIs to take risks." According to Pinsky, growth in loan origination for community development loan funds is beginning to slow, with a growth rate in 2002 of 14 percent—still high, but not the 35-40 percent annual growth seen in the mid-1990s.[91]

The industry's desire to further expand to meet the demand for community development finance in the face of reduced allocations from Washington has led to widespread internal debate. The CDFI industry has grown, but it is still a small player in the financial world. As one CDFI director put it, at $14 billion in assets the entire CDFI industry is smaller than many departments at the $1.264 trillion Citigroup. These numbers bring up another critical issue: not only has the community development finance world changed, but the conventional finance world has as well.[92]

The 1990s were a decade of rapid consolidation in the financial services industry, leading to the creation of trillion-dollar conglomerates such as Citigroup. This consolidation brought mixed results for CDFIs. On the one hand, mergers frequently led to the announcement of record Community Reinvestment Act commitments. Large CRA commitments were seen as an easy way to ensure federal approval of the mergers and forestall possible interventions by community groups, which might otherwise oppose the loss of local banks. Consequently, one result of industry conglomeration was the creation of a much larger financing pool for community investment, including investments in CDFIs. In this regard, in the first 15 years of CRA, from 1977 through 1991, total CRA commitments by banks totaled $8.8 billion. Yet from 1992 through 2000, bank CRA commitments totaled $1.09 trillion—$696 billion of which occurred in 1998, the year of the mergers of NationsBank and Bank of America, Citibank and Travelers, and U.S. Bank and First Chicago.[93]

On the other hand, the disappearance of local banks also had a negative effect on community investment. Local banks, although they did not make as many community investments under the auspices of CRA, were often better able to accommodate community needs than big financial conglomerates. As Margaret Lund of Northcountry Cooperative Development Fund put it, "We used to have more local partners...we don't have what we had 10 years ago. Today I say you can try this bank or that bank. I used to be able to say, 'You call this person and they will help you out.' Now it is 'maybe they'll do it if they have a good day and the home office says it's OK.'"[94]

Another development has been a change in the way affordable housing and community development loans are conducted. CDFIs used to directly provide these loans because banks would not. Now banks have become active community lenders, so the role of CDFIs has shifted from providing complete financing to providing riskier secondary finance. For instance, with affordable housing loans, the bank most often will take the first lien (meaning they are paid back first in case of foreclosure) and lend 70 percent of the value of the purchase, with the CDFI providing the remaining 30 percent. This means that CDFIs can stretch limited resources further since they're providing only 30 percent of each loan. However, CDFIs are also put at greater risk because in case of foreclosure, they are paid only after the primary lender (i.e., the bank) is fully reimbursed for its loan. As one study puts it, "Given the unlikelihood that banks will completely supplant the need for CDFI, the model ... that is becoming increasingly common is that of a partnership, with conventional financial institutions providing capital to businesses both directly and through CDFIs, while CDFIs provide those businesses with technical assistance. It is not clear, however, how equal such partnerships are."[95]

A final challenge has been the rise of so-called fringe banking services, such as "payday" loans (cash advances on paychecks), check cashing services, and pawn shops, which a substantial percentage of low-income people use either in lieu of—or in addition to—traditional banks and credit unions. Fringe banking affects community development banks and credit unions by cutting into their potential deposit base, and by extension their ability to make loans. According to Katy Jacobs of the Center for Financial Services Innovation, an institute established in 2004 by ShoreBank with support from the Ford Foundation, as many as half of inner city residents in some cities may be users of fringe banking services. These companies offer "quick cash with few questions asked," providing low-income customers with ready access to credit, but at a high cost. For instance, a typical two-week loan of $300 might carry $45 worth of fees, the equivalent of a 400 percent annualized interest rate.[96]

In the past decade, the number of payday lending branches has increased from 300 to 15,000. The estimated 2003 loan volume of these vendors was $25 billion nationwide, up from $10 billion in 2000. CDFIs have responded by offering competing products. For instance, North

Side Community Federal Credit Union of Chicago operates a program called "Hot Funds, Cold Cash" that makes loans that average about $500 and last one year as an alternative to payday loans. A major obstacle to CDFIs is that the companies offering fringe services have greater access to capital, enabling them to have longer hours and more locations than community development financial institutions.[97]

The combination of reduced allocations to the CDFI Fund, growing financial conglomerates, and the desire to more effectively compete against the rising fringe financial industry creates pressure for CDFIs to conform their practices to the expectations of financial markets in order to raise more capital. This brings other issues: namely how to balance growth and community service goals. One option, advanced by Okagaki and Moy, is for CDFIs to embrace greater standardization of loan documents, due diligence, and origination procedures so that loans can be more easily bundled and sold as securities on the secondary market.

Securitization would enable CDFIs to reduce risk exposure and access more private capital, but may reduce the flexibility community financial institutions have to customize their services to meet community needs. As Pinsky explains, "CDFIs are without doubt constrained by their resistance to capital market compliance. Just the same, CDFI leverage derives from CDFI alignment with community needs instead of capital markets." The National Community Capital Association has sought to attack the issue by creating an industry-rating system that allows the industry as a whole to maintain control over the standards that are applied. It is also beginning to encourage CDFIs that develop special expertise to market to other CDFIs. For instance, if this model were to take hold, the New Hampshire Community Loan Fund, which has spent 20 years providing loans for manufactured housing (mobile home) co-ops, might underwrite similar loans for other community loan funds. Such pooling of expertise can save training and staffing expense while increasing the business volume for the CDFI that directly originates the loans.[98]

Standardization, securitization, and pooling of resources can lower costs and further increase the impact of CDFIs. In theory these cost savings can free up funds for CDFIs to originate more high-risk loans. For instance, Neighborhood Reinvestment Corporation (NRC), a national intermediary, greatly cut its loan origination and administration costs by securitizing its subsidized 3 percent mortgage loans with Fannie Mae and Freddie Mac. As NRC Vice President Charles Tansey explains, "We reduced the cost of subsidizing 3 percent mortgages from $15 million to $2 million. This frees up $13 million to do the really hard stuff."[99]

At the heart of the discussion is whether participants in the CDFI industry will respond to greater access to capital markets by using the savings from securitized loans to support added "non-conforming" activity (loans they cannot sell on the secondary market) or, instead, aim for maximum return within well-defined affordable housing markets. While choosing the latter would certainly benefit many low-income homebuyers, arguably such loans might have a more limited community development impact. As a December 2004 paper by Gregory Ratliff and Kirsten Moy of The Aspen Institute indicates, while scale is important, "Achieving scale is only one way to achieve impact ... many organizations can and should look at other measures, e.g., the depth of the transformative effects of their work."

For instance, unsecured business loans are much more difficult to standardize than housing, yet small business development is a central element of most community development strategies. As Tansey explains, an organization that chooses to pursue a high-impact, low-return road "needs to convince the community to give the money it needs." Will funders be convinced of the need to support a market niche of riskier models of community development when a safer alternative exists? While established CDFIs may be able to convince funders to support this activity, smaller and newer CDFIs may have difficulty doing so. Pinsky himself believes that a shaking out period is likely to ensue. He estimates that perhaps 15 percent of CDFIs will fail to survive, but that the remainder will adapt, with the industry emerging much larger and stronger than it is now.[100]

Still, while the CDFI industry faces major challenges, it is important not to lose sight of the big picture—one of rapidly increasing community development activity. As Pinsky notes, despite the difficulties CDFIs face, "The CDFI industry has never been stronger in capitalization, portfolio performance, public perception, government relations, and positioning vis-à-vis conventional finance. For many in the private and government sectors, CDFIs represent the leading edge in financing for economically disadvantaged people and communities."[101]

One of the most prominent CDFIs is the Durham, North Carolina-based Center for Community Self-Help. Founded in 1980, Self-Help includes both a community development credit union (Self-Help Credit Union) and a community development loan fund. Though Self-Help has become a leading home mortgage lender in the community development community, it initially made no home loans at all. As CEO Martin Eakes says, "When Self Help first started we were interested only in starting small businesses ... [but we] found that for minority, and rural and women entrepreneurs to have the kind of stake to get started in a business they had to first be able to own a home. So, we became these preachers for the importance of owning a home." To date, Self-Help has lent $102 million to 1,891 families to finance home purchases, 65 percent to people of color, 40 percent to rural communities, and 43 percent to female-headed households.[102]

Self-Help has made $173 million in business loans, 48 percent of which are to minority businesses, 46 percent to rural businesses, and 50 percent to women-owned businesses, supporting a total of 14,492 jobs. Self-Help also has provided $75 million in loans to finance childcare centers, school spaces, and assisted living facilities, supporting another 5,363 jobs in the process.[103]

Last but not least, Self-Help spurred the creation of a national affordable housing homeownership program, the first time a community development credit union had led such an effort. Partnering with Fannie Mae, Ford Foundation, Bank of America, and Chevy Chase Bank, $2 billion in loans were made from 1998 to 2003 to 30,000 families, 46 percent of whom were people of color. Through this partnership, Self-Help credit enhances the mortgages and sells them to Fannie Mae. This replenishes the banks' ability to make affordable housing loans by reducing the number of "non-conforming" loans (i.e., loans they cannot sell on the secondary market) they must carry on their books. Chevy Chase and Bank of America's branch networks give the program its national reach. Families receiving loans have all been at or below the area median income, except in high-cost markets where they must earn less than 115 percent of area median income. The foreclosure rate on these loans has been 0.7 percent, versus 1.1 percent for all loans. Based on this success, the program was renewed for an additional $2.5 billion to serve another 35,000 families between 2003 and 2008.[104]

ShoreBank, the nation's first community development bank, is another industry leader. Founded in the South Shore area of Chicago in 1973, it has grown to have affiliate organizations in Cleveland and Detroit and over $1.5 billion in total assets. ShoreBank has also created a rural development affiliate in Washington State, partnered with Northern Michigan University to develop a community development corporation that works in Michigan's Upper Peninsula, and even started a community development venture capital fund to invest in sustainable development internationally. Over its 30-year history, ShoreBank has financed the purchase and renovation of 42,000 apartments. In 2003 alone, ShoreBank provided financing for more than 4,300 houses and apartments, disbursed $51 million in business loans, and made $71 million in loans that in one form or another met ShoreBank's environmental goals (such as loans to improve energy efficiency, produce organic products, and/or incorporate environmentally friendly elements into building or production design)—all while earning a small profit.[105]

When ShoreBank started out, however, its success was far from assured. As Richard Taub of the University of Chicago put it, creating a community development bank "was a really courageous act because, at that time, the notion was that you couldn't lend money in these communities." Scale was central to ShoreBank's success. As Taub explains, "What you really have to do is make a lot of loans, get the whole neighborhood stronger." The Shore Bank founders were fortunate in that the neighborhood retained many people with skills and steady income. As Taub cautions, "It becomes a different issue when you're in a very homogeneously, severely impacted community. Then it's difficult to find people who are going to invest and spend money and be able to handle that money well and run businesses and stay in the process and not have to worry about being shot or attacked every time they walk out on the corner."[106]

Community development loan funds, venture capital funds, and microenterprise loan funds round out the community development finance industry. Assets under management of community development loan funds have risen from $1.742 billion in 1999 to $3.6 billion in 2003. Venture funds have increased over the same period from $150 million to over $500 million, assisted by bank investments, which provide 40 percent of the industry's equity capital.[107] Unlike banks and credit unions, community development loan funds and venture capital funds do not have federally-insured deposit accounts, which can make attracting funding more challenging, but also gives these groups greater freedom to choose how they use their funds. For instance, Northcountry Cooperative Development Fund lends to a wide variety of worker co-ops, consumer food co-ops, and consumer housing co-ops in an 11-state region in the mid-western United States; Partners for the Common Good has a national strategy oriented to non-profit services and non-profit social enterprise lending, as well as supporting international micro-enterprises.[108]

The Rural Community Assistance Corporation (RCAC) is an example of a rural development loan fund. It finances projects in eleven Western states. Since its founding in 1988, the group has closed 291 loans totaling $114.2 million and has leveraged $621 million for rural projects. These loans supported more than 4,800 water and wastewater hook-ups for rural citizens, more than 6,500 housing units, and over 487,000 square feet of community and program space.[109]

Acción USA concentrates on microenterprise loans to support small independent businesses in eight U.S. states. From 1997 to 2002, the number of loans it has originated increased from 998 loans worth $3.5 million to 3,795 loans worth $18.4 million. The effect of these loans on individuals' lives can be substantial. A study Acción USA conducted of 849 borrowers in 1998 found that borrowers who had received two loans in an average period of 17 months had, on average, increased their take-home income by 38 percent or $455 per month, while their profits had risen by 47 percent and business equity had climbed by 42 percent.[110]

Community development venture capital or "CDVC" funds invest equity in the firms they support. This investment focus gives them greater flexibility than other more customer-driven forms of community development finance to direct their monies according to each fund's own community development vision. In some cases, state and municipal government gets involved. For instance, the City of San Diego has invested $2.5 million in an "emerging technology" fund, which targets "small businesses that increase employment in Low Income Communities and that expand economic opportunity among historically underserved groups in San Diego County." An example of a private community development venture fund is SJF Ventures (originally "Sustainable Jobs Fund") of North Carolina, which invests in the recycling, manufacturing, and environmental industries. According to Julia Sass Rubin of Rutgers University, a majority of community development venture capital firms target manufacturing because manufacturing jobs provide decent wages and benefits for individuals with lower education and skill levels.[111]

Assessing the newer funds' impact is difficult because their main focus is on long-term returns. Nevertheless, the available evidence is suggestive. According to Rubin, as of December 31, 2000, three of the four oldest venture funds—the Development Corporation of Austin, Kentucky Highlands Investment Company, and Northeast Ventures— together created more than 4,000 jobs at an average cost of $10,000 per job. By comparison, the SBA estimates that jobs created by the federal government's Small Business Investment Companies program cost $35,000 per job. As Rubin notes, "These figures are even more impressive in light of the fact that the jobs created were primarily in manufacturing, with livable wages and benefits, and located in economically depressed rural regions."[112]

In short, all segments of the community development finance industry have had considerable expansion in both the scale and scope of their activity. Few analysts would have predicted such growth a decade ago when the CDFI Fund, which has provided an average of less than $100 million in federal funds a year, was signed into law. Of course, as with all investments, community development investments carry risk. Not all can be expected to be successful, although loss rates for CDFIs are generally equal to or lower than comparable private investments. A more critical issue is resolving how CDFIs can and should relate to mainstream financial institutions. As one loan fund director said, "The prevailing mood is that the only way you play with financial institutions is to play their way. We are not strong enough to counter that. We need a stronger vision of what we are proposing as an alternative."[113]

ESOPs and the Growth of Shared Ownership

There is nothing more American than everyone's right
to participate in the decisions which affect them.

Issue Brief of The ESOP Association[114]

Employee stock-ownership plan (ESOP) companies are for-profit enti-
ties in which employees own part or all of the companies for which they
work. Since 1974, when federal pension legislation created tax breaks that
encouraged their formation, the number of ESOP companies has increased
from around 200 firms to somewhere between 9,500 and 11,000 today,
involving more than eight million employee-owners.

Although largely unnoticed by the general public, an important development in the American economy over the past three decades is that
employees are increasingly coming to own their place of employment.
This is a thriving sector, with a significant potential for asset accumulation. In 1974, about 200 employee stock ownership plans (ESOPs) covered fewer than 100,000 people. In that year, spurred by Senator Russell
Long (D) of Louisiana, Congress introduced legislation encouraging the
formation of ESOPs, as part of a more comprehensive pension bill known
as Employee Retirement Income Security Act (ERISA). Basic statistics
regarding the employee ownership sector are below:[115]

Employee Ownership: Basic Statistics	
Number of employee stock ownership plans, 2004	9,500-11,000
Number of plan participants (employee-owners), 2004	8.2-10.8 million
Estimated value of ESOP plan holdings, 2002	$297 billion[116]
Employees who own stock in the company where they work, 2002	37.67 million
Value of total employee stock holdings (including ESOPs), 2002	$555 billion
Employees granted stock options in the company where they work, 2002	14.3 million
Estimated productivity gain of ESOPs with worker participation	4-5%
Average account value of ESOP per capita, Washington State, 1998	$32,200
Average retirement account value, Washington State, comparison group	$12,700

ESOPs provide a way for employees to accumulate assets, invest in the businesses where they work, and become partial or full owners and thereby enjoy the equity gains of their labor. As John Logue and Jacqueline Yates of the Ohio Employee Ownership Center explain, ESOPs are created through a pension plan with two very unusual features: 1) most of the employee pension money is invested in the company where the workers are employed, and 2) they may borrow against future corporate earnings to purchase company stock. Money or stock the company contributes to fund the plan—either directly or to repay a loan—is tax deductible.[117]

In 1984, to further sweeten the pot, Congress allowed owners of closely held "C" corporation businesses to sell to an ESOP or worker co-op, such that it owns 30 percent or more of total company shares, and can defer capital gains tax, as long as the sale proceeds are reinvested in stocks or bonds of domestic companies. In so doing, Congress provided owners with an easy mechanism to cash out, while helping ensure that local businesses remained in the communities in which they had prospered after the original owners retired.[118]

In response to these tax law changes, employee ownership has drastically expanded. The National Center for Employee Ownership (NCEO) estimates that as of December 2003 there were approximately 11,000 ESOPs with some 8.8 million members. Jacquelyn Yates of Kent State University conducted a study using data from 1999 through 2001, based on the Form 5500 pension reports that ESOPs file with the IRS and came up with a smaller number—9,478—but with a higher participant estimate of 10.8 million. These numbers represent close to a 100-fold increase from the levels of three decades before. According to Joseph Blasi and Douglas Kruse, the accumulated worker assets in these ESOP plans total nearly $300 billion; if one includes all forms of employee stock ownership, workers in July 2002 owned $555 billion in employer stock—equal to 5.4 percent of the total value of the stock market.[119]

In addition to ESOPs, a host of other employee stock ownership mechanisms have also developed and expanded. NCEO estimates that the number of employees receiving stock options on an annualized basis has risen from one million in 1990 to somewhere between eight and ten million as of 2003, as stock options once given only to high-level management were increasingly distributed to other employees as well. In their analysis of the National Opinion Research Center's 2002

General Social Survey, Blasi and Kruse find that out of 108 million employees in the national economy, 23 million reported owning stock in the company they work for through ESOPs, 401(k) pension plans, or employee stock purchase programs; 14.3 million hold stock options. According to the 2003 National Organizations Survey 51.9 percent of publicly held companies provided company stock to a majority of their employees, with 16.4 percent reporting they provided stock options to a majority of their workers in the previous year.[120]

Evidence suggests that employee ownership can lead to higher profits and productivity. Both a 1985 Government Accountability Office (GAO) study and Logue and Yates' 2001 book find that a combination of employee ownership and employee participation in decision-making can produce substantial productivity gains.[121] A review of over 70 surveys by Blasi, Kruse, and Bernstein found that productivity is an average of four percentage points greater for a company with broad-based employee ownership and high employee ownership than one without—meaning an average 4 percent greater production per labor-hour for these firms compared to their conventional counterparts. Shareholder value, even after subtracting the dilution effect of the options, averages two percentage points higher, resulting in a 14 percent greater return on equity. In the 1990s, broad-based employee stock option distribution grew fastest in the computer industry and biotechnology, which were leading sectors of the 1990s economic boom. Blasi, Kruse, and Bernstein calculate that non-executive workers in the top 100 "high tech" firms in the United States earned $78 billion through the exercise of stock options between 1994 and 2001, an average of $425,000 per employee. They further contend, "that most corporations in America would enjoy more motivated workers and larger profits if they embraced partnership capitalism centered around employee stock options."[122]

It is worth noting that even when stock options are distributed to the majority of employees, their distribution has been significantly less equitable than with ESOPs where the law requires that ESOPs be distributed to nearly all employees.[123] In the most equitable area where stock options are regularly employed—namely, the high tech sector—the top five officers combined own an average of 14 percent of the company through stock grants and options, compared with 19 percent for everyone else inside the company. For the top 100 companies outside the high tech sector, the numbers are downright dismal. The top five officers average 14 percent through stock grants and options—all other managers and employees 2 percent. In short, in today's economy, capital may be shared, but these are hardly equal shares. The mean value of employee stock holdings for those who own stock is over $84,000, but the median is only $10,000—the higher mean reflects the skewing effect of the small percentage of employees who get larger stock options and grants.[124]

So far, we have looked at ESOPs as if they were just another employee benefit. Certainly at many firms, particularly large public companies where the percentage workers own is low and thus has very limited impact on corporate governance, this is often the case.[125] At companies where workers own a majority of their firm through an ESOP—roughly 3,000 according to NCEO President Corey Rosen—the ESOP not only provides an important economic benefit, but also helps anchor jobs in local communities and build more democratic workplaces.[126] Still, even if all the ESOP does is to provide a pension benefit, it can still have an important wealth-building effect. For instance, a 1998 Washington State study showed that the average pension value at an ESOP company was $32,200 versus $12,700 in the control group of non-ESOP companies. The pension benefit came on top of wages, as worker median wages typically exceeded those of non-ESOP companies in similar industries.[127]

But the ESOP, at least in theory, can be very different than a 401(k) employee stock purchase plan (or a stock option plan), because in the ESOP each worker owns, in essence, a percentage of a collectively held trust. An employee can often exercise a degree of individual control over how his or her shares are invested in a 401(k) and can decide when to buy and sell stock in an employee stock purchase plan. With a stock option, after the stock is vested the worker can choose when and whether to sell the stock. With an ESOP, except for the dividend payments that some companies pay out, the employee only receives the benefit after leaving the company (if vested, which can take up to five years).[128] There is no other way for an individual to exit the plan. This provides, *potentially*, a strong incentive for workers to band together, as their benefits depend greatly on how the company performs.[129] Whether this potential of higher employee commitment is realized depends on many factors, including the size of the ownership stake the ESOP has in the company and especially the degree to which company management makes employee ownership meaningful by facilitating employee participation.

Particularly within the organized ESOP sector—that is, for the thousand-plus companies that participate in such organizations as The ESOP Association, the National Center for Employee Ownership, and the Ohio Employee Ownership Network—the creation of a distinct, more participatory ESOP culture is evident. Often referred to as the "ownership culture," ESOPs that have adopted it have made significant changes in the way they do business. Although these changes often fall short of workplace democracy, this sector of the ESOP world has succeeded in increasing worker participation, further raising productivity and helping stabilize jobs and community in the process.[130]

Where are these more participatory ESOPs? One place is within The ESOP Association's membership. For some, this may seem surprising because The ESOP Association in the 1970s and early 1980s had been skeptical of those who advocated greater worker participation in ESOPs. For instance, in the late 1970s, when Congress amended ERISA to require that ESOP plan participants be able to instruct their pension trustee on how to vote on so-called "major issues" such as closings and mergers (on all other issues, management retained the right to instruct a trustee to vote the employees' shares as management saw fit)—the ESOP Association vociferously opposed—and nearly succeeded in overturning—this minimal democratic requirement.[131]

But times have changed. In 1982, only 20 percent of The ESOP Association members were majority ESOP companies; by 2000 that figure was 68 percent. And the emphasis placed on employee ownership culture has grown markedly. As Blasi and Kruse note, "The irony is that most of these firms were created by mostly conservative small businesspeople selling their union and non-union companies to the workers using the enabling legislation signed into law by President Ronald Reagan." For the association's president, J. Michael Keeling, defining features of this new culture include a board that "thinks about the ownership structure" and which is "strategically dedicated to shared ownership." According to Keeling, while ESOPs are similar to other companies in many respects, there are some key differences. The shared ownership culture is one. Another is their dedication to protecting the core workforce. As Keeling says, while CEOs on Wall Street are often financially rewarded for downsizing, "CEOs of ESOPs agonize over lay-offs. To say that they do all they can to save a job is not too far-fetched."[132]

The founding CEO of Chatsworth Products, Joe Cabral, who served as chair of The ESOP Association board in 2003-04, is representative of this new culture. Chatsworth Products was founded as a spin-off of a larger company. The firm, which employs a mostly Latino and Asian workforce and sells data storage equipment to Silicon Valley firms, grew tremendously during the Internet boom of the 1990s. When the Internet stock bubble burst in 1999, company sales crashed as well, but the company still held off for 18 months before laying-off any employees. For those who ultimately had to be laid off, the average value of the ESOP account they took with them on separation was greater than $100,000.[133]

By and large, the new ESOP culture does not include extending formal democratic representation rights to workers, although there is a slowly growing minority of companies within The ESOP Association that do. Most notably, in 1987 only 9 percent of surveyed companies had employee representatives on the board; by 2000, 21 percent did.

Figure 7 provides a map showing the distribution of association members by state. As can be seen, ESOP Association members are found in every state of the country.[134]

Figure 7: The ESOP Association Membership distribution, 2003 Directory

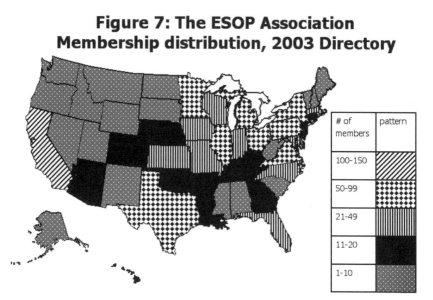

Note: DC is included with Maryland.

Dividing association members by industry, we find that although member companies exist in many sectors, the three top industries are manufacturing, distribution (wholesaling), and construction. In The ESOP Association's 2000 survey, these three categories account for 63 percent of all members. The heavy concentration of members in industrial regions is likely a product of manufacturing sector dominance. The average number of members per firm has increased somewhat over time, but not dramatically. In 1982 the average firm size was 441 employees; in 2000 it was 574 employees.[135] In short, what you typically find among ESOP Association members is that a more participatory ownership culture is relatively common in mid-size, privately held, manufacturing firms.[136]

To check these figures, we also examined a database of majority-owned ESOPs from the National Center for Employee Ownership (based in Oakland, California). This database, updated in 2003, is derived from records compiled by a national newspaper clipping service and verified using both Dun & Bradstreet data and IRS Form 5500 filings. A total of 711 companies are listed; NCEO Executive Director Corey Rosen estimates that the database covers only about one-quarter of all majority ESOP companies. As can be seen in Figure 8, similar patterns are evident.[137]

Figure 8: Majority ESOPs, Partial Listing NCEO, 2003

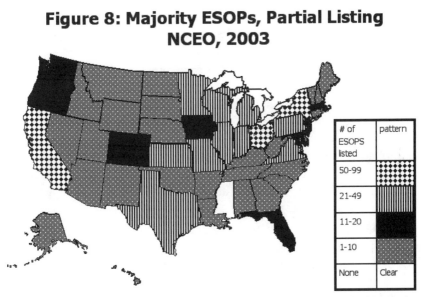

# of ESOPS listed	pattern
50-99	
21-49	
11-20	
1-10	
None	Clear

Note: DC is included with Maryland.

Broadly speaking, there appears to be similar sectoral variation in the NCEO database as there is among The ESOP Association's membership. A December 2004 analysis by NCEO staff found that roughly half of the listed firms are in manufacturing, 15 percent in construction and contracting, 8 percent in distribution and wholesaling, 8 percent in engineering and architecture, and 7 percent in banking and insurance.[138] The regional distribution of ESOPs is also roughly similar, but the NCEO database does list a greater number of firms coming from the Pacific Northwest, even though the database size is smaller. Another difference is that in the NCEO database, the state of Ohio has the single largest concentration of majority ESOPs with almost 10 percent of the total, which is likely a sign of the successful activity of the Ohio Employee Ownership Center in promoting employee ownership in that state. One other compelling finding from the NCEO data concerns the cause of ESOP formation. Of the 265 businesses in the database where a reason for ESOP formation is listed, nearly two-thirds involve instances of family business owners transferring the business to their employees—more evidence of the important role played by the 1984 law signed by President Reagan that allowed family business owners to defer capital gains if they transferred ownership of at least 30 percent of the company to their employees.[139]

There has also been significant research that demonstrates that ESOPs help promote community and employment stability. As Douglas Kruse of Rutgers said in testimony to Congress in 2002, "Employee ownership is associated with greater employment stability, which does not come at the expense of local efficiency." In fact, as Kruse explains, ESOPs maintained greater employment stability, while also having better stock market performance than comparable non-ESOP companies. ESOPs are able to do this, Kruse suggests, partly because of their strategy of adjusting work hours before resorting to lay-offs, much like the case of Chatsworth Products cited above. Kruse also finds that ESOPs have higher business survival rates and higher employment growth rates than comparable non-ESOP firms.[140]

ESOPs are far less likely to move under one or another form of economic pressure—an important fact for communities seeking to build a stable tax base that can help maintain support for public services in a global economy with increasing capital mobility. For instance, the nonprofit Northland Institute cites the employee-owned Antioch Company plant in St. Cloud, Minnesota as an example of the wealth-building potential of an ESOP. By 2002, after a decade of employee ownership, the value of the shares owned by Antioch's 250 St. Cloud employees had increased to more than $8 million. As the Northland Institute explains on its web site, "The company's ESOP-funding obligation more firmly anchors the company in St. Cloud. If Antioch were to close their St. Cloud plant and/or move their facility to any other location, they would have to buy out the shares of all laid-off employee-owners. Instead, the company is in the process of making a significant expansion locally."[141]

In short, knowledge of where ESOPs are located, what industries they are in, where majority ESOPs are concentrated, how much wealth ESOPs generate for their members, the productivity benefits of employee ownership, how they anchor capital in communities and help stabilize the local tax base, and why ESOPs are formed is quite substantial. One area where knowledge is weaker, however, is in what it all means on the shop floor.

As Logue and Yates explain, Congress in ERISA did not take a position on whether ESOP-owned companies should be democratically run. For ESOPs that are public companies, employee-owners have the same voting rights as all other shareholders. However, with privately held ESOPs the law permits the ESOP trustee, most often selected by management, to vote workers' shares on all matters except a few specifically defined "major issues," such as merger, acquisition, and dissolution. Thus, at most privately held ESOP companies, employee-owners do not elect the board of directors or vote on many other issues. A small but slowly growing minority of ESOP companies do choose to "pass through" voting on all matters to employees, allowing employees, rather than management, to tell the trustee how to vote the ESOP's shares.[142] Still, as of 2000, among ESOP Association members, only 7 percent passed through voting rights on all items, while 82 percent passed through voting only where required to by law. In Ohio, perhaps because of the employee participation efforts of the Ohio Employee Ownership Center, pass-through voting rights for employees are more common. A 1992-93 survey of Ohio ESOPs found pass-through voting at 42 percent of surveyed ESOPs, up from 14 percent only seven years before, while the number of majority-owned ESOP companies had climbed from 15 percent to 30 percent.[143] Moreover, although growth of formal democratic mechanisms outside of Ohio has increased only slowly, at a managerial level the majority of privately held ESOPs have evolved to employ a wide variety of informal mechanisms to facilitate greater employee consultation and sharing of financial information.[144]

A good example of the results of informal employee participation is the ownership culture at Schreiber Foods, which became a 100 percent ESOP-owned company in 1999. Based in Green Bay, Wisconsin, Schreiber is the United States' largest private label cheese producer with 4,500 employees and $2.5 billion in annual sales. The character of Schreiber Foods, explains Senior Vice President of Human Resources Jeff Ottum, comes from the dairy farmers who helped create the company with an attitude of hard work and a long time horizon. Schreiber is dedicated to providing space for two-way communication between management and workers, informing employees about company financials, and leading by example, but does not engage in "open book management" (sharing all financial information) and has not taken any steps to implement formal employee representation in firm governance. Although not a small company, Schreiber in many ways exemplifies the kind of middle America small business class that makes up the core of managers in the privately held ESOP sector—eager to promote a shared sense of ownership, but reluctant to yield control. As David Binns, Vice President of the Beyster Institute, explains, "Gradually, managers tend to cede greater information and authority, but it's a slow process."[145]

ComSonics, an older ESOP established in 1975, illustrates Binns' point. The Virginia-based firm, founded in 1972, manufactures and repairs cable television equipment. Although an ESOP was formed in 1975, the company made no effort to instill an ownership culture for the first ten years; company financial performance during this time was adequate, but less than stellar. In 1985, however, the company became a 100 percent ESOP-owned company at the same time as the founding CEO was beginning to plan for retirement. In these circumstances, promoting a sense of employee ownership became a management priority. In 1987, an employee ESOP Communications Committee was established and its Chair made an automatic member of the company board. ComSonics management also decided to implement open book management and to pass through to employees the ability to instruct the ESOP trustee how to vote their shares. Today, the company has $16 million in annual revenues and employs 190 people. From January 2000 through December 2003, ComSonics' stock price rose 3.5 percent, exceeding both industry and stock market averages.[146]

At Carris Reels, a Vermont company that makes metal reels for the wire and cable industry, the exiting CEO took the unusual step of not only providing voting rights, but also set up corporate bylaws so that each member has an equal vote. Maryland Brush is an ESOP whose workers are represented by the Steelworkers union. Since 1990, the board has had three management representatives, three employee representatives, and one jointly selected outside representative.[147]

But how does the average worker experience the ESOP? To address this question, we analyzed a database provided to us by Ownership Associates, an ESOP consulting firm. The database includes responses of over 3,000 surveyed ESOP employees. In all but one firm, at least 50 percent of eligible employees completed the surveys. Additionally, the database includes responses from a small number of worker co-op employees, which, while too small a sampling to be statistically significant, allows for comparison of the ESOPs against a more egalitarian enterprise form. Another data shortfall is the lack of a non-ESOP control group. Nonetheless, the data do suggest key areas of ESOP strength and weaknesses. For the below table, 4 is average, 1 low, and 7 high. For ease of presentation, we rephrased the questions into shorter phrases.[148]

	Co-op Average	ESOP Average
Good working conditions	5.86	5.68
Change is possible	5.62	5.37
Employees share benefits	5.34	5.17
Rules are fair	5.58	5.09
Fair to employees	5.86	5.01
Information shared	5.47	4.97
Participation encouraged	5.24	4.64
Feel I am an owner	6.42	4.62
Understand co-op/ESOP	5.85	4.61
Employees satisfied	5.42	4.59
Managers accountable	4.76	4.54
Pay system fair	4.81	3.93
Real say	4.79	3.88
Pay is fair	3.78	3.61

In general, the co-ops score higher than the ESOPs. However, it is important to note that the ESOPs get above average marks in most categories. The ESOPs got above a "5" on fairness, working conditions, ability to make change, and sharing of benefits—and fall just short of a "5" on information sharing. Not surprisingly, both co-op and ESOP members are dissatisfied with their personal pay. However, the fact that ESOPs also get below a "4" on the issues of pay system fairness and of having a "real say" illustrate areas of concern. While the ESOP "ownership culture" surely results in a fairer workplace, the 3.88 figure for "real say" is a clear indication that workers are aware that many ESOP workplaces are not truly democratic. At the same time, it is important to note a couple of key areas where the co-op average was significantly below the ESOP average:

	Co-op Average	ESOP Average
Merit not rewarded *(Low score indicates better result)*	4.59	3.61
I will benefit from company success	4.80	5.41

The weaknesses shown by the co-ops surveyed illustrate some of the challenges more egalitarian firms can face, including a tendency to insufficiently reward achievement and an inadequate connection between personal and company success. By contrast, the surveyed ESOPs scored significantly better in these areas.

Most importantly, the Ownership Associates data provides at least suggestive evidence that ESOPs, in addition to providing workers with financial benefits in terms of wages and retirement income, are perceived by employees themselves to benefit the everyday worker, even in situations that fall well short of industrial democracy. When combined with the benefits that ESOPs provide in terms of productivity, job stability, and community economic stability, the argument for greater support is compelling. Expanding state programs such as the Ohio Employee Ownership Center (OEOC) could help business owners transfer their businesses to ESOPs, thus helping anchor capital locally. With an annual budget of under $500,000, the OEOC has helped retain or stabilize 13,654 jobs at 69 companies since 1987; OEOC's work might help explain why from 1993 to 2001 the number of employee-owned companies in Ohio increased by 37 percent versus 23 percent nationally. Other efforts—such as the proposal Rep. Dana Rohrabacher (R) of California introduced in the 2001-2002 session of Congress (HR 2416) to create additional tax incentives for those companies that choose to provide majority ownership and pass through full voting rights to plan members—also deserve renewed consideration.[149]

With over 8 million members, ESOP companies can hardly be considered experimental. As Yates and Logue's preliminary 2004 survey confirms, ESOPs have proven an effective vehicle for integrating economic and community-based functions across sectoral boundaries, meeting (albeit imperfectly) a number of important objectives. As they write, "Many of these goals are economic, but some, such as voice for members, a focus on local economic development and community, decent work for employees, and training and education for members, are both highly valued and broadly distributed."[150]

Community Land Trusts
and Collective Asset Formation

This is, in effect, a balancing act between two kinds of
fairness, fair access for one group of homeowners versus fair return for another.

John Emmeus Davis and Amy Demetrowitz

*A community land trust is a non-profit organization that buys land on
behalf of the community and holds it in trust. By taking the land out of the
marketplace and capturing the equity gain on the community's behalf, the
land trust serves as an effective wealth-building approach. Most community land trusts lease homes out to residents using a limited-equity model,
allowing residents to gain a minority share of the equity gain, but capturing most of the gain in the trust, thereby ensuring affordability is maintained for the future members.*

A key feature of the community land trust model is its promise of
"permanent affordability." As Davis and Demetrowitz explain, achieving permanent affordability is hardly a simple matter. Nevertheless, as
their case study of the 20-year history of the Burlington Community
Land Trust of Vermont demonstrates, the land trust model has enabled
current members to achieve a limited accumulation of equity while
assuring that new members can buy into the trust at equivalent prices
to those who entered earlier. Basic sector statistics are below:

Community Land Trusts: Key Statistics [152]	
Number of incorporated community land trusts, 2004	112
Housing units, 1991	fewer than 2,000
Housing units, 2001	5,792
New housing units, 2001	309
Total residents in land trusts, 2001	11,947
Estimated growth rate, 2002	5.2%
Percentage of residents with income less than 50% of area median	82%
Percentage of residents who are non-white	32%

The most common type of land trust in the United States comes from the environmental movement, which has used the trust mechanism (often known as "conservation trusts") to preserve open space. In a conservation trust, the homeowner cedes (either by sale or donation) certain development rights to the trust. In the event the property is sold, the buyer must accept the deed restrictions, which typically limit future development on environmentally valuable land. As of 2003, 1,526 regional and local trusts owned land rights on over 9.3 million acres of land nationwide.[153]

The community land trust's origins come from abroad, especially the Gandhi-inspired village land ownership model that emerged in post-independence India. Still, a community land trust, which most commonly aims to preserve affordable housing, operates in much the same way as a conservation trust. Only in this case, the restriction concerns a formula that restricts the price for which a seller may sell her home, thereby limiting the accumulation of private equity and preserving affordable housing for the next generation of buyers. In so doing, the community land trust creates an important mechanism to build wealth in low-income communities.[154]

The first community land trust in the United States was formed in Albany, Georgia in the late 1960s, when a 5,000-acre land parcel was purchased by a group led by Robert Swann and Slater King, a cousin of Martin Luther King, Jr. The trust then leased this land to former black sharecroppers, providing these African-American farmers the ability to farm the land securely and affordably. Swann, and the Institute for Community Economics he helped to form, later adapted the model to the urban housing market.[155]

To describe the functioning of a community land trust, it is helpful to compare it to homebuyer assistance programs, which might provide, for instance, a zero-interest downpayment loan to an income-eligible family that is forgivable if the family resides in the house for a number of years. Affordable housing in this case is provided for one family *once*—at the cost of perhaps $25,000—and that one family reaps the entire benefit of the accumulated equity when they sell.[156]

With a community land trust, a large portion of the equity is kept within the community trust, as the non-profit trust maintains ownership of the land. The buyer receives a 99-year lease with a restricted deed requiring that the buyer, when re-selling the property, give the trust the option to buy the house back at a price set by a predetermined formula. The formula varies, but typically the seller gets the value of the principal payments and down-payment plus 25 percent of the accumulated equity, while the trust retains the other 75 percent of the accumulated equity. As a result, the land trust can re-sell the property at a below-market price, keeping the housing affordable and stretching affordable housing dollars farther. For the same reason, land trusts are often a very effective barrier to gentrification. Davis and Demetrowitz, in their study of 97 re-sales in Burlington, found initial house-hold buyer income was 69.4 percent of the area median; on resale, it was 67.8 percent—nearly identical. Meanwhile, the average person who sold realized a profit of $5,000 to $8,000 after an average of six years of residency, a con-siderable gain compared to the likely alternative of apartment rental.[157]

As of 2004, there were 112 incorporated community land trusts (and about 20 unincorporated land trusts) in the United States spread across 32 states and the District of Columbia. In 1991, fewer than 2,000 households lived on community land trust property; by 2002 that number had increased to over 6,000 households and nearly 12,000 people. The map in Figure 9 shows the states where land trusts can be found. Primary areas of concentration are in New England and the Pacific Northwest. Because the larger community land trusts tend to be concentrated in these areas, the degree of concentration is even greater than a glance at the map would indicate. As of 2001, the date the most recent survey of the sector was taken, the Institute for Community Economics (ICE) estimated that 57 percent of all members of community land trusts resided in these two regions.[158]

Figure 9: Community Land Trusts, 2004

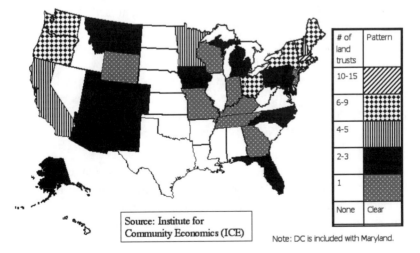

# of land trusts	Pattern
10-15	
6-9	
4-5	
2-3	
1	
None	Clear

Source: Institute for Community Economics (ICE)

Note: DC is included with Maryland.

The community land trust model shares some features of limited equity cooperatives, which have 400,000 members in the United States, a majority of whom live in New York City. As with community land trusts, limited equity cooperatives restrict personal equity accumulation while maintaining affordability through the use of a formula mechanism. But community land trusts differ from cooperatives in some important aspects. One difference is board structure. While the housing cooperative board consists solely of resident representatives, the typical community land trust board consists of one-third residents, one-third community members who do not reside in trust property, and one-third elected or appointed local government officials. The trust model thus reduces resident control but greatly facilitates expansion, as the mixed board helps ensure that those who are seeking to expand the provision of affordable housing are represented. The non-profit structure also helps the trust obtain the foundation and city support needed to raise funds, purchase land, and increase the stock of affordable housing. Community land trusts are very flexible. While most cooperatives own only a single apartment building or townhouse complex, community land trusts own property throughout a city or region. Some land trusts, including the New Columbia Land Trust of Washington, D.C., Burlington Community Land Trust in Vermont, and Dudley Neighbors, Inc., in Boston, have even set up limited equity cooperatives.[159]

New Columbia Land Trust initially focused on limited equity cooperatives because D.C. city law gives tenants the first right to purchase apartments as a cooperative if a landlord wishes to sell. A spring 2004 study indicated that Washington, D.C. had 57 limited-equity co-ops that provide housing for 2,269 households. In the first three years after its founding in 1990, the New Columbia Land Trust was able to raise $316,000 and acquire land to develop a single family home and form four small limited equity cooperatives. Now the group is developing more limited equity condominiums and fewer cooperatives, but still does both. As of 2004, New Columbia owns 15 pieces of property with a total of 51 housing units.[160]

James DeFilippis outlines one potential disadvantage of limited equity cooperatives, namely that members have the temptation to pull up the ladder beneath them by voting to change the rules to realize greater equity gains for themselves. Most often, such a change is prohibited by the terms of government financing, at least until the mortgage is fully paid. But the trust model presents an even easier solution, as community land trust leases preclude this option.[161]

In some cases, community land trusts embrace a much broader mission than providing affordable housing. For instance, New Jersey's North Camden Land Trust also has job creation as one of its goals; the trust meets this goal by being the majority owner in a construction company that employs Camden residents on its housing rehabilitation jobs. In Duluth, Minnesota, the Northern Communities Land Trust founded a "deconstruction" service that salvages and recycles building materials; the start-up venture employs seven and aims to both reduce the land trust's construction costs, as well as provide employment for residents. The Burlington Community Land Trust has broadened its activities to include such projects as creating a park and building a community technology center. A survey of ICE members found that, as of 2001, in addition to providing housing, seven of the 52 surveyed community land trusts promoted economic development, seven helped develop non-profit facilities, and six provided construction job training or development.[162]

By stabilizing neighborhoods and having a system that recycles affordable housing from one generation to the next, community land trusts develop locally controlled assets that make an important contribution to community economic stability. A key challenge for the sector is moving to greater scale. As Julie Orvis of the Institute for Community Economics, the leading community land trust trade association, points out, some community land trusts have been able to use federal HOME Community Housing Development Organization (CHDO) and CDBG (Community Development Block Grant) dollars to begin to grow to scale. Where they have, much larger projects have become feasible. For instance, in Boston, the Dudley Neighbors, Inc. community land trust has become the owner of 170 of the 500 housing units developed by the neighborhood's community development corporation. State policy can also make a difference. The Vermont Housing Finance Agency, for instance, has established a "Perpetually Affordable Housing Program" that provides reduced-rate mortgages for low-income purchasers of resale-restricted homes. Access to this state support is one reason why six of the nation's largest community land trusts and more than one in four of community land trust members nationally reside in that state.[164]

Cooperatives: Building Anew
for New Times

> The pioneers at Rochdale did not start simply to get a
> fair price; they were there to start a social movement.
>
> Frank T. Adams, 2002 Eastern Conference on
> Workplace Democracy[165]

*Cooperatives are an established wealth-building strategy that can be
found in many economic sectors, including banking (credit unions), agriculture, electricity generation and transmission, telecommunications,
housing, and child care. Areas of growth include consumer-owned natural
food stores, purchasing cooperatives owned by groups of independent businesses, and worker-owned cooperatives. In every case, cooperatives operate
on the basis of the core democratic principle of "one person, one vote."*

For a sector of its size, cooperatives—often called "co-ops"—maintain a
remarkably low profile. How large is the cooperative sector? For the past
eleven years, the National Cooperative Bank has published a listing of the
top 100 cooperatives in terms of annual revenue, which it labels the "Co-op
100." In 2003, cooperatives listed in the Co-op 100 earned $117 billion in
revenue and had an asset base of $284 billion.[166] The numbers of the Co-op
100 only begin to tell the story of the scale of cooperative enterprise in the
U.S. economy. For instance, in ten years, the credit union sector added over
20 million members and more than *doubled* in terms of deposits, loans, and
total assets. In 2003 more than 9,000 member-owned credit unions with a
total of over 84 million members held $545 billion in deposits, made loans
worth $388 billion, and had assets of over $629 billion.[167]

Even these numbers fail to encompass the scope of cooperatives,
large and small, that are found throughout America in a number of different sectors including agriculture, electricity, telecommunications,
health care, housing, retail, and child care, to name but a few. All told,
the National Cooperative Business Association (NCBA) estimates that
there may be as many as 48,000 cooperatives in the United States with
a total of over 120 million members. Additional statistics regarding the
cooperative sector are in the table below.[168]

Cooperative Sector: Additional Statistics [169]

Americans who get their electricity from electric cooperatives	36 million
Electrical cooperative market share in United States	11.8%
Percent of total agriculture production marketed by cooperatives	30%
Number of purchasing cooperatives, 1996	50
Number of purchasing cooperatives, 2001	250
Date of formation of U.S. worker co-op federation	May 2004
Retail food cooperative sales, 2002	$750 million
Number of food co-op members, 2002	1.9 million
Number of members of REI co-op, 2002	1.8 million
Number of housing co-op members, 2004	3 million

What is a co-op? A cooperative can be any business that is governed on the principle of *one member, one vote.* In other words, unlike a stock corporation, everyone makes an equal investment in purchasing shares and therefore has an equal say. Although antecedents exist (including a mutual fire insurance company established by Benjamin Franklin in 1752 that continues to operate in Philadelphia to this day), the first modern cooperative was a retail co-op founded by 28 people in Rochdale, England in 1844. Originally selling butter, sugar, flour, oatmeal, and tallow candles, business expanded rapidly in scope and scale as the co-op succeeded in elevating food standards—rejecting then-common tactics such as watering down milk. By 1880 Rochdale had over 10,000 members and more than 500,000 people had joined food co-ops in Britain; by 1900 British food co-op membership totaled 1.7 million. [170]

While 1.9 million people in the United States have directly followed the Rochdale example and are members of food co-ops in roughly 300 communities today, the concept of consumers getting together on a one-person-one-vote basis to create businesses and meet collective needs has proved to have far wider applicability. Nationwide, in addition to 84 million credit union members and nearly two million food co-op members, *consumer co-ops* also include more than three million people living in housing co-ops, 36 million household members of electrical utility co-ops, two million members of telecommunications co-ops, and 1.8 million members of Recreational Equipment, Inc., (REI), an outdoor equipment retailer. [171]

A second type of cooperative is the *producer co-op.* Producer co-ops, as one co-op web site puts it, "provide goods and services for producers and are owned by the producers."[172] These cooperatives are most commonly found in the agricultural sector, where family farmers pooled resources to market their products to effectively compete against corporate agriculture. One of the oldest agricultural co-ops, Sunkist, was founded in 1895 by 60 struggling citrus farmers; today, Sunkist has 6,500 members with over $1 billion a year in sales. Cooperatives are so common in agriculture that there are actually more co-op members than family farmers, since many farmers belong to more than one co-op. All told, about 30 percent of total U.S. agricultural production is marketed by cooperatives, which allows family farmers, despite the obstacles they face, to effectively maintain market share in the otherwise corporate-dominated farming sector. Outside of agriculture, two prominent producer co-ops are Ace Hardware (owned by local hardware stores) and the Associated Press (owned by local newspapers).[173]

A third type of cooperative is the *purchasing co-op*. Purchasing co-ops help independent businesses pool resources to negotiate better supply contracts, thereby lowering their costs to more effectively compete against larger national chains. For instance, through the VHA, Inc. co-op, member non-profit hospitals purchased over $20 billion worth of equipment in 2003. Other prominent purchasing co-ops include the is.group (which jointly purchases office supplies for independent office supply stores) and AMAROK (which purchases drywall on behalf of over a hundred independent distributors). By winning the lower supply costs that national chains enjoy, purchasing co-ops provide a critical mechanism for smaller businesses to band together to gain the advantages of larger scale while maintaining individuality and sensitivity to local conditions.[174]

The last major type of co-op is the *worker cooperative*, an employee-owned business where each worker gets an equal say. In small cooperatives, every worker might also be a board member. In larger cooperatives, workers typically elect board members from among themselves to oversee co-op-wide matters. Worker cooperatives first gained prominence in the United States in the 1880s as the Knights of Labor promoted direct worker ownership of businesses; however, as the Knights of Labor declined, so did worker-run businesses. In recent years, inspired in part by the successes of worker cooperatives in Spain, there has been a resurgence of interest in worker-owned businesses in the United States. In the Basque region of Spain, the Mondragón network of worker cooperatives had, as of 2003, grown to have nearly 34,000 worker-owners with annual sales in excess of $10 billion. The

U.S. worker co-op sector is more modest, but worker cooperatives today can be found in many lines of business, including fair trade coffee, printing, copy stores, food stores, bookstores, home construction, taxi cabs, bakeries, and health care. This resurgence led to the creation of a national trade association, the U.S. Federation of Worker Cooperatives and Democratic Workplaces, at a conference held in Minneapolis in May 2004.[175]

The breadth of the cooperative sector is great, but its community impact is not always obvious. Large cooperatives in particular are often criticized for being indistinguishable from large corporations, yet they provide important community benefits beyond those provided by conventional firms. Minnesota, home to the nation's highest concentration of cooperatives, also has some of the largest, including the Cenex Harvest States grain cooperative with $9.4 billion in revenues in 2003 and the Land O' Lakes dairy cooperative, with $6.3 billion in revenues. According to a 2003 U.S. Dept. of Agriculture (USDA) study of Minnesota credit unions, agricultural co-ops, electrical co-ops, and housing co-ops, one benefit stemming from these cooperatives' local ownership is that they contribute $600 million a year more to the state economy than comparable non-cooperative businesses would.[176]

Cooperatives have become so much part of the backbone of the communities they serve that their presence seems unremarkable. This is particularly true in rural America. The map in Figure 10, for instance, shows the extent of U.S. rural electric cooperatives.[177]

Figure 10: Electrical Co-ops
percent of total customers by state, 2002

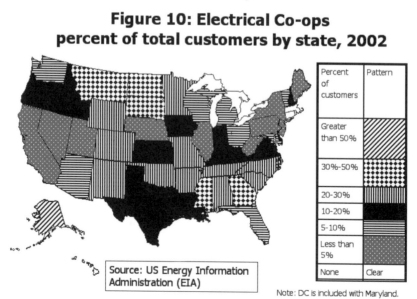

Percent of customers	Pattern
Greater than 50%	
30%-50%	
20-30%	
10-20%	
5-10%	
Less than 5%	
None	Clear

Source: US Energy Information Administration (EIA)

Note: DC is included with Maryland.

In 1935, prior to the passage of the Rural Electrification Act that facilitated the expansion of rural electric cooperatives, only 10 percent of rural Americans had electrical service at a time when 90 percent of urban Americans did. Today 95 percent of rural Americans have electric service and nearly half of those rural electric lines were built by cooperatives. Cooperatives, still the leading suppliers of electricity in rural America, may be taken for granted, but statewide rural electric cooperative associations and a number of individual electric cooperatives have adopted a new role as regional economic developers. The reasons for this are clear: they need to promote economic development to have enough customers to cover their costs. These costs are high since, as a result of the lower density of rural areas, rural electric co-ops have only seven customers per mile compared to 34 customers per mile for investor-owned utilities. Rural electric cooperatives are one of the few rural institutions with the capital base and regional scope necessary to effectively promote economic development. In 1985 in Iowa, 70 rural electric cooperatives and a few municipal electric companies founded a development consortium known as the Iowa Area Development Group. By 2000, they had assisted with over 850 business expansions, resulting in $2.5 billion in capital investment and 26,000 jobs. Additionally, the consortium had provided 57 direct grants for more than $16 million in projects that led to 2,900 new jobs. All money for these grants came directly from the electric cooperatives' earnings. Egg production was one focal point of development. In the 1950s, Iowa was first in the nation in egg production, but the state had fallen to 24th by the late 1980s; with targeted marketing and national promotion, Iowa production rebounded to second in the country by 1999. The group has also provided support for the food processing industry and affordable housing.[178]

The Federation of Southern Cooperatives/Land Assistance Fund (FSC/LAF) provides another example of rural cooperative development. Founded in 1967 by 22 cooperatives in the Southern "Black Belt" (as of 2003 it had 65 members), the FSC/LAF was founded to provide African-American farmers with a mechanism to obtain and retain land. In the 1960s, many African-American sharecropping families were thrown off the land after participating in civil rights activities as mild as listening to a speaker at a rally. The federation provided a means for these farmers to get land of their own and the credit necessary to productively farm the land. Over 35 years, the federation helped 5,000

African-American farmers save more than 175,000 acres of land. In addition, the federation has helped develop credit unions; supported other businesses such as a quilting cooperative in Alberta, Alabama (the Freedom Quilting Bee); and financed $26 million worth of new and reconstructed affordable housing, including four multi-family rental projects with a total of 126 units. Finally, the FSC/LAF has played an important advocacy role; for example, it assisted with a class action lawsuit against the U.S. Department of Agriculture (USDA) for failing to provide African-American farmers the extension and credit services white farmers received. As of July 2003, affected farmers had received $648 million in settlement money for their claims.[179]

While the electrical cooperatives and the Federation of Southern Cooperatives work primarily in rural America, the cooperative presence in urban America is also growing. For example, community development credit unions have increased their asset base from $600 million in 1999 to $2.7 billion in 2003. Other expanding areas of urban cooperatives include food co-ops, purchasing co-ops, and worker co-ops.

The food co-op sector provides a fascinating phoenix-like tale of rebirth and regeneration. A few decades ago, food cooperatives had become major players in the supermarket industry in some cities. For instance, in 1970 the Greenbelt Consumer Cooperative, with stores throughout the Baltimore-Washington metropolitan region, managed 22 supermarkets, 10 service stations, five pharmacies, and seven furniture stores and had $50 million in annual sales (close to $250 million in 2004 dollars). In the San Francisco Bay Area, Consumers Cooperative of Berkeley operated 12 supermarkets—including one with the highest sales per square foot of any grocery store west of the Mississippi River—and many other enterprises, including service stations, pharmacies, a hardware store, a garden nursery, and a wilderness supply outlet. By 1980, annual sales figures had reached $83.6 million (a little over $200 million in 2004 dollars). These co-op giants overshadowed the smaller natural food stores that had emerged in the late 1960s and 1970s across the country. Yet by the end of the 1980s, both the Greenbelt and Berkeley co-ops had declared bankruptcy. Meanwhile, times were not so good for the fledgling natural food co-ops either. Indicative of the despair was a roundtable discussion by four participants on the sector held in *Cooperative Grocer* in 1987. The title: "Why co-ops die."[180]

Yet a decade and a half later, prospects look brighter. Out of the trials and tribulations of the 1980s emerged a food co-op sector that has broadened its community base while becoming much smarter about business operations. On the business side, the industry developed a members-only web site to share best practices, a financial data sharing program known as CoCoFiSt (Common Cooperative Financial Statements), and regional trade associations. On the community side, cooperatives have begun to break out of the "counter-culture" box. For instance, managers and members of Weaver Street Co-op in Carrboro, North Carolina (near Chapel Hill) noticed that Latinos were under-utilizing their store. The food co-op responded by developing employee training programs in Spanish and recruited Latino employees to reach out more effectively to this community.[181]

As a result, the retail food co-op sector is once again growing, with many cooperatives doubling their floor space or adding new stores or operations, such as a restaurant or café. The chart below only shows those co-ops whose expansion projects have been profiled in *Cooperative Grocer*, and thus does not purport to be comprehensive.[182]

Food Co-op Expansion: 2000-2003	
Co-op Name	**City**
Bloomingfoods	Bloomington, IN
Bluff City Co-op	Winona, MN
Chequamegon	Ashland, WI
Community Food Co-op	Bozeman, MT
Community Mercantile	Lawrence, KS
First Alternative	Corvallis, OR
New Pioneer	Coralville, IA
North Coast	Arcata, CA
Ocean Beach People's	San Diego, CA
People's Foods	Portland, OR
Puget Consumer Co-op	Seattle, WA
Quincy Natural Food	Quincy, CA
The Food Co-op	Port Townsend, WA
Tidal Creek Food Co-op	Wilmington, NC
Valley Natural Foods	Burnsville, MN
Weaver Street	Carrboro, NC

Taken together, retail food cooperatives would constitute the fourth largest "chain" in the natural foods industry. As of 2001, food co-op sales were $750 million, compared to $2.27 billion for Whole Foods, $1.9 billion for Trader Joe's, and $900 million for Wild Oats. In 2002, food co-op sales increased by an additional 12 percent. Meanwhile, retail food cooperatives, cognizant of the history of the failed Berkeley and Greenbelt co-ops, are taking action and banding together to preserve and extend their strength. In April 2004, by a vote of 89 to 2 (with 3 abstentions), 94 retail food co-ops with 111 stores and $626 million in annual sales voted to merge eleven regional associations into one national association, the National Cooperative Grocers Association (NCGA), which had previously existed merely as a coalition of regional groups. The newly restructured association is planning to begin a national purchasing program for retail food cooperatives in 2005.[183]

Purchasing cooperatives are another area of increased co-op activity. For instance, VHA Inc., with more than $20 billion a year in negotiated sales, serves the hospital sector and has played a major role in helping non-profit hospitals survive the 1990s onslaught of for-profit competition. Most often, purchasing cooperatives are set up for defensive purposes. As NCBA President Paul Hazen said, "Small non-profit hospitals didn't create the 'bigness' situation, but they had to respond to it if they were going to survive. They did that in the only way they could—by forming a purchasing cooperative that gave them the critical mass they needed to compete." Between 1996 and 2001, the number of purchasing cooperatives quintupled from around 50 to over 250.[184]

Purchasing cooperatives play a large role in the hardware and home construction industries. In the hardware industry, Ace Hardware and True Value had combined sales of over $5 billion in 2002, but this number underestimates their impact. According to one analyst, as of 1998 the 15,000 stores supplied by Ace and TruServ conducted $27 billion in business. A large purchasing cooperative in the construction industry is AMAROK, a drywall purchaser. Founded in the mid-1990s with only seven members representing 0.1 percent of the industry, it has grown to include 115 companies in 45 states with 9 percent of the market. Today, it carries out $1.2 billion in purchases a year—making AMAROK one of the United States' leading purchasers of drywall. Before AMAROK existed, a drywall shortage would likely mean that suppliers would ship to Lowe's and Home Depot before they sent stock to independents.

With AMAROK, suppliers are much quicker to respond to the independents' requests.[185]

Another purchasing cooperative is Carpet One, now the largest U.S. retailer of flooring products. As of 2001, there were 1,100 Carpet One stores in all 50 states, as well as Canada, Australia, New Zealand, and Guam, doing a combined business of $2.8 billion. Independent office-supply stores have formed the "is.group" cooperative to compete more effectively against Office Depot, Office Max, and Staples. Even franchisees of major chain restaurants such as Kentucky Fried Chicken, Taco Bell, and Dairy Queen have formed cooperatives so that, as Hazen says, "they are not held hostage to the franchisor's prices for the inputs the franchisee is required to buy."[186]

Christina Clamp of Southern New Hampshire University notes that purchasing cooperatives provide "a good strategy for stabilizing small proprietors on urban and rural main streets ... [and] holding on to family-owned businesses." Much as agricultural cooperatives helped small farmers persevere early in the twentieth century, today's purchasing cooperatives help local businesses resist and respond to the encroachment of big box stores. Alan Greenberg, Co-Chair of the Carpet One co-op, states this point as follows, "Give the independents the tools and buying power, and they can outperform anyone because of the power of local ownership."[187]

While purchasing co-ops play a support role to small businesses, worker cooperatives represent a very different kind of co-op that directly empowers employees. The movement to build worker cooperatives in the United States is small but growing. Estimates of the sector's size range between 300 and 500 cooperatives, most of which have well under 100 employee-owners. Rainbow Grocery in San Francisco, which has approximately 200 worker-owners and generates about $30 million in annual sales, is thus considered a fairly large enterprise in the worker cooperative world. The nation's largest worker cooperative is Cooperative Home Care, a Bronx-based home health care group with 780 worker-owners.[188]

While worker cooperatives tend to be small, increasing numbers of worker co-ops and worker co-op models are being generated. In Madison, Wisconsin, Union Cab is a worker-owned cab company with 150 members and $3.75 million in annual revenues. Collective Copies is a worker-owned copy store in Amherst, Massachusetts. The store was so successful that in 2000 members opened a second store in nearby Florence, which has exceeded initial projections. In San Francisco, Alvarado Street Bakery produces bread products that are sold across the United States. In New York City, surviving employees of the World Trade Center's Windows on the World restaurant started a new worker co-op restaurant.[189]

The worker cooperative movement has also taken big steps to overcome the historical obstacles it faces. Problems that have stymied worker co-op development in the past include a tendency to insufficiently reward achievement; exaggerated suspicion of management, which can make resolving organizational issues more difficult; insufficient attention to long-term, bottom-line performance; and long, poorly facilitated meetings.[190] The willingness of worker cooperatives to confront these issues and develop strong management marks an important shift from some cooperatives' past reluctance to do so. Where worker cooperatives are well managed, they are often very strong and stable businesses with high levels of worker dedication.

Tim Huet of Arrizmendi contends that while many worker cooperatives founded in the 1970s self-destructed, the ones that survived became stronger as a result. According to Huet, "The cooperatives who wanted to learn and help their community stayed and they became the basis of growing a new generation." Learning perhaps from the experience of retail food co-ops, worker cooperatives in 2004 rejected the option of establishing regional federations and chose to set up a national federation instead. Federation goals include networking, building a database, lobbying on behalf of members, and providing technical assistance to new cooperatives. Worker co-op leaders are optimistic about their prospects. As Bob Stone from *Grassroots Economic Organizing*, an industry publication, put it at a 2002 conference, "the key is that co-ops have a social mission to communities that has a role in displacing the Wal-Mart economy globally." While worker cooperatives have not displaced the Wal-Mart economy, they are, together with their consumer and purchasing cooperative brethren, providing a mechanism that builds wealth and economic capacity at the local level.[191]

Municipal Enterprise:
Local Government as Developer

You see a lot more community leaders—mayors, chambers of commerce, commissioners—who are saying, "Our salvation is not getting the branch plant, the next Mercedes Benz; we have to focus internally on what we need....It's a change of mind set."

Ray Daffner, Manager, Entrepreneurship Initiative, Appalachian Regional Commission[192]

Municipal enterprises are businesses owned by local public authorities that provide services and often revenue in cities across the United States. Spurred by political resistance to tax increases and public pressure to provide for jobs in an unpredictable global economy, local governments have increasingly turned to new strategies to raise revenues and to promote local economic stability.

Widespread privatization and government downsizing is frequently seen as the norm in the United States. Yet the trend often is in just the opposite direction. Driven by increasingly difficult fiscal conditions and greater economic instability as a result of exposure to the global market, municipal governments have taken on a much more active role in community economic development.[193] Some are now creating new municipal enterprises. Others are expanding existing enterprises. Municipalities are also increasingly using other techniques to more actively promote local development, including investing in convention center hotels to spur tourism and using their ownership of real estate assets to support transit-oriented development. As a number of experts have noted, the outlines of a new strategy are emerging. While city officials continue to offer generous incentives for businesses to relocate, a different approach that relies on using cities' own investment capacity to cultivate locally based development and asset accumulation is becoming more prominent. The table below shows basic statistics on municipal enterprises.[194]

MUNICIPAL ENTERPRISES: BASIC STATISTICS[195]	
Municipal enterprises identified in Minnesota study, 2002	2,597
Municipal enterprises per surveyed Minnesota city	5.57
Municipal enterprises per city in 2001 National League of Cities study	4.49
Municipal power company income, nationally, 2002	$39.5 billion
Estimated 2002 general fund contributions of municipal power companies	$2.3 billion
Municipal utilities providing telecom services, 2001	230
Municipal utilities providing telecom services, 2003	357
Lease revenue contributed to general fund in City of San Diego, FY2004	$31.4 million
Income of Washington D.C. Metro from transit-oriented development, 2003	$6 million
Number of city-owned hotels opened since 1995	9

What do cities gain through municipal enterprise efforts? There are, of course, long-standing debates regarding the costs and benefits of public enterprise, the extent to which government can and should act to discourage market choices which have negative social effects (such as pollution) and encourage ones with positive social effects (such as recycling), the ways government can help reduce private sector information collection and transaction costs, the role of government in addressing structural issues of market failure, and so on. We do not wish to dwell on these debates here. What is clear is that when done well, municipal enterprise and related public entrepreneurial activity have the potential to make local economies more responsive to public needs, generate good jobs for underserved members of the labor force, and broaden citizen access to resources and opportunities. They can also provide cities and other local governments with an important source of revenue in difficult fiscal times.[196]

Of course, some municipal enterprises are simply poorly disguised tax increases: a way to substitute user fees for previously free public services, for example. It is also possible for a public enterprise to develop a rosy business plan and fail to perform according to expectations. Still, politicians who promote unsuccessful business efforts do so at their peril. Although officials are not always held to account, the local scale of the enterprises increases accountability because residents are more likely to notice unsatisfactory outcomes and vote accordingly.[197] Moreover, the risks must be weighed against the benefits. Today public intervention enjoys broad support from Republicans and Democrats alike for a simple reason: because they meet the needs of the communities they serve.[198]

What services do municipal enterprises provide and how prevalent are they? This is an area where data remains relatively scarce. The prevalence of municipal enterprise, however, is not in doubt. General surveys document the widespread use of "enterprise funds"—that is, services that are run by local governments "on a business-like basis." These enterprise activities include public utilities, environmental services (e.g., solid waste and drainage), facility management (e.g., convention centers), recreation facilities (e.g., golf courses), and transportation services (e.g., ports and airports), among others. A National League of Cities survey conducted in 2001 found an average of 4.49 enterprises in the 326 cities surveyed. A 2000 study of 124 large cities by Beverly Bunch of the University of Illinois-Springfield found an average of 4.44 enterprises, an increase of 12 percent for the cities surveyed from a decade before.[199] However, beyond the overall numbers, the data we have regarding enterprise performance is limited. Further, by focusing solely on enterprise funds, these studies miss a wide range of enterprising activities by local governments that take place outside the scope of enterprise funds—most notably, real estate development and the operation of city-owned convention hotels.

One state where more comprehensive research has occurred is Minnesota, which provides us with a good starting point for further discussion. A 2004 Minnesota state government study found a total of 2,597 enterprises in 466 towns and cities, or an average of 5.57 enterprises per city as of 2002. It is likely that the 387 non-responding cities had slightly fewer enterprises.[200] The League of Minnesota Cities estimates that the average city in Minnesota runs five enterprises. Although Minnesota has a somewhat greater number of enterprises than the national average, the trends there reflect broader national patterns. The majority of its municipal enterprises are found in utilities, including water, sewage, electricity, and cable. Other forms of city businesses include environmental enterprises (solid waste, recycling), city-owned facilities (hospitals, arenas, community centers, nursing homes, cemeteries, marinas), public safety enterprises (such as ambulances), transportation businesses (parking garages, airports, transit), recreation services (golf courses, pools), community development enterprises (economic development agencies and housing authorities), and various other forms, including 233 city-owned liquor stores. The chart in Figure 11 provides a sectoral breakdown of these businesses.[201]

Figure 11: Minnesota Municipal Enterprises

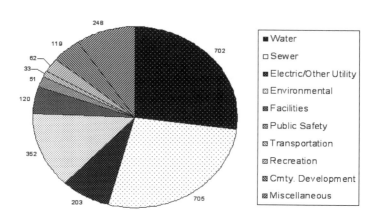

Legend:
- Water
- Sewer
- Electric/Other Utility
- Environmental
- Facilities
- Public Safety
- Transportation
- Recreation
- Cmty. Development
- Miscellaneous

Hutchinson, Minnesota, a small city of 13,581, demonstrates the impact that municipal enterprise can have. Its businesses transferred more than $1.2 million to the city's general fund in 2002—amounting to 12.8 percent of the city's $9.4 million in income for the year. One business is the city hospital with 600 employees. In 2001 the hospital bought the adjacent shopping center with a plan to convert it into health-related businesses. Hutchinson also has a recycling business that collects organic material for its Creek Side Soils brand of compost and colored mulches (sold to golf courses, individuals, and retailers). The city has an electric plant on the Crow River that generates power for residents and for sale to other cities. The city also owns a liquor store, the local cemetery, and an airport. Gary Plotz, city administrator for the past 26 years, acknowledges "the incongruity of a city owning and operating many services in an area of predominately Republican voters," but says, "the appeal of low costs and reliable service may blunt philosophical objections."[202]

Not all municipal enterprises make money and, indeed, in many cases, are not intended to do so. For instance, transit systems almost always lose money and most municipalities purposefully subsidize parks and recreation to reduce the exclusionary aspects of user fees. But some types of municipal enterprises make considerable contributions to municipal finance, as seen in the table below:[203]

	Net Revenue Transfers, Minnesota		
	1998	2002	Increase
Public Utilities	56,075,204	85,039,262	51.7%
Environmental	2,105,432	7,196,283	241.8%
Public Safety	225,190	573,062	154.5%
Liquor Stores	11,454,318	14,067,766	22.8%

As the Minnesota data shows, public utilities especially can be a significant source of municipal income. Nationwide, there were 2,007 publicly owned electric companies, which had total sales revenue of $39.5 billion in 2002. Public power exists in 49 states—every state except Hawaii—and provides electricity to 43 million people. On average, public power costs about 10 percent less than electricity provided by private companies. According to an American Public Power Association (APPA) study of 573 public utilities, the median net revenue transfer to municipalities was 5.8 percent of revenues. By contrast, the median tax payment of investor-owned utilities was 18 percent less or 4.9 percent of gross revenues. This means that public power contributes close to $2.3 billion a year to their public owners or approximately $350 million a year more than those same localities would likely receive in taxes if they had investor-owned utilities instead.[204]

While many public utilities exist in small rural communities, millions of municipal utility customers live in urban areas. Many urban areas, including Los Angeles, Long Island (New York), Sacramento, Jacksonville, Orlando, Nashville, Memphis, San Antonio, Austin, and Cleveland have public power systems, some of which are quite large. Los Angeles' Department of Water Power (DWP), for instance, is of an entirely different scale of municipal enterprise from that of Hutchinson, Minnesota. As of 2003, the DWP had over 8,000 employees, $2.1 billion in annual revenues, and more than a million customer households. The DWP has a checkered past. In the early 1900s, it was well known for involvement in corrupt land and water dealings, made famous by the 1974 award-winning film *Chinatown*. But its more recent history illustrates a much more positive record. For instance, when electricity shortages hit California in 2001, the DWP's ownership of power facilities ensured that its customers did not suffer rolling blackouts, while California's investor-owned utility customers did. As a result, DWP customers enjoyed both lower prices and much better service. Indeed, in 2002 and 2003, the DWP won awards for providing the best electrical service to mid-level business customers in the entire western United States.[205]

Public utilities' primary line of business, naturally, is power generation, transmission and/or distribution, but they are also increasingly investing in telecommunications, including cable television, broadband (high-speed internet) services, local and long distance telephone service, fiber leasing, and data transmission. According to a study by Kent Lassman and Randolph May of the libertarian Progress and Freedom Foundation, from 2001 to 2003 the number of public utilities offering telecommunication services increased by 54 percent from 230 to 357. As the map in Figure 12 indicates, publicly owned telecommunications services can be found in most U.S. states. Regional concentrations are primarily found in the Midwest, the South, and the West Coast.[206]

Figure 12: Municipal Enterprise Public Telecom service providers, 2003

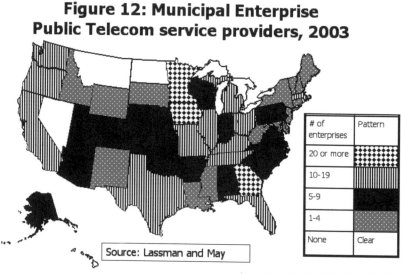

# of enterprises	Pattern
20 or more	
10-19	
5-9	
1-4	
None	Clear

Source: Lassman and May

Note: DC is included with Maryland.

One early innovator was Glasgow, Kentucky, whose public utility started construction of a telecommunications network in 1988. The Glasgow Electric Plant Board (EPB) says, "A conservative estimate of the money the EPB has saved its customers is over $30 million" since 1988. Another benefit for Glasgow residents has been top-rate broadband service, which has helped attract new businesses such as Johnson Controls and International Paper to the city.[207]

Some critics suggest that public ownership of telecommunications is financial folly. Although Glasgow in 2002-03 showed a modest surplus in both its Cable TV division and its LAN (local area network)-telephone division, a 2004 article by Thomas Leonard of the libertarian Progress and Freedom Foundation approvingly cites a 1997 study that judges that Glasgow "would likely involve permanent subsidies" and contends that "municipal governments that are using their taxpayers' money to enter the telecom business are not investing their money wisely."[208]

Are the critics right? Undoubtedly, broadband service is a long-term investment without a quick return, yet the continued growth of the municipal sector casts doubt on critics' claims. Even if the cities investing in broadband were suffering large losses, one might expect those cities to continue their projects because of sunk capital costs. But in such a situation, it seems unlikely that hundreds of other cities would follow their lead or that private firms would feel threatened enough to press for legislation to ban further municipal entry into telecommunications.[209]

Jim Baller, a municipal utilities lawyer, says part of the confusion stems from the fact that municipal enterprises have different ends and time horizons than for-profit firms. The goal, Baller says, is not simply "to produce a profit, but ... [to] develop an asset that encourages businesses to come into the community and create jobs and tax revenue ... under the criteria of a public works project, many of these projects are extremely successful." For instance, a January 2004 APPA study found that a public utility's broadband network in Barbourville, Kentucky helped land that city a U.S. Immigration and Naturalization Service call center in 1999, bringing the city 300 new jobs, and that Cedar Falls, Iowa's public broadband network helped to attract a Target distribution center, bringing 1,100 new local jobs.[210]

An October 2003 paper authored by Doris Kelley of the Iowa Association of Municipal Utilities did a paired comparison of Cedar Falls, which has a municipal company providing broadband versus neighboring Waterloo, which relied on private providers. Her main finding: "Since 1996, several companies have relocated from Waterloo or expanded to the Cedar Falls Industrial and Technology Parks .... In the same time frame, Cedar Falls has not lost a business to relocation." Kelley also quotes Waterloo Mayor John Roof as saying, "I believe it has hurt us economically to not be able to provide fiber optics to business-es locating in our city." [211]

Municipal utilities' entry into telecommunications is only continu-ing to grow. For example, in July 2004, Provo, Utah, decided to develop a city-owned communications network. Provo's power company will be among the nation's first municipal utilities to own the fiber-to-the-home infrastructure. It then plans to lease capacity to different service providers, much as a shopping center owner leases commercial space to vendors. Provo's plan follows a similar effort started in March 2001 by the Grant County Public Utility District in Washington State, which resulted in a 42 percent participation rate of residents and business in three years. [212]

In addition to telecommunications, another growing area of munic-ipal enterprise activity is in environmental businesses, such as projects that recover and sell landfill gas to generate energy. The methane recov-ery operation in Riverview, Michigan (southeast of Detroit), illustrates the trend. In the mid-1980s, Riverview contracted with DTE Energy to build a gas recovery facility at its Riverview Land Preserve. The plant now generates 40,000-megawatt hours of electricity a year, enough to meet the energy needs of over 3,700 households. Riverview's royalties covered its start-up costs after two years of operations and now con-tribute to the city's cash flows. [213]

In Glendale, California, Glendale Water and Power estimates that "methane gas from local landfills is used as a fuel source for approxi-mately 6 to 8 percent of our locally produced electricity." Other cities operating landfill gas recovery projects include Phoenix, Los Angeles, Omaha, and Orlando. In Minnesota, net revenue transfers from envi-ronmental enterprises to city general funds more than tripled in four years—from $2.1 million in 1998 to $7.2 million in 2002. A 2004 study by the Energy Information Administration indicates that the number of landfill gas recovery projects operating nationwide has increased from 14 in 1994 to 390 by 2002. [214]

Municipalities also earn significant income through business invest-ment activity in real estate. The city of San Marcos, California—a 55,000-person suburb about 45 minutes north of San Diego—supports city services through real estate leasing revenues. Since 1994, the city has developed a shopping center, which it leases to private businesses. It also leases out other land, restaurant storefronts, and office buildings. The city even rents out the surplus space in its City Hall building. Leasing brings San Marcos $2.4 million in annual revenue, making it the city's third leading revenue source—after sales tax and car taxes. The city of San Diego itself leases out 700 properties, including valuable real estate at Mission Bay and Sea World, which were expected to generate $54.7 million in Fiscal-Year 2004 and to contribute $31.4 million to the city's general fund, an amount equivalent to 4.2 percent of all general fund revenues. Other cities and local government districts with sizeable real estate holdings include Portland, Maine; Alhambra, California; Fairfield, California; Cincinnati, Ohio; San Antonio, Texas; Louisville, Kentucky; Hartford, Connecticut; Boston; and the Port of Los Angeles.[215]

Many cities focus their real estate investments to encourage greater use of mass transit—a strategy better known as "transit-oriented development" or most often, simply "TOD." The idea behind TOD is to build greater densities near rail stations and major bus lines in order to encourage transit use and reduce traffic congestion and pollution. Of course, to the extent the development succeeds, real estate around the station can become very valuable, with the city or transit system earning a return as a result. Cities that make use of transit-oriented development include San Francisco, Portland, Dallas, Atlanta, Boston, St. Louis, and Washington, D.C.[216]

While "TOD" is a relatively new term, organizing development around transit nodes is a very old concept and was the norm in U.S. cities before World War II. Ironically, modern-day transit-oriented development is a product of the automobile. Because cities such as San Francisco and Washington built transit systems after World War II and needed to transport commuters from the suburbs, they acquired considerable land around transit stops to provide for surface parking lots. As Elisa Hill of the Washington Metropolitan Area Transit Authority (WMATA) explains, "When we started, we got larger plots. In many areas, they wouldn't subdivide, so it was all or nothing. It turned out to be a good investment. [At one station] in Greenbelt, we got 78 acres plus a huge yard." Even as early as the 1970s, entrepreneurial transit officials realized that if surface lots were replaced with stacked parking, the surplus land could be used for high-density residential and commercial development, increasing income to the transit system directly through land leases or sales and indirectly through increased rider fare revenue.[217]

Washington D.C.'s Metro system provides the nation's leading example of transit-oriented development. Since 2002, both the District of Columbia and Prince George's County in Maryland have adopted official policy statements that emphasize TOD's importance. Even before these accelerated efforts got under way, in 2003 the Washington D.C. Metro system already was collecting over $6 million a year in lease payments. Additionally, approximately 10 percent of total ridership (roughly 90,000 daily riders) comes from the development of high-density residential and commercial projects in the vicinity of Metro stations. As Robert Grow, Director of Government Relations at the Greater Washington (D.C.) Board of Trade points out, TOD also leads to a higher tax base and reduces municipal costs, since by reducing sprawl, "you don't have to extend the public services (sewer lines, etc.) so far." Arlington County, Virginia was one of the first to fully exploit the potential of TOD, having focused real estate and commercial development in transit station areas since the mass transit system began operating in the 1970s. Located across the Potomac River, over 50 percent of the county's tax base is now concentrated in transit corridors. Office space in these areas has increased from 4.1 million square feet in 1969 to 30 million in 2003, while housing in the immediate vicinity has increased from 4,300 units to 34,000. The effect of this development on local government revenues is significant. As Robert Brosnan, Planning Director for Arlington County explains, "We have the lowest tax rate [in the region]. The tax burden is high, but the rates—we've been lowering them. We have AA bond rates. We can float bonds for schools, parks. You get a lot of service without raising taxes."[218]

In the past, money that WMATA earned from leases was simply contributed to the operating budget. Money in newer transit-oriented projects, however, is being placed in a capital improvement fund. WMATA officials hope ultimately to raise $250 million for this purpose. And Washington's transit-oriented development efforts are about to get much bigger, as WMATA begins its largest TOD project yet, the Anacostia Waterfront Initiative. If successful, the project will develop over five million square feet of office space and thousands of new housing units as part of a broad effort to revitalize the Southeast and Southwest quarters of the capital. The Anacostia site is just one of seven sites in the Washington D.C. metropolitan area on which WMATA was seeking bids in 2004.[219]

While efforts at transit-oriented development have been building over decades, city-owned convention center hotels are a more recent development. Typically, cities have provided subsidies to encourage private convention hotel construction, much as cities use economic incentives to attract other kinds of business. However, many cities have entered the hotel business because of a combination of factors, including tax law changes in 1997 that facilitated city leasing of hotels; increasing industry pressure to develop hotels to complement convention centers; and, importantly, difficulty in finding willing private investors. Typically, the city creates a special authority, which enters into a partnership with a major hotel chain such as Hyatt or Marriot. The hotel chain oversees construction and obtains a 15-year management contract from the city, while the city provides tax-free bond financing. For the hotel chain, this arrangement lowers operating costs substantially. For the city, the costs of borrowing and risks of ownership are offset, at least in theory, by increased tax and tourism revenue, as well as the value of owning the hotel itself. Although derided by some as "hotel socialism," city-owned hotels have already opened in Austin, Houston, Chicago, Omaha, Overland Park (Kansas), Sacramento, Marietta (Georgia), Oceanside (California), and Myrtle Beach (South Carolina). In a twist on the same theme, the Maryland Economic Development Corporation invested in a resort hotel in Cambridge, Maryland, on Maryland's Eastern Shore. Additional projects are anticipated. Denver and Vancouver, Washington (near Portland, Oregon) are already building what will be their city-owned convention hotels. Projects are also under consideration in San Antonio, Phoenix, and Washington.[220]

How will the finances work out? It is too soon to say; results vary by city and by hotel. Some city hotels are doing well. A July 2004 article in *The Houston Chronicle* touted a record 45 percent increase in hotel convention bookings in the first year following the opening of the city-owned downtown hotel. One study, authored by Heywood Sanders, a leading critic of public sector hotel development, finds that earnings fall well short of projections, although his article concedes that at this point we can only draw "preliminary" lessons.[221]

In another study, two writers for the *Fort-Worth Star-Telegram* found mixed results, with Sacramento generating "enough revenue in its first year of operation to cover its yearly bond debt, pay its bills and give a little money to the city," while Overland Park, Kansas was losing money.

A quick look at the two cities that have had city-owned hotels the longest—Marietta, Georgia and Oceanside, California—shows starkly divergent results. Marietta has had a number of management problems and has regularly lost money. By contrast, Oceanside has seen annual lease and tax income rise from $73,000 in 1994 to $315,000 in 2001 while the real estate value of the hotel property has soared from $1.1 million to over $15 million.[222]

As shown above, increasing local government enterprise activity can be found in both urban and rural areas—and is led by both Republican and Democratic mayors. City involvement in business, per se, is rarely the goal. Rather, whether it is developing telecommunications, creating environmental businesses, investing in real estate to support transit-oriented development, or entering into the hotel business, municipal enterprise is employed as a tool for local economic development. Not all efforts are successful. But in a surprising number of cases, municipal enterprise provides an effective means to create jobs, meet public needs, and spur investment.

Local Asset-Based
Investment Strategies:
Pensions, Loan Funds,
and Venture Capital

Many officials now believe that in some instances pension funds can be a tool for economic development ... to the extent trustees can accomplish other goals without sacrificing performance, it makes sense to investigate opportunities for 'economically targeted investments' (ETIs).

Doug Hoffer, report to the State of Vermont,
February 2004 [223]

In the past two decades, city and state governments have adopted a wide set of policy tools to spur local economic development, including creating loan funds that help start up local businesses and venture capital funds that give cities and states an equity stake in the outcome of their public investments. Increasingly, state and city governments invest billions of dollars of their pension fund holdings in economically-targeted investments that seek to build a locally owned and controlled asset base while still protecting the risk-adjusted pension return.

In the past two decades, city, county, and state governments in the U.S. have increasingly sought to invest directly in local business, either through economic development programs that make loans or investments in local businesses, or through direct targeting of pension fund investments. As with municipal enterprise, changes in state and municipal policy are driven by many factors, including difficult fiscal conditions and job instability resulting from globalizing market forces. Basic statistics regarding these investment efforts are provided in the table below:

LOCAL AND STATE GOVERNMENT INVESTMENT STRATEGIES: BASIC STATISTICS[224]	
Percent of cities surveyed investing city money in equities, 1989	20.4%
Percent of cities surveyed investing city money in equities, 1996	56.3%
Percent of cities surveyed with venture capital funds, 1989	5.4%
Percent of cities surveyed with venture capital funds, 1996	33.2%
Percent of public sector pension holdings of total pension holdings, 1998	28.4%
States that have allocated state dollars to venture and loan funds, 2000	31
States whose pension funds have investments in private equity, 2002	31
Estimated public sector pension fund holdings, 2002	$2.3 trillion
State pension funds in economically targeted investments (estimate), 2004	$43.6 billion

The strategies of local governments have shifted gradually over the past two decades. A classic 1988 study by Peter Eisinger discussed the rise of what he termed the *entrepreneurial state*, characterized by city development policies that sought to "foster new business formation, business diversification, and new industries." Such policies offered the potential to increase local capital formation and reduce the use of tax abatements and related incentive payments to attract business from other cities. A more recent study by Susan Clarke and Gary Gaile confirms this trend. As Clarke and Gaile write, "cities are rethinking traditional strategies in favor of orientations emphasizing job creation and new locally based growth." One key area where the rise of city- and state-level entrepreneurship is most notable is in their increased willingness to make equity investments. Clarke and Gaile found that 35.9 percent of cities surveyed first used direct municipal equity investments between 1989 and 1996 and that 27.8 percent of cities first developed venture capital funds during that period. By 1996, 56.3 percent of cities surveyed were using equity investments and 33.2 percent were using venture capital funds as part of their economic development strategy.[225]

State and municipal loan and venture funds provide perhaps the most common form of public investment efforts. Direct ownership in the form of municipal enterprise can sometimes generate controversy. However, state and municipal governments invest in firms and take equity positions in the projects they support with little discussion in the press. Indeed, this process has become almost mundane and commonplace. It is rare to find a city or county government that does not seek to use policy tools such as equity and loan investments to support the creation of local business, promoting local asset development in the process. Most commonly, this is done through the use of an arms-length, non-profit, largely self-supporting "economic development corporation" in which city officials provide limited financial support and partner with business and other government officials to develop local business support services.[226]

One example is the Philadelphia Industrial Development Corporation (PIDC), whose board is mutually appointed by the Mayor and the local Chamber of Commerce president. The PIDC administers the Pennsylvania Industrial Development Authority loan program for the City of Philadelphia. Through this loan program, the PIDC can lend up to 50 percent of second mortgage costs to finance "owner-user, labor-intensive warehouse, distribution and manufacturing firms located, or planning to locate, in Philadelphia. In 2002, the PIDC estimates that the 142 loans it made helped retain or create 7,000 jobs."[227]

The Tri-County Economic Development Corporation of Butte, Glenn, and Tehama Counties of Northern California, which manages a total of seven loan funds, provides an example of similar activity in a rural region. Between 1988 and 2000, the Tri-County EDC made loans totaling $7.6 million, leveraging $44 million in private funds, and creating over 1,100 jobs.[228] Another example comes from the Northeast Council of Governments of Aberdeen, South Dakota, which created a revolving loan fund in 1989. By 2004, the group had originated over 100 business loans ranging in value from $5,000 to $250,000, with a fund balance of $2.3 million.[229]

In addition to loans, economic development corporations often make equity investments in the firms they assist. For instance, the Development Corporation of Austin, Minnesota, in which the City of Austin participates as a sustaining member, considers "investments as low as $5,000 and as high as $500,000" in local companies, with the majority of investments falling within the $50,000-$200,000 range.[230] In New York City, the Queens County Overall Economic Development Corporation, a partnership between the state, city, borough, and local business sector, operates the Prospect Street Discovery Fund, which makes equity investments in the amount of $1 to $9 million in local firms in many industries including "interactive media, medical devices, telecommunications, biotechnology, robotics and computer-related products."[231]

A recent trend has been the creation of local venture funds that invest from $500,000 to $2 million, a range typically too large for individual investors to fill yet too small to interest traditional venture funds. Cities that have pursued this option include Worthington, Minnesota; Whitefish, Montana; Las Cruces, New Mexico; Shreveport, Louisiana; Fairfield, Iowa; Tulsa, Oklahoma; Greenville, South Carolina; Morgantown, West Virginia; and Portland, Maine.[232]

Another important policy change has been the increasingly active targeting of state and local pension fund monies, something that a decade ago would likely have prompted much greater opposition both on grounds of risk and of inappropriate government "picking of winners and losers." Edward A. H. Siedle, a former staff member of the Securities & Exchange Commission, underlines the degree of the shift. "This is an entirely new development," Siedle said. "In the early 1990s, some states did not even let their pension funds invest in publicly traded stocks, much less private equities." Yet by the end of the 1990s, a 2000 National Governors' Association study identified 31 states that allocated state funds to promote increased access to capital and 19 that invested pension funds in private equity.

Two years later, a *Pensions and Investments* industry survey found 31 state pension funds had investments totaling $12.15 billion in venture capital. If anything, the numbers have since increased. For instance, in February 2004, Oregon announced the creation of a $100 million state venture fund and Vermont released a study that supported increased state use of economically targeted pension investments. In April 2004, Florida's Republican Governor Jeb Bush announced that Florida's state employee retirement fund would invest up to $1 billion of its $102 billion employee pension fund in the next three to five years in venture capital to entice biotechnology firms to the state. In justifying his policy, Bush gave a classic exposition of the need to anchor capital locally: "What breaks my heart is when a talented entrepreneur is trying to find financing and is told he's got to go Austin, Texas, or St. Louis, Missouri, or San Francisco to find it."[233]

Although many state venture fund investments are too new to be fairly evaluated, the evidence so far is favorable in terms of community impact. As with private venture capital, returns vary. An example of this volatility is the Texas Growth Fund, whose first installment upon cashing out had a 21 percent return and placed in the top quartile of all venture funds, while the second installment lost 15 percent and finished in the lowest quartile. Other funds have had more consistently favorable results. For instance, CVM Equity of Colorado, which has invested $15 million to date, has made rural investments that have helped create 350 jobs and developed eight new private companies, and has had its first two funds close in the top quartile of venture funds. The Oklahoma Capital Investment Board invested $26 million between 1993 and 1996 in 12 companies. According to a National Governors' association study by Robert Heard and John Sibert, these investments earned a rate of return of 29 percent while "helping to create an environment in the state that is conducive to high-tech entrepreneurship."[234]

Why has this change in public investment activity occurred? Partly it stems from the need to create jobs and build community economic stability in a global economy. It is also a response to tighter fiscal conditions. As Hoffer's Vermont report indicates, "Geographically targeted investments in venture capital, small business loans, and affordable housing improve the tax base that supports both the employment and the pension security of public employee participants and beneficiaries."[235] And, of course, to the extent their local investment and asset-building efforts succeed, the state also enjoys greater tax revenues.

Another factor that has played an important role in encouraging state and municipal pension funds to engage in more targeted investment activity has been union interest in the job creation aspects of economically targeted investments. According to a 1998 study, total pension fund holdings in the United States are $7.4 trillion dollars, of which $2.1 trillion are held in public funds.[236] By 2002, public pension funds' value had climbed to $2.3 trillion, despite a volatile stock market.[237] Because the pensions represent a good portion of public employees' retirement savings, worker representatives often serve as trustees on the pension fund boards. For instance, Sean Harrigan, a vice president of the United Food and Commercial Workers served, until the fall of 2004, as president of the CalPERS Board of Administration in California.[238]

Until the early 1990s, labor rarely used its pension clout.[239] One reason, according to Robert Pleasure, former Executive Director of the AFL-CIO Center for Working Capital, was that many unions had adopted the position that, "Pensions are the bosses' business. We don't want to know how, as long as we get our pension." When labor union leaders began to take a more active stance they encountered resistance, from some who argued that pension legislation, especially in the private sector, greatly limits pension trustee discretion; ERISA (Employment Retirement and Economic Security Act) pension rules mandate, as Pleasure puts it, that trustees seek the greatest "risk-adjusted rate of return," as well as providing more general protections to support the interests of pension plan beneficiaries. Although ERISA does not directly apply to the public sector, many states have enacted similar, albeit generally less restrictive, legislation.[240]

Still, within the restrictions, pension plan trustees retain considerable flexibility. In 1994, the U.S. Department of Labor issued an interpretive bulletin that economically targeted investments are permissible under ERISA, provided they are not expected to result in "a lower rate of return than available alternative investments with commensurate degrees of risk or [are] riskier than alternative investments with commensurate rates of return."[241]

In 1991, the AFL-CIO Executive Committee took the position of urging union trustees to advance such goals as the "promotion of local economic development," by directing a greater percentage of state and local pension funds to equity investments that support businesses within their regions. Increasingly, union trustees have sought to better leverage their pension investments to achieve multiple aims, including job creation and affordable housing construction.[242]

Billions of dollars are at stake. A January 2004 study by the state of Maryland found that 38 states invested a total of 4.7 percent of their assets—or $51.86 billion—in private equity, a form of capital where the fund can have more influence and greater flexibility in targeting investments.[243] In California, CalPERS trustees—and trustees of the California teachers' pension fund—have further pledged to invest 2 percent of their assets in poor and underserved areas in the state, a combined fund commitment of $5 billion. Other states and cities with high levels of economically targeted investments include Massachusetts, New York City, and Wisconsin. Massachusetts invests $1.5 billion in its Alternative Investments Portfolio. New York City has $920 million in targeted investments, including $200 million in affordable housing. Wisconsin targets 10 percent of its $56.8 billion pension fund into real estate and private equity.[244]

Economically targeted investment estimates vary. The last comprehensive survey, conducted by the U.S. General Accounting Office in 1993, found that pension funds in 29 states had $19.8 billion in targeted investments, or roughly 2.4 percent of total assets. Today, conservatively estimated, economically targeted investments have more than doubled to $43.6 billion.[245]

In short, increases in city and state promotion of local asset building are readily apparent—both through economic development agency loans or equity investments and pension fund investments. Such efforts are driven by many factors, including the desire to promote local economy stability in a fluctuating global economy, greater union interest in using public pension leverage for job creation purposes, and desire by state officials to more effectively leverage existing assets within tight fiscal constraints. As cities and states continue to seek to bolster local tax bases and find viable niches in the global economy, these efforts will in all likelihood continue to grow.

International Asset-Based and Cross-Sectoral Strategies

A diverse array of significant scale, community-building economic entities flourishes throughout Asia,
Africa, Europe and the Americas....The most innovative among them are locally-anchored activities that
produce jobs and promote equity while structurally
embedding or rooting economic assets ... in institutions that are accountable to the community.

Aziza Agia[246]

The international asset-based and cross-sectoral strategies reviewed
here provide illustrative models that suggest possibilities for future efforts
in the United States. In Bangladesh, the Grameen bank has shown how a
micro-enterprise loan fund can meet the financing needs of millions of
people. In Great Britain, Japan, and Canada, effective models of multi-
divisional consumer cooperatives with hundreds of thousands or even mil-
lions of members have been developed. Both Spain and Italy have exten-
sive worker cooperative networks that link smaller worker cooperatives
together, with Spain's Mondragón network having over 34,000 worker-
owners. China's town and village enterprises—which have been a central
component of China's economic growth model—illustrate the wide variety
of potential uses for municipal enterprise.

Although our focus in this report is on wealth building in the United
States, the forces driving these asset-based efforts—most notably, economic globalization and growing fiscal constraints on government—
are not unique to America. It should therefore not be surprising that
the emergence of these strategies is not unique to the United States
either. Indeed, while the growth of U.S. asset-based strategies over the
past three decades is impressive, international achievements are in
some instances even more far-reaching. A 2004 report of The
Democracy Collaborative and The National Center for Economic and
Security Alternatives outlines some of the key developments, which
have potential implications for future wealth-building efforts here.

Particularly notable are growing efforts under way in connection with consumer cooperatives, worker ownership, municipal enterprise, and community development finance.[247]

Each of these areas is reviewed in turn. The table below provides some basic statistics:

INTERNATIONAL, CROSS-SECTORAL ASSET-BUILDING EXAMPLES: BASIC STATISTICS[248]	
Total sales, The Cooperative Group consumer co-op, Great Britain, 2002	$13 billion
Total sales, Co-op Atlantic, Canada, 2002	$500 million
Membership, Co-op Kobe, Japan, 2002	1.45 million
Total sales, Mondragón worker cooperative network, Spain, 2003	$10 billion
Membership, Italian worker cooperatives, Italy, 2002	342,000
Employment in town and village enterprises, China, 1996	135 million
Number of clients served at Grameen Bank since its founding in 1976	3.36 million
Total Grameen bank loans disbursed since founding	$4.27 billion

Consumer cooperatives are one of the most widely used asset-based strategies internationally with more than 100 million members worldwide.[249] Three countries with particularly large consumer co-op sectors are Great Britain (which is also the birthplace of the modern cooperative movement), Canada, and Japan. Great Britain is home to the world's largest single cooperative, The Co-operative Group, which runs a broad range of member-owned enterprises and employs over 75,000 people. Financial figures in 2003 showed annual sales of over £8 billion (at press time, $14 billion) and consolidated operating profits of £327 million. The Co-operative Group operates over 1,700 food stores, 300 pharmacies, 39 department stores, 27 auto dealerships, Britain's largest funeral home company, Britain's largest travel agency, a company providing banking and insurance for over six million people, a property management firm, an engineering firm, and a dairy products company.[250]

Canada's eastern provinces have a much smaller population base, but Co-op Atlantic, a federation of independent cooperatives, has a significant presence, as it employs 600 directly while member cooperatives employ over 5,000. The co-op federation and its members sell a variety of products including food items, hardware, petroleum, building supplies, and agricultural equipment. Sales in 2002 exceeded $500 million.[251]

Japan's Co-op Kobe has over 1.45 million members and operates a wide variety of businesses, including medical, insurance, housing, university, student, teacher, workplace, and neighborhood cooperatives. As of 1996, it employed nearly 16,000 people and operated 175 retail stores and dozens of other facilities, including three resort villages. When the Kobe region suffered an earthquake in 1995 that killed more than 6,000 people, the cooperative was credited with playing a leading role in reconstruction at the same time that the government was being criticized for its relatively slow response.[252]

One notable difference between international efforts and consumer cooperatives in the United States is the prominence of large, multi-divisional structures, which have allowed cooperatives to extend member control over a considerable asset base in the face of corporate competition. In Britain, hundreds of previously independent cooperatives merged to form The Cooperative Group over the last half century. In Atlantic, Canada, 28 cooperatives merged in 2000 to form the 45,000-member Consumer's Co-operative retail food co-op to more effectively compete against corporate chain markets. The merger has been effective, as membership increased by 6,000 to 51,000 within the following two years. To some extent, there are signs that cooperatives in the United States are beginning to be willing to give up some autonomy in exchange for greater effectiveness. This trend is evident in the formation in 2004 of a national retail food cooperative trade association, the effort to create a joint retail food co-op brand, and the five-fold increase in purchasing cooperatives from 1996 to 2001.[253]

Employee ownership is another area where international efforts are prominent. Internationally, the most common form of worker ownership is not the ESOP; it is the worker cooperative. Spain and Italy provide two leading examples.

In Spain, the Mondragón system of cooperatives has over 34,000 worker-owners, annual sales in excess of $10 billion (9 billion Euros), and total assets of over $16 billion, making the Mondragón federation the largest single company in the Basque region and Spain's seventh largest business enterprise. The Mondragón federation is divided into a number of different industrial groups, many of which lead their sectors. For instance, the Mondragón cooperatives are Spain's leading producer of domestic appliances and machine tools; the Mondragón supermarket chain (Eroski) is Spain's largest domestically owned retail food distributor; and Mondragón firms are Europe's third leading supplier of automotive parts. Mondragón also controls an extensive system of credit unions—the Caja Laboral Popular—providing critically important financing for its enterprises.[254]

The Italian network of worker cooperatives is even larger: 342,000 people are worker-owners of cooperatives. The cooperatives are major players in a number of industries. For instance, Italy produces three-quarters of the world's brand-name eyeglasses, a large percentage of which are produced by worker cooperatives. Nationwide, the cooperative activity accounts for about 10 percent of GDP. In Italy's fastest growing industrial region, Emilia-Romagna, cooperative activity is twice this level.[255]

Cooperatives have had considerable success in transforming formerly depressed economic regions such as the Basque Country and Emilia-Romagna into their nations' leading industrial regions. The Italian cooperatives' efforts are exemplary in this regard. Emerging from a deep recession in the 1970s, by 2000 Emilia-Romagna had Italy's highest per capita income and ranked 10th out of 122 regions in the European Union. As of 2002, its unemployment rate was 3.3 percent, one of the lowest in the European Union.[256]

European worker cooperatives are structured quite differently than U.S. worker co-ops. In some respects, they resemble U.S. employee stock ownership plan companies. For instance, Mondragón mixes democratic accountability with the acceptance of broad managerial discretion that might be anathema to many American worker cooperatives. Mondragón cooperative committees conduct performance reviews of managers and can hire and fire managers, but they do not have the authority to question individual managerial decisions. One of the primary motives for revisions of the Mondragón Cooperative Corporation's corporate structure in 1986 was to facilitate alliances with non-cooperative entities in order to improve competitive efficiency. Many Italian worker cooperatives also participate in a federative structure, known as La Lega, which, like Mondragón, links member cooperatives through interlocking directorships and financing arrangements. These mechanisms allow worker cooperatives in Spain and Italy to act at a scale that within the world of worker ownership only ESOPs have been capable of in the United States. At the same time, unlike most ESOPs in the United States, Mondragón and La Lega cooperatives have maintained the central elements of cooperation, including workplace committees and worker-elected boards.[257]

Chinese town and village enterprises provide an international practice that suggests other possibilities that municipal government might explore. In China, town and village enterprises are widely credited as primary agents for the rapid economic growth China has experienced since adopting a more market-based approach in 1978. As of 1996, these enterprises were responsible for one-third of Chinese gross domestic product. Town and village enterprises primarily exist in small cities that dot the Chinese countryside. They tend to be structured as labor-intensive industrial enterprises that operate in a wide variety of industries, including coal mining, canned goods, radios, telephones, electric fans, clothing, and construction materials (such as gravel, wood, and polished granite). The size of these enterprises tends to be fairly small—as of 1996, the average village enterprise employed 26, while the average township enterprise employed 73. From 1980 to 1996, the number of these enterprises increased from 1.4 million to 23.4 million, with total sector employment reaching 135 million. As of 1995, they provided 21 percent of total employment. By 1997, they were responsible for 46.2 percent of China's total exports.[258]

Scholars have noted that key factors of town and village enterprises' success have been hard budget constraints (i.e., local governments, unlike national governments, do not have the ability to manipulate prices or credit) and their ability to respond flexibly to changes in market demand due to their small scale. These enterprises are not without drawbacks, however, one of which is limited access to outside capital (forcing them to rely on reinvestment of earnings). Since 1997, the need for external capital has led to government efforts to convert many town and village enterprises into either cooperatives or private enterprises, but they remain major players in the Chinese economy.[259]

One obvious difference between town and village enterprises in China and municipal enterprise in the United States is that the Chinese economy had many more instances of market failure requiring municipal intervention than the American economy does. Nonetheless, the Chinese experience does illustrate the potential for municipalities to operate in non-traditional markets. There are also some broad areas of similarities. For instance, U.S. municipal enterprises share with their Chinese town and village enterprise counterparts the strengths of flexibility and the need to successfully compete in the marketplace. Of course, like their Chinese counterparts, U.S. municipal enterprises run the risk of corruption (although American municipal enterprises have not had corruption on the scale of corporate scandals such as those at Enron or World Com). In terms of financing, American municipal enterprises benefit from their ready access to tax-free municipal bonds, which provide low-interest bond financing; however, like their Chinese counterparts, American municipal enterprises do need to rely primarily on internal earnings for equity.

Community development finance, especially with micro-enterprise development, provides one further example of significant international asset-based efforts. The well-known Grameen Bank of Bangladesh, in particular, has become a highly influential model that has been emulated by microenterprise loan funds throughout the world. For instance, Acción USA, which follows an adapted form of the Grameen model of small scale lending, has seen its activity expand from 998 loans worth $3.5 million in 1997 to 3,795 loans worth $18.4 million in 2002.[260]

The Grameen network works on the basis of four key principles: group-based lending (where group members guarantee each other's loans, thus serving as a peer enforcement mechanism), community outreach, a focus on lending to women, and a weekly repayment schedule—this last feature enables fund managers to spot and address problems quickly and helps break up what would otherwise be larger monthly payments for borrowers. The Grameen is structured as a cooperative bank, with borrowers owning 93 percent of the shares and the government the remaining 7 percent. Between its founding in 1976 and 2004, Grameen has disbursed over $4 billion in loans to over three million clients (95 percent of whom are women) with a repayment rate of 97 percent. Grameen has also sponsored businesses in a number of industries including fisheries, agriculture, renewable energy, and even cellular and Internet services.[261]

In sum, the preliminary work done on international activity suggests that there are many areas of parallel development emerging abroad. Further research is likely to suggest possibilities for further global development and yield insights on the application of asset-based strategies in the United States.

Conclusion

This study, as we have noted, is the first attempt to comprehensively examine the development of new asset-based approaches and their strategic interaction. The approaches are united by their emphasis on building wealth as a way to work toward solving social and economic problems. In diverse ways, these strategies provide income, savings, direct services, and jobs; by building the tax base, they indirectly support public services. And because they move beyond strictly economic activity to include cultural, educational and other activities, these strategies cross and blur common sectoral lines of demarcation.

We began this work with a discussion of the scope and proliferation of new organizational forms that use wealth-building approaches to help achieve important public purposes. It is worth briefly reviewing these developments: Forty years ago there were fewer than 200 employee-owned companies in the United States and only a smattering of community development credit unions. The community development finance industry did not yet exist. There were few community development corporations and no significant community land trusts. State public pension funds did not employ economically targeted investments. The notions of "social enterprise," "individual development accounts," and "enterprising government" had not yet been invented.

Today over eight million employees go to work at roughly 10,000 businesses where they own all or part of the company through employee stock option plans. In 2002, these plans reached a value of $297 billion. There are now over 4,000 community development corporations. The 1999 industry census reported that CDCs regularly developed 37,500 units of affordable housing and 12 million square feet of commercial real estate a year—numbers certain to be adjusted upward when the 2005 survey results become available. As of 2002, roughly 700 community development financial institutions were managing more than $14 billion worth of assets. In 2002 alone their efforts provided financing for new or renovated affordable housing for over 34,500 housing units and helped local micro-enterprises create or maintain over 34,000 jobs. More than half of states now allocate a portion of their pension funds to economically targeted investments totaling an estimated $43.6 billion.

There have also been other areas of growth. Although the sector is still small, today over 100 community land trusts provide permanently affordable housing for more than 6,000 families, a tripling of the level of only a dozen years before. Individual Development Account programs now number roughly 500 nationwide with a total of more than 20,000 participants. A census of social enterprises has not yet been undertaken, but trade association member figures indicate that active social enterprises already minimally number several hundred, with a combined business volume in excess of $500 million. The cooperative sector, which has a much older pedigree, has also increased in size. The top 100 cooperatives on the National Cooperative Bank's annual survey generated $117 billion in revenues as of 2003. Recent years have been marked by rapid growth in purchasing, food, and worker cooperatives.

The influence of the asset approach is evident in the policies and approaches adopted by federal, state, and local governments that encourage various forms of wealth-building. At the federal level, ESOPs now receive indirect tax support estimated at roughly $2 billion a year. The level of support the federal government has provided to community development corporations through housing allocations and tax credits is estimated to be $3.94 billion in Fiscal-Year 2005. The average of just under $100 million a year provided to community development financial institutions through the CDFI Fund has been limited but significant. The federal government's American Dream Demonstration pilot program has given an important boost to individual development account (IDA) advocates. Although the support level—at $25 million a year—is modest, this program may well set a precedent for subsequent expansion of asset support programs for low-income individuals, as has been proposed by President Bush, former Senator Edwards, and others.[262]

Changes at the state level have been even more far reaching. Traditionally concerned with narrowly conceived returns, public pension managers and trustees have increasingly adopted a more nuanced approach. The new approach continues to seek maximum returns, but allows both for investments in private equity placements where pension funds can have a greater direct say in governance issues, and for the economic targeting of a portion of investments. Today a majority of state governments funnel billions in pension fund and other investments to support economic development. California state pension funds alone have shifted $5 billion in this direction.

At the local level, municipalities and other local government districts (such as public transit authorities) have used a variety of asset-building approaches to expand their tax base and promote local economic development. Municipal enterprise has been extended into new areas such as broadband service provision and convention hotel ownership. Participatory leasing arrangements provide cities with a real estate income stream. Transit-oriented development projects generate revenue for localities and ridership to support public transportation systems. Cities, counties, and states have also increasingly used loan funds, venture capital funds, and business incubators to develop the local tax base while providing local jobs and promoting greater community economic stability.

The precise scope of the various asset-based efforts, taken together, is difficult to estimate; reliable data do not exist in a number of areas. There is no doubt, however, as to the growing significance of the various efforts. The graphs in Figure 13 highlight just a few of the changes:

Figure 13: Growth of the Asset-Based Model

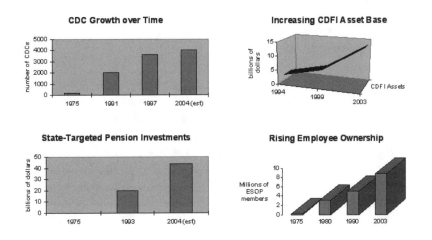

The growth has also been significant in terms of the value of holdings that constitute the emerging asset-based economy. In 1960 the sum of the assets of all credit unions, community development financial institutions, ESOPs, and economically targeted investments by state pension funds was roughly $6 billion. Even if one included cooperatives and the limited stock holdings of workers through stock purchase plans at the time, the total would likely have remained well under $100 billion. As of 2004 the total assets of these sectors exceeds $1.5 trillion, a sum that is more than 10 percent of the annual gross domestic product and equal to nearly 4 percent of the $37.8 trillion in total U.S. financial and stock assets.[263]

We have noted two factors that help explain the emergence of the new wealth-building approaches. One is increasing political resistance to raising taxes. Fiscal constraints and the absence of sufficient tax revenues to meet the demand for services have forced governments and nonprofits alike to become more creative in using investment income to produce revenues and support services. A second factor is the rise of a more integrated global economy—one in which capital is more footloose and can move fleetingly across international borders. In such an economy, investing in businesses that are anchored to the local communities where they operate becomes ever more important to maintain jobs and sustain a tax base capable of supporting important social services.

The growth of the various asset-based strategies is substantial, but their development also raises many questions. For our purposes, the most important of these involve overall impact, cross-sectoral cooperation, and the general policy implications of the approach.

Clearly, relative to the size of the national economy, these efforts, while growing, remain only modest first steps in a possible new direction. On the other hand, there are other important tests of current and potential impact—particularly when considered from the vantage point of possible contribution to more expansive future policies. One key test is: *do they make a difference in the communities where they are employed?* Here the answer is emphatic and affirmative. Not every asset-based initiative can, does, or will succeed, but what has been accomplished to date is significant. One obvious example discussed at length in the report illustrates the possibilities: the New Community Corporation has played a major role in helping spur the revitalization of Newark. It houses over 7,000 people, and its enterprises employ 1,600 neighborhood residents and generate over $50 million in economic activity. Many CDCs, including New Community, began work after their cities or neighborhoods were devastated by riots in places where few others dared to tread. Nationally, there is little doubt that CDCs have contributed to the revival of many urban and rural communities.

Similar positive economic development effects have been demonstrated by other asset-based approaches. In St. Cloud, Minnesota, the purchase of a closed-down factory by an ESOP in 1992 resulted in 280 jobs for that community and 280 new employee-owners; nine years after the purchase, their shares were worth $8 million or nearly $30,000 per person. In San Francisco the three social-purpose businesses of Golden Gate Community Inc. and the other dozen or so businesses supported by REDF (formerly, the Roberts Enterprise Development Fund) were able to employ over 1,600 people over four years, with 70 percent either employed elsewhere or still employed at an REDF business more than two years after their initial hire. In Chicago the activity of ShoreBank, now the nation's leading community development bank, has greatly contributed to neighborhood revival through the creation of a community development lending community in that city, in which mainstream banks, as well as ShoreBank, now participate.[264]

One can cite similar examples for cooperatives, community land trusts, municipal enterprises, state and local venture funds, and targeted state pension fund investments. What is important and unique about such asset-based strategies is that they are able, at least partially, to fund themselves. And, in the case of ESOPs, municipal enterprises, and cooperatives, their social benefits—including anchoring jobs in communities and improving the local tax base upon which public services depend—rest on the success of their self-financed, regular business activities.

A critical challenge for practitioners and outside groups and foundations is how to develop greater linkages across sectors in a manner that can broaden and deepen the overall impact and support base of the various strategies. Ideally, an integrated wealth-building approach would encompass mutually reinforcing government, community, and individual wealth-building efforts. It might include direct government asset-based efforts that promote local job stability (such as local investment policies and municipal enterprise), matched savings programs, and community-based wealth-building efforts. Each of these strategies can have a positive impact on community development on its own; in combination the potential for anchoring jobs and promoting community development could be greatly enhanced.

Figure 14: An Integrated Wealth-Building Approach

Key Components

Putting the Pieces Together

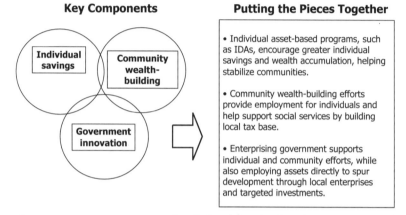

- Individual asset-based programs, such as IDAs, encourage greater individual savings and wealth accumulation, helping stabilize communities.

- Community wealth-building efforts provide employment for individuals and help support social services by building local tax base.

- Enterprising government supports individual and community efforts, while also employing assets directly to spur development through local enterprises and targeted investments.

In some areas, cross-sectoral collaboration is already common as, for instance, between CDCs and CDFIs, which share both common roots (the civil rights movement) and a common focus on community economic development. Some organizations, such as The Reinvestment Fund of Philadelphia and Coastal Enterprises of Portland, Maine, actually combine financing (CDFI) and development (CDC) work in-house.[265]

In a number of other areas, different asset-based approaches have also worked in a coordinated manner for mutual benefit. For instance, as its name suggests, the Northcountry Cooperative Development Fund provides financing to cooperatives. Many CDCs administer IDA and micro-enterprise programs on behalf of their communities. Economically targeted investments by state pension funds have also worked in several areas to support the activities of community development groups. In December 2003 New York City Comptroller William Thompson announced that the City would set aside $12.5 million from the teachers' pension fund and another $12.5 million from the general city employees' pension fund to invest in a revolving loan fund to support affordable housing—much of which will almost certainly end up supporting CDC projects.

The National Cooperative Bank Development Corporation (NCBDC) provides another example. As of December 2003, NCBDC had $70 million in loans invested in a variety of activities, including affordable housing (both cooperative and CDC-developed), food cooperatives, health care, and community development. NCBDC has also entered into a partnership agreement with Local Initiatives Support Corporation (LISC) to develop affordable assisted living housing in Illinois, and partnered with the U.S. Department of Education and Philadelphia's The Reinvestment Fund to raise $45 million for charter school facility development.

At the local level, some community foundations have also adopted a broad cross-sectoral community development focus. The Northland Foundation of Minneapolis supports a broad range of wealth-building efforts: ESOP formation, social enterprise, and individual development accounts. The New Hampshire Community Loan Fund has likewise taken a multi-tiered approach that involves an IDA program, loans that support the creation of worker-focused businesses (such as worker-owned cooperatives), funding for community facility building, affordable housing funding, and small business development support.

New directions for public policy are important in all of this.[266] There are many precedents to build upon: Pilot IDA programs have demonstrated the ability of the poor to save in matched savings programs. Further expansion of these efforts as envisioned in the ASPIRE Act legislation is merited. The non-profit social-enterprise sector is perhaps too new an area for it to have a developed listing of potentially useful government programs. However, government support for this sector, for instance, by increasing the pool of equity capital for social enterprise, either through tax credits or an equity fund similar to today's CDFI Fund, would help promote these entities.

In the case of CDCs and CDFIs, the policy environment, although far from ideal, has been relatively favorable. On the other hand, recent funding cutbacks to the CDFI Fund threaten to reduce the ability of community development finance institutions to provide support for projects that build locally based assets. Raising the annual allocation level to the CDFI Fund to its previous level of $118 million would likely leverage an additional $1 billion of private money. Another critical policy initiative is the creation of a National Low Income Housing Trust Fund: the National Low Income Housing Coalition is currently backing a proposal to develop a trust fund to finance the construction of 1.5 million homes over 10 years.

The community land trust sector has lacked significant government support to date. The Vermont Housing Finance Agency's "Perpetually Affordable Housing Program," which provides reduced-rate mortgages for low-income purchasers of resale-restricted homes, has helped the land trust movement reach significant scale in Vermont, and might serve as a model for other states. We suspect that such state efforts, coordinated with existing community development corporation support systems—including the federal Community Housing Development Organization (CHDO) program, as well as non-governmental intermediaries such as LISC and Enterprise—could make a significant contribution in this area.

Probably the most important step to take in support of ESOP development would be to encourage the formation of state employee ownership centers. Today, only two states—Ohio and Vermont—have these. The Ohio center, which has existed for 15 years, provides a strong model to emulate. Its track record demonstrates that at very low cost (its annual allocation is less than $1 million a year) it is possible to both expand the use of employee ownership and to employ it more meaningfully—resulting in higher employee participation and higher productivity. At the federal level, Representative Dana Rohrabacher's (R. - Calif.) proposal to create a sub-category of ESOPs that receive additional tax benefits in exchange for giving workers more rights strikes a good balance, as it encourages firms to adopt a high participation, high performance model, without generating a backlash by forcing them to do so.

One key step that would assist cooperatives would be to make it easier to raise outside equity by eliminating the requirement that cooperatives reduce their net earnings by the amount they pay out in dividends to non-members on preferred (non-voting) stock. Even more important would be the creation of a fund to provide technical assistance to worker cooperatives. A one-time allocation of $1.5 million in Canada has led to rapid expansion there, helping create new jobs in 79 depressed urban communities at a dollars-per-job ratio that is well below those of other government job-creation programs.

In connection with municipal enterprise, an important policy initiative would be the elimination of restrictions that in some states prohibit entry into telecommunications, especially as municipalities have played a positive role in breaking down the digital divide between urban and rural communities. We also believe that states and municipalities can expand upon current efforts to target their investments to further transit-oriented development and otherwise support local asset-based approaches.

At the local level, inclusionary zoning, in which developers gain the right to place more units on a property in exchange for setting aside a portion of the development to provide affordable housing, can be an effective means to support community development at relatively low cost. Such zoning can also be integrated effectively with other asset-based approaches. For instance, when combined with broader transit-oriented development strategies, inclusionary zoning can help promote community-building and smart growth policies at the same time.

While in many cases the policy needs are quite specific, it may well be that a common policy agenda can be forged that would garner broader political support "across the board" for diverse elements a new wealth-buiding paradigm. Such an agenda might include technical assistance, loans, loan guarantees, preferential public financing, and perhaps additional tax credit provisions.

Figure 15: Wealth-Building Paradigm — Summary of Key Issues

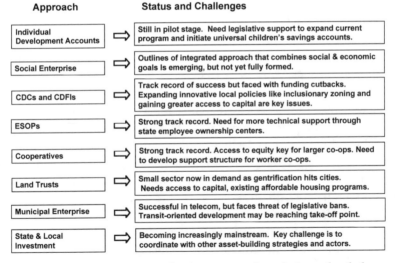

Approach	Status and Challenges
Individual Development Accounts	Still in pilot stage. Need legislative support to expand current program and initiate universal children's savings accounts.
Social Enterprise	Outlines of integrated approach that combines social & economic goals is emerging, but not yet fully formed.
CDCs and CDFIs	Track record of success but faced with funding cutbacks. Expanding innovative local policies like inclusionary zoning and gaining greater access to capital are key issues.
ESOPs	Strong track record. Need for more technical support through state employee ownership centers.
Cooperatives	Strong track record. Access to equity key for larger co-ops. Need to develop support structure for worker co-ops.
Land Trusts	Small sector now in demand as gentrification hits cities. Needs access to capital, existing affordable housing programs.
Municipal Enterprise	Successful in telecom, but faces threat of legislative bans. Transit-oriented development may be reaching take-off point.
State & Local Investment	Becoming increasingly mainstream. Key challenge is to coordinate with other asset-building strategies and actors.

Non-government actors are also important: foundations clearly have a role to play by supporting asset-based research and policy development efforts; helping disseminate information through reports, web publications, and conferences; and in directly funding asset-based programs, both in individual sectors and through cross-sectoral efforts.[287]   An encouraging sign in this respect is the wide variety of asset-based efforts that have received support from community foundations. The Rhode Island Community Foundation, for instance, has focused on a wealth-building strategy that supports affordable housing efforts and the development of women-owned small businesses. The Peninsula Community Foundation, located near Silicon Valley, has been a local leader in the IDA movement through its "Assets for All" program, which has provided financial education for 1,324 individuals. The East Bay Community Foundation of the San Francisco-Oakland Bay Area has focused its efforts at supporting transit-oriented development around Bay Area Rapid Transit (BART) stations in Oakland, Pleasanton, and Dublin.

Universities can also help support wealth-building efforts through directed research, education, purchasing, and even by pursuing investment policies that encourage new organizational forms that employ asset strategies.[268] One example of the potential effect of university partnerships is illustrated by the University of Pennsylvania's "Buy West Philadelphia" program. In this program, the university's concerted efforts to purchase more products locally led to $57 million in local purchases in 2000, up from only $1 million 13 years before. Organizations such as the Partnership for Nonprofit Ventures at Yale University are also doing important work in promoting information sharing, business plan development, and the building of a community of non-profit social enterprise leaders.

Of course, most important in all of this are the practitioners. While the achievements of the asset-based approach have been significant, even the most successful practitioners realize that meeting the challenges that remain will require considerable—and, at times, difficult—practical, on-the-ground struggle. The Mid-Bronx Desperadoes have been widely celebrated for their success at reviving the South Bronx; their CEO, Cicero Wilson, underscores the need for a comprehensive approach: "Often, the CDC attitude is we do it because the community needs it. You've got to do both ownership/income and provide the service....Assets are not just money in the bank, but rather what's producing income each year."[269]

A new and potentially important wealth-building paradigm is clearly emerging in diverse sectors and communities, but it is not yet fully formed. We believe there are many opportunities for those working in disparate areas to join together to network, exchange information, share best practices, further build internal capacity, and develop a common policy agenda that can lead to increased public and policy support. We look forward to working with others to deepen our common knowledge, refine our practices and policies, and help build a broader understanding of an increasingly important strategy for dealing with the challenging new fiscal and global environment we now face.

Endnotes

1   Robert D. Putnam, "Tuning In, Tuning Out: The Strange Disappearance of Social Capital in America." *PS. Political Science and Politics.* Vol. 28, no. 4 (Dec. 1995): 664-683, quote on p. 666.

2   Michael Sherraden. *Toward a Universal and Progressive Asset-Based Domestic Policy,* Speech at the Meeting of the Labour Party. Brighton, England: Center for Social Development, October 2, 2001, page 1.

3   Trina Williams, "The Homestead Act: A Major Asset-building Policy in American History." Working Paper 00-9. St. Louis: Center for Social Development (Washington University), 2000, pages 5-6. See also Homestead National Monument of America, "The Homestead Act." http://www.nps.gov/home/homestead_act.html. The land was nearly, but not completely, free, as homesteaders had to pay small government fees. On the GI Bill, see U.S. Department of Veterans' Administration. "The GI Bill from Roosevelt to Montgomery." http://www.gibill.va.gov/education/GI_Bill.htm. Accessed August 12, 2004.

4   Estimates of number of IDA participants and programs from Leslie Parrish, New America Foundation, Interview, August 13, 2004, and Renee Bryce-La Port, Corporation for Enterprise Development, Interview, August 16, 2004. Estimates of number of state IDA programs from Center for Social Development, Washington University, *Summary Tables: IDA Policy in The States,* Tables 4, June 2004. For analysis of American Dream demonstration program, see Center for Social Development (CSD), *Savings Performance in the American Dream Demonstration.* St. Louis, CSD, October 2002, pp. iv-v, 15-28.

5   See Sherraden, *op. cit.* See also Judy Watts. "Helping the Poor Build Assets." Washington University in St. Louis Magazine. http://magazine.wustl.edu/Fall00/helpingpoor.html. Accessed August 12, 2004. Michael Sherraden, "Financial Services in Low-Income Communities." Presentation at conference on *Bootstrap Capitalism,* Washington, D.C.: Sept. 17, 2004.

6   Sherraden, *op. cit.,* page 2. Lillian G. Woo, F. William Schweke, and Dave Bucholz. *Hidden in Plain Sight.* CFED: Washington, D.C., 2004, pages 4-13. Robert Reich, The Work of Nations, New York: Albert A. Knopf, 1991. See pages 225-240 for Reich's discussion of the central role education plays in training "symbolic analysts" in the global, information-based economy.

7   See Woo, Schweke, and Bucholz, *op. cit.,* page 13. See also Larry Beeferman, *Asset Development Policy: The New Opportunity.* Waltham, MA: Asset Development Institute, October 2001.

8   Michael Sherraden, "Financial Services in Low-Income Communities." Presentation at conference on *Bootstrap Capitalism,* Washington, D.C.: Sept. 17, 2004. Although the United States' income distribution is highly unequal, the inequality of wealth is still greater. According to Beeferman, in 1998 the top 10 percent of households in the United States had 62.8 percent of all household assets. Beeferman, *op. cit.,* p. 20. In a 2004 study, Edward N. Wolff found that 10 percent of households had 71.5 percent of total net worth. See Edward N. Wolff, "Changes in Household Wealth in the 1980s and 1990s in the U.S." *Working Paper 407.* Annandale-on-Hudson, NY: The Levy Economics Institute and New York University, May 2004, page 30 (table 2). Income distribution is also unequal, but less so. According to the U.S. Census Bureau, the top 20 percent of households in the United States earned 50.1 percent of all household income. See U.S. Census Bureau. *Historical Income Tables – Households: Table H-2. Share of Aggregate Income Received by Each Fifth and Top 5 Percent of Households (All Races): 1967 to 2001,* http://www.census.gov/hhes/income/histinc/h02.html. Accessed August 11, 2004.

9   Center for Social Development (CSD), *Savings Performance in the American Dream Demonstration.* St. Louis, CSD, October 2002, pp. iv-v. and 15-28.

10 Leslie Parrish, New America Foundation, Interview, August 13, 2004. Larry Beeferman, *The Promise of Asset-Development Policies.* Waltham, MA: Asset Development Institute: January 2002. Larry Beeferman and Sandra Venner, *Promising State Asset Development Policies: Promoting Economic Well-Being Among Low-Income Households.* Waltham, MA: Asset Development Institute, April 2001. CSD, *Summary Tables: IDA Policy in the States.* St. Louis: Washington University, December 2002, page 18. Estimates vary of how many states have IDAs; some studies have cited as many as 40 (Michael Sherraden, "Financial Services in Low-Income Communities." Presentation at conference on Bootstrap Capitalism, Washington, D.C.: Sept. 17, 2004).

11 The map here is based on Center for Social Development, Washington University, *Summary Tables: IDA Policy in The States,* Tables 4, June 2004, which lists 38 states, Puerto Rico, and D.C. as having some form of IDA program. From that list, we subtracted Rhode Island, New Mexico, and Utah (all of which the chart indicated were stalled) and Mississippi, where the chart indicated the program was no longer operational. Estimates of the number of IDA participants from Parrish and also Renee Bryce-La Port, Corporation for Enterprise Development, Interview, August 16, 2004.

12 List of foundations provided in interview by Robert Zdenek, an IDA advocate. Interview, Robert Zdenek, October 25, 2004. Funding numbers are taken from Karen Edwards, "State Policy Update." *Assets.* Spring 2003: page 4.

13 Michael Sherraden. "From Research to Policy: Lessons from Individual Development Accounts." St. Louis: Center for Social Development, 2000, pages 8, 28. Interview: Leslie Parrish, New American Foundation. August 13, 2004. Renee Bryce-La Port, *op. cit.* New America Foundation, "IDAs and Matched Savings Accounts." Washington, D.C. Feb. 27, 2004. http://www.assetbuilding.org/AssetBuilding/index.cfm?pg=docs&SecID=50&TopID=2. Accessed Aug. 12, 2004.

14 Jared Bernstein notes that the focus on individual savings in IDA programs can potentially reduce working class solidarity. See Jared Bernstein, "Asset Based Policies for the Poor: A Perspective from the Left." St. Louis: Center for Social Development (Washington University), Sept. 2000.

15 In 2003, the Atlanta Cooperative Development Center won an IDA grant that encouraged people who saved money through IDAs to invest that money either in co-op housing share payments or co-op business. Gloria Bromell-Tinubu, Personal Correspondence, May 2003.

16 Heather McCullock and Lisa Robinson, *Resident Ownership Mechanisms,* Policy Link: New York, December 2002, page 92. For more information on the land trust, see www.catchhousing.org.

17 Larry Beeferman and Sandra Venner. "Promising State Asset Development Policies: Promoting Economic Well-Being Among Low-Income Households," Asset Development Institute (Waltham, MA), January 2002. http://www.centeronhunger.org/ADI/promisingfinancial.html. Accessed August 12, 2004.

18 Sarah Dewees and Lou Florio, *Sovereign Individuals, Sovereign Nations: Promising Practices for IDA Programs in Indian Country.* Fredericksburg, VA: First Nations Development Institute, December 2002.

19 Leslie Parrish, Personal Correspondence, August 31, 2004. Quote from Robert Kuttner, "Concluding Remarks." Presentation to *Bootstrap Capitalism* conference, Washington, D.C.: Sept. 17, 2004. Reid Cramer, Papia Debory, Leslie Parrish, and Ray Boshara, *Federal Assets Policy Report and Outlook 2004.* Washington, DC: New America Foundation, February 27, 2004, pages 1, 8.

20 The original request was for 900,000 accounts, but this was pared back by Congress in 2004 to 300,000 (Interview, Leslie Parrish, August 13, 2004). Michael Sherraden, "Financial Services in Low-Income Communities." Presentation at conference on *Bootstrap Capitalism*, Washington, D.C.: Sept. 17, 2004.

21 Similar legislation has been reintroduced in Congress in 2005. Regarding the ASPIRE Act, see New America Foundation, *The ASPIRE Act; Summary of the Bill.* Washington, D.C.: New America Foundation, 2004. See also www.AspireAct.org. The ASPIRE Act was introduced in the Senate by Sen. Santorum (R-PA) and Sen. Corzine (D-NJ) and in the House by Rep. Ford (D-TN), Rep. Petri (R-WI), Rep. Kennedy (D-RI), and Rep. English (R-PA).

22 As quoted by Charles King, "Building a National Gathering of Social Entrepreneurs." Keynote address to the 3rd National Gathering of Social Entrepreneurs. Seattle, WA: Nov. 29-Dec. 2, 2001. A revised version is also available in printed form. See Charles King, "The Need for a New Paradigm: Social Entrepreneurship" in Community Wealth Ventures, *Powering Social Change.* Washington D.C. 2003, pp. 20-23.

23 Murray S. Weitzman, Nadine Jalandoni, Linda Lampkin and Thomas H. Polark, Independent Sector, *The New Nonprofit Almanac and Desk Reference.* San Francisco: Jossey-Bass, 2002, p. 33.

24 The definition of "social enterprise" remains in flux. For some, it includes for-profit businesses with a social mission. (Michael Shuman, Personal Correspondence, Jan. 19, 2005). The Social Enterprise Alliance limits itself to the non-profit sector, but defines "social enterprise" to include strategic alliances. Specifically, they define "social enterprise" as: "Any earned-income business or strategy undertaken by a nonprofit for the purpose of generating revenue in support of the non-profit social mission." See Social Enterprise Alliance, "Social Enterprise Lexicon." http://www.se-alliance.org/resources_lexicon.cfm. Accessed Jan. 1, 2005. While we acknowledge that many for-profit businesses provide important social benefits and many non-profits raise significant amounts of revenue from strategic alliances, we see both of these as conceptually distinct from the asset-based strategy of social-purpose businesses outlined above.

25 Beth Bubis, President of the Social Enterprise Alliance, points out that some social-purpose businesses do not pay their "employees," instead viewing employment training as part of their programs. Many others, including the case studies cited below, view paying a wage itself to be an important part of their training process. Clearly, whether or not the client is also an employee may affect whether or not the client does in fact feel like a participant. Beth Bubis, Personal Correspondence, November 23, 2004.

26 Michael Shuman, Personal Correspondence, Jan. 19, 2005. See also REDF, "FAQs about Social Entrepreneurship," *Social Enterprise Magazine Online.* 2003. http://pages.zdnet.com/mark/1p/faqs.html. See also Kirsten Burns, President, "The Roberts Enterprise Development Fund is now 'REDF.'" www.redf.org/about_intro.htm. Web sites accessed September 6, 2004.

27 Industry survey is by Community Wealth Ventures; the survey included responses from 72 non-profit organizations that operated social ventures. We used median figures—not the much higher mean figures—since we believe the medians better represent the size and scope of the typical social enterprise. Community Wealth Ventures and the Social Enterprise Alliance joint-

ly maintain the industry directory. It should be cautioned that this directory, although the most comprehensive that exists right now, is widely seen as failing to encompass a large number of social enterprises. In calculating the number of ventures on the Social Enterprise Alliance/Community Wealth Ventures' database, we have excluded strategic alliances, since, in our estimation, these most often represent a new form of fundraising, rather than business enterprises that are operated directly by the non-profit organization.

28 Civic organization is a designation applied to a variety of nonprofit organizations that tend to be social or fraternal in purpose and are often membership-based. Examples include alumni associations, fraternities and sororities, and youth organizations. See Weitzman, Jalandoni, Lampkin and Polark, *op. cit.,* p. 114.

29 Lester M. Salamon, "The Resilient Sector: The State of Nonprofit America." *The State of Non-Profit America.* Lester Salamon, ed. Washington D.C.: Brookings, 2002, pp 31-32. Note that the Independent Sector and Urban Institute's non-profit almanac gives much higher figures for fee income. The difference concerns how government payments for services (such as Medicare) are treated. Salamon treats this as government income; the non-profit almanac treats this as fee income. If one uses this alternative formulation, non-profits gained 68 percent of their revenues from fees in 1998. See Weitzman, Jalandoni, Lampkin and Polark, *op. cit.,* p. 135. For the health sector, reliance on fee income fell from 53 percent in 1977 to 52 percent in 1997. For education, fee income fell from 67 percent in 1977 to 65 percent in 1997. For the arts, reliance on fee income fell from 47 percent in 1977 to 46 percent in 1997. For the religious sector, reliance on fee income increased somewhat from 14 percent in 1977 to 16 percent in 1997.

30 Samantha Beinhacker, Deputy Director, Yale School of Management-The Goldman Sachs Foundation Partnership for Non-Profit Ventures. Interview, July 8, 2004. Beth Bubis, Personal Correspondence, June 3, 2004 and November 23, 2004.

31 Janelle Kerlin. *National Center for Charitable Statistics/Guide Star National Nonprofit Database,* Washington D.C.: NCCS, 2004. It should be noted that NCCS is in the process of cleaning the data, so it is likely that some non-profits will be reclassified after the data cleaning is complete, changing the overall numbers. In addition, the dataset itself has certain limitations because it is limited to 501(c)(3) public charities *only.* It also excludes all 501(c)(3) groups that fail to file a Form 990, for any reason. In particular, it under-represents groups that have exemptions from filing, including most organizations with gross receipts of under $25,000 and many religious organizations.

32 Calculations by authors; numbers in this paragraph are rounded to ensure easier readability.

33 Calculations by authors; database itself is available on line at http://63.124.148.154/resources_ search.asp. There are also links from the web pages of both Community Wealth Ventures and the Social Enterprise Alliance.

34 Calculations made by authors, based on cross-tabulation data provided by Ed Barker of Community Wealth Ventures. Community Wealth Ventures, Inc (02-745). Table Q2, pages 4-7, Table Q6, page 12, and Table Q9_1, pages 20-22.

35 Source is Yale School of Management-The Goldman Sachs Foundation Partnership on Nonprofit Ventures, National Business Competition for Nonprofit Organizations, 2003-2005, Three Year Competition Entrant Demographics, Englewood Cliffs, New Jersey: Yale-Goldman Sachs, Partnership 2004. Provided to author by Samantha Beinhacker, Deputy Director of Yale-Goldman Sachs Partnership, December 2, 2004.

36 For information on Greyston, see their web site, www.gresyton.org. For funding information, see *Greyston Times*, Fall 2003/Winter 2004, p. 10. http://www.greyston.org/06-news/gtimes1103.pdf. Quote of Julius Walls from Julius Walls, "A Successful Social Enterprise Responds to the Market." *Powering Social Change*. Washington, D. C.: Community Wealth Ventures, 2003, pp. 26-29, quote on p. 29. See also Partners for the Common Good, "Borrower Profile: Greyston Foundation." Washington, D.C. The organization was also featured in January 2004 on *60 Minutes*. See www.cbsnews.com/stories/2004/01/09/60minutes/main592382.shtml. Web sites accessed July 9, 2004. Beth Bubis, Personal Correspondence, November 23, 2004.

37 Sara Terry, "Genius at Work." *Fast Company*. Issue 17. September 1998. Document is available on-line at www.fastcompany.magzaine/17/genius.html. Information on MCG Jazz and overall finances from Nicole Wallace, Turning Music Into Money." *The Chronicle of Philanthropy*, May 27, 2004. See also, www.manchesterguild.org/home/aboutusFlash.html, www.mcgjazz.org, and www.bidwell-training.org. All web sites accessed July 9, 2004.

38 REDF, "Employment Counts: 11.04." San Francisco: REDF, November 2004. www.redf.org/download/other/employ_counts_041215.ppt. Accessed January 11, 2005. Golden Gate Community, Inc. "What a Difference A Job Makes…The Long-Term Impact of Golden Gate Community, Inc. Employment," volume 1, no. 1, January 2002, www.redf.org/download/ggcinewslettervol1.doc. See also GGCI's website at www.ggci.org, which has links to all of its programs and businesses. REDF also has a lot of data on GGCI and other non-profits organizations with whom it partners, at www.redf.org. All web sites accessed July 9, 2004.

39 REDF, *loc. cit.* Financial figures are from Guidestar, www.guidestar.org/search/report/financial.jsp. Quote from Deborah Sexton, "Nonprofit Print Shop Builds Business With Aggressive Marketing." US Screen Printing Institute. http://www.usscreen.com/articles/index.php?art=196. Web sites accessed July 9, 2004.

40 Thad Williamson, David Imbroscio, and Gar Alperovitz, *Making a Place for Community*, Routledge: New York, 2003, pp. 245-246. Michael R. Burns, "Self-Sufficiency: How Important Is It?" *Powering Social Change*. Community Washington, D.C.: Wealth Ventures, 2003, pp. 30-33. 99.6 percent figure on page 30.

41 For more on the capacity of non-profit business to create and retain assets in communities, see Christopher Gunn, *Third Sector Development: Making Up for the Market*. Ithaca, NY: Cornell University Press, 2004, pp. 52-53.

42 Burton Weisbrod. "The Nonprofit Mission and Its Financing." Burton Weisbrod, ed. *To Profit or Not To Profit*, New York: Columbia University Press, 1998, pp. 1-21, example on page 2. Angela M. Eikenberry and Jodie Drapal Klover, "The Marketization of the Nonprofit Sector: Civil Society at Risk?" *Public Administration Review*, March/April 2004, vol. 64 (2), pp. 132-140. Pablo Eisenberg, "The Public Loses Out When Charities Become Too Businesslike." The *Chronicle of Philanthropy*, June 10, 2004. On issues of commercialism in non-profits, see also Brenda Zimmerman and Raymond Dart, "Charities Doing Commercial Ventures: Societal and Organizational Implications" in Kevin Shawn Sealey et al., editors, *A Reader in Social Enterprise*. Boston, MA: Pearson Custom Publishing, 2000, pp. 295-373.

43 Weisbrod *op cit.*, p 15. Frank A. Sloan, "Commercialism in nonprofit hospitals." Burton Weisbrod, ed. *To Profit or Not To Profit*, New York: Columbia University Press, 1998, pp. 151-168, quote on p. 166. Dennis Young and Lester Salamon. "Commercialism and Social Ventures," *The State of Nonprofit America*, Lester Salamon, ed.,Washington, D.C.: Brookings, 2002, pp. 423-446; quote on p. 436.

44 Michael Shuman and Merrian Fuller, "Profits for Justice." *The Nation.* January 24, 2005.

45 Sheena Bonini and Jed Emerson, *The Blended Value Map: Tracking the Intersects and Opportunities of Economic, Social, and Environmental Value Creation,* October 2003. Lopez cited by Bonini and Emerson on page 125. Quote of Bonini and Emerson on page 60. Accessed at www.blendedvalue.org. As Young and Salamon note, Europe provides an example of a region where social enterprise has flourished, in part because they never had the chasm between non-profit and for-profit forms that the United States has traditionally maintained. See Young and Salamon, *op. cit.,* pp. 442-443.

46 Paul Grogan and Tony Proscio, *Comeback Cities: A Blueprint for Urban Neighborhood Renewal.* Boulder, CO: Westview, 2000, quote on page 73.

47 The industry figure, based on a 1998 survey (published in 1999) found 3,600 CDCs, including 400 CDFIs. See National Congress for Community Economic Development (NCCED), *Coming of Age.* Washington DC: NCCED, 1999. If growth continued at the same pace after the survey as it had before, there would be 5,000 CDCs by now, so 4,000 may be an underestimate. John Nelson, Co-Director of Wall Street Without Walls, also estimates there are 4,000 CDCs. See www.bos.frb.org/commdev/conf/orient/bios.htm. Grogan and Proscio indicate that "95 percent of the top 133 cities" have at least one CDC. Grogan and Proscio, *op. cit.,* p. 70. Regarding board membership, one factor that encourages community participation on CDC boards is that the U.S. government has set aside 15 percent of approximately $2 billion in annual affordable housing development monies for community housing development organizations that meet this community participation requirement. See www.hud.gov/offices/cpd/affordablehousing/library/building/ch08.pdf. Accessed July 14, 2004.

48 Employment and asset numbers are conservative estimates based on authors' extrapolations from NCCED's 1998 survey database. For employment, we took the median employment figure (rather than mean, which is four times higher, since we figure that non-surveyed CDCs are likely smaller) and multiplied it by the number of estimated CDCs. For annual turnover, by adding up information collected on the different funding sources, we found that the 800 CDCs who responded to those questions had annual turnover of approximately $500 million—given that these CDCs represented only a fourth of the industry at the time, $1 billion again appears to be a conservative estimate. Most data is from NCCED, *op. cit.* 1999 estimate of CDC staff in 23 large cities is from Christopher Walker, *Community Development Systems and Their Changing Support Systems,* Washington, DC: Urban Institute, 2002, LISC and Enterprise data was provided by LISC and Enterprise staff to authors. Kevin Kelly, Personal Correspondence, January 18, 2005.

49 Calculation by authors based on subtracting figures from 1995 survey (based on 1993 data) from the 1999 survey (based on 1997 data). See NCCED, *op. cit.* and NCCED, *Tying It All Together.* Washington, DC: NCCED, 1995. Business numbers come directly from the 4th Census database that NCCED provided to authors. Not all known CDC businesses were listed on the database. For instance, Bedford-Stuyvesant CDC, which is known to own enterprises, did not respond to the survey. New Communities CDC, another leading entrepreneurial CDC, responded to the survey, but did not disclose its business holdings, which are considerable.

50 Aaron Bernstein with Christopher Palmeri and Roger O. Crockett, "An Inner-City Renaissance." *Business Week,* Oct. 27, 2003, pages 64-66, 68. Grogan and Proscio, *op. cit.,* quotes on pages 69, 87. Walker, *op. cit.,* see especially, pp. 1, 7-10. Quote on page 8.

51 See Walker, *op. cit.,* pages 1, 4. The authors gratefully acknowledge the assistance of LISC and

Enterprise staff in providing this data. Figures for 2004 were not available at press time. However, based on preliminary numbers, it appears that financing in 2004 will be greater than in 2003.

52 LISC, *What to Expect from New Markets Tax Credits,* Tampa, FL: January 8, 2003. Mark Pinsky, National Community Capital Association, Interview, July 21, 2004.

53 Grogan and Proscio, *op. cit.,* quote on page 13. Stoecker, *loc. cit.* James DeFillipis, *Unmaking Goliath: Community Control in the Face of Global Capital.* New York: Routledge, 2004, quote on page 53.

54 National Low Income Housing Coalition, *Losing Ground in the Best of Times: Low Income Renters in the 1990s,* Washington, D. C.: NLIHC, 2004, pp. 12-14, 17. www.nlihc.org/pubs/ index/htm# losingground. Stoecker, loc. cit. Robert Zdenek, Personal Correspondence, October 27, 2004.

55 LISC, *The Whole Agenda: The Past and Future of Community Development.* New York: LISC, 2002.

56 See, for instance, NCCED's report on the first industry census of CDCs, conducted in 1988. NCCED, *Against All Odds: The Achievements of Community-Based Organizations.* Washington, D.C.: NCCED, March 1989.

57 LISC, *The Whole Agenda: The Past and Future of Community Development.* New York: LISC, 2002; quote on p. 19. *www.lisc.org/resources/2002/03/development_775.shtml?Social+&+ Economic+Development.* Andy Mott, Moving to Scale in Improving America's Housing. Washington, D.C.: Center for Community Change, 2003, quote on p. 5.

58 Being in a CDC-managed shopping center can be a competitive advantage for the supermarket. For instance, when Pathmark was preparing to renovate its Newark store in 2000, New Community's Hispanic Development Corp. held focus groups to assist with the design. See Michael Porter, *The Changing Models of Inner City Grocery Retailing,* Boston: ICIC, 2002, p. 13. Interview by Joe Guinan, Mary Abernathy of New Community, Aug. 26, 2003; Dale Robinson Anglin, Director of Resource Development, New Community, Interview, December 9, 2004 and Personal Correspondence, April 25, 2005. Robert Zdenek, Personal Correspondence, October 27, 2004. The $50 million figure is likely conservative, as the number does not include all operations of all New Community for-profit and non-profit subsidiaries. Revenue figure calculated based on the 2002 Form 990 filings of the parent organization (New Community Corporation) and also New Community Hudson Senior Housing Corporation, New Community Harmony House Corporation, New Community Employment Services Corporation, New Community Health Care Inc., New Community Roseville Towers Housing Corp., and New Community Urban Renewal Corp. Accessed at www.guidestar.com, January 2, 2005.

59 Dale Robinson Anglin: Interview, December 9, 2004 and Personal Correspondence, April 25, 2005. See also New Community Corporation's web site at http://www.newcommunity.org/main.htm. Hispanic population data is from Robert Anthony Watts, "Not the Old Newark," www.livingcities.org/new_look/redesign_stock /pdf/not_the_old_newark.pdf. Accessed July 15, 2004. Kristin Rusch, *The Emerging New Society.* College Park, MD: The Democracy Collaborative, 2001, pp. 2-6. Interview by Joe Guinan: Mary Abernathy of New Community, August 26, 2003.

60 Watts, *loc. cit.* Grogan and Proscio, *op. cit.,* page 13.

61 Stephanie Lessans Geller, NCESA. Interview of Raymond Codey, May 19, 1997. Rusch, *op. cit.,* p. 6. Ted Sherman, "Newark nonprofit stretched for cash." *The Star-Ledger.* Newark, N.J., Aug. 22, 2004, p. 19. Nikita Stewart and Jeffrey C. Mays, "For Newark groups, it pays to be connect-

ed." *The Star-Ledger.* Newark, N.J.: Sept. 12, 2004. Jeffrey Kraus, "Generational Conflict in Urban Politics: the 2002 Newark Mayoral Election." *The Forum* 2 (3): article 7, 2004. Dale Robinson Anglin: Interview, Dec. 9, 2004. Robert Zdenek, Personal Correspondence, Oct. 27, 2004.

62 List compiled from Barbara Abell, *Supermarket Development: CDC's and Inner City Economic Development.* Washington, D.C.: NCCED, 1998, Barbara Abell, Overcoming Obstacles to CDC Supermarket Development, A Guide. Washington, D.C.: NCCED, 2001, and Barbara Abell, Interview, June 1, 2004 and Nov. 15, 2004. For more information on the West Oakland development, see National Council of Churches, "NCC Honors Oakland Religious Leaders as Examples of 'Light' in the Community." *News from the National Council of Churches.* November 15, 2001. http://www.ncccusa.org/news/01news98.html.

63 Loretta Tate, President, Marshall Heights CDC, Interview, June 25, 2004.

64 According to Dwain Brown, Director of The Retail Initiative at LISC, The Retail Initiative helped finance two projects in New York, two projects in Chicago, one in San Diego, one in Dallas, one in Philadelphia, and one in New Haven. Not all of these projects are listed on the table of CDC projects above, as the chart above only reflects those projects where CDCs gained at least a minority ownership stake in the final project. (Dwain Brown, Interview, May 28, 2004.)

65 Dwain Brown, Interview, May 28, 2004. Dwain Brown, Personal Communication, February 12, 2003. Interview, Barbara Abell, June 1, 2004. ICIC, *op. cit.,* p. 29. See also Andrew Cuomo, *New Markets: the Untapped Retail Buying Power in America's Inner Cities,* Washington, DC: HUD, July 1999. Robert Zdenek, Personal Correspondence, Oct. 27, 2004. One federal funding source that has supported some CDC retail development projects, as well as other CDC business development activity, is the Urban and Rural Community Economic Development Program of the U.S. Office of Community Services. Funding in Fiscal-Year 2004 was $26.9 million. For further details, see the program's website at http://www.acf.hhs.gov/programs/ocs/ocsfs2004. htm#CED. See also the congressional testimony regarding the program of Mary Nelson, Executive Director of Bethel New Life CDC at http://edworkforce.house.gov/hearings/108th/edr/liheap070803/nelson.htm, July 8, 2003.

66 For a review of some of the common criticisms made of CDCs, see Thad Williamson, David Imbroscio, and Gar Alperovitz, *Making a Place for Community.* New York: Routledge, 2003, pp. 217-218. See also Randy Stoecker, "Comment on William M. Rohe and Rachel G. Bratt's 'Failures, Downsizings, and Mergers among Community Development Corporations': Defending Community Development Corporations or Defending Communities?" *Housing Policy Debate* (2003), volume 14, issues 1 and 2, pp. 47-56. Quote is on page 49. The authors acknowledge the contribution of Robert Zdenek for drawing attention to the networking example provided by the Cleveland Housing Network.

67 Domenic Moulden, Interview, June 25, 2004.

68 Domenic Moulden, Interview, June 25, 2004. See also Manna CDC's web site at www.mannadc.org/mannacdc/front.htm. Institute study is cited in Walker, op. cit. p. 15.

69 *Ibid.*

70 *Ibid.* On the gap between non-profits and communities that can develop in the absence of careful community surveying, see Rebecca J. Kissane and Jeff Gingerich, "Do You See What I See? Nonprofit and Resident Perceptions of Urban Neighborhood Problems," *Nonprofit and Voluntary Sector Quarterly,* vol. 33, no. 2, June 2004, pp. 311-333.

71 *Ibid.* Robert Zdenek, Personal Correspondence, Oct. 27, 2004.

72 *Ibid.* Note that the Washington, D.C. law, while beneficial to tenants seeking to convert their properties into cooperatives, is not without loopholes. As one reviewer pointed out, it is possible for landlords to evade this provision by retaining a minority share of the building (Brendan Leary: Personal Correspondence, August 11, 2004).

73 Cicero Wilson, Interview, December 9, 2004. Cicero Wilson, Presentation to the National Congress on Community Economic Development, Los Angeles, CA, Oct. 7, 2004. Mid Bronx Desperadoes, "MBD New Horizons Shopping Center," www.mbdhousing.org/documents/ MBDNewHorizonspdf.pdf. Mid Bronx Desperadoes, "Background," www.mbdhousing.org/ background.html. Accessed Jan. 13, 2005. Grogan and Proscio, *op cit.,* pp. 15-30.

74 Jeff Mosley, Rural LISC, Interview, January 27, 2005. Rural LISC, "Helping Neighbors Build Communities. Washington. D.C.: Rural LISC, Dec. 31, 2004 (mimeo). Organization profiles available on Rural LISC's web site: see Coastal Enterprises, Inc. http://www.ruralisc.org/cei_ strategies.htm "Quitman County Development Organization, Inc." http://www.ruralisc.org/ qcdo_strategies.htm. Accessed February 1, 2005.

75 Mary Brooks, *Housing Trust Fund Progress Report 2002.* Frazier Park, CA: Center for Community Change, 2002, pp. 1-3, 7, and 53. See also Mary Brooks, *Winning at the Local Level: 5 Housing Trust Fund Campaigns Tell Their Stories.* Frazier Park, CA: Center for Community Change, 2004.

76 Andy Mott, *op. cit.,* pp. 38-43, 49, 54. Quote on page 49. Note that according to Matt Achhammer of the National Low Income Housing Coalition, over 150 CDCs have endorsed the organization's campaign for a national housing trust fund. Matt Achhammer, Interview, January 26, 2005.

77 Porter, *op. cit.,* p. 19.

78 Mark Pinsky, "Taking Stock: CDFIs Look Ahead After 25 Years of Community Development Finance." *Capital Xchange.* Harvard University, Joint Center for Housing Studies and The Brookings Institution, Center on Urban and Metropolitan Policy, December 2001, quote on p. 13.

79 On mutual aid societies, see Suzanne McVetty, "Help is at Hand: Immigrant Aid Societies: Part I," *Ancestry Magazine,* 14 (4): July/August 1996, www.ancestry.com/library/view/anc-mag/2157.asp and Gary Mormino and George Pozetta. "The cradle of mutual aid: Immigrant cooperative societies in Ybor City, *Tampa Bay History* 7/2 (Fall/Winter 1985), pp. 36-58. www.lib.usf.edu/ldsu/digitalcollections/T06/journal/v07n2_85/v07n2_85_036.pdf.   On African-American community development credit unions, see CDFI Coalition, What are CDFIs?" www.cdfi.org/whatare.asp. Accessed July 11, 2004. See also Lehn Benjamin, Julia Sass Rubin, and Sean Zielenbach, "Community Development Financial Institutions: Current Issues and Future Prospects." *Seeds of Growth: Sustainable Community Development: What Works, What Doesn't and Why.* Washington, D.C.: The Federal Reserve Systems' Third Community Affairs Research Conference, March 27-28, 2003. Regarding CDFI numbers, see CDFI Fund, "718 Certified Community Development Financial Institutions as of September 1, 2004." http://www.cdfifund.gov/docs/certification/cdfi/CDFI-state.pdf.. Accessed on Sept. 21, 2004.

80 Statistics based on data from the CDFI Fund, *loc. cit.* Pinsky, *op. cit.,* p. 25. Social Investment Forum, *2003 Report on Socially Responsible Investing Trends in the United States;* Washington, D.C.: Social Investment Forum, Dec. 2003; Social Investment Forum, 1999 Report on Social

Investing Trends in the United States. Washington, D.C.: Social Investment Forum, Nov. 1999. The Aspen Institute, *1996 Directory of U.S. Microenterprise Programs,* Washington, D.C.: The Aspen Institute, 1997, p. xv-xvii. The Aspen Institute, *2002 Directory of U.S. Microenterprise Programs.* Washington, D.C.: The Aspen Institute, 2002, pages xv-xix. CDFI Coalition, "CDFI Fund Awards." http://www.cdfi.org/cdfifunds.asp. Accessed Sept. 21, 2004. For job and housing figures, see CDP Data Project 2002, calculations by authors.

81 Some CDFIs founded around the same time came more directly out of the cooperative sector and placed a greater emphasis on encouraging cooperative or community ownership. Examples include the Alternatives Fund of Ithaca, New York (founded in 1970), the Cooperative Fund of New England, based in Amherst, Mass. (founded in 1975) and Northcountry Cooperative Development Fund of Minneapolis (founded in 1978). (Margaret Lund, Personal Correspondence, November 22, 2004.) For additional information on the history of these three groups, see www.alternatives.org/alternativesgroup.html, www.cooperativefund.org, and www.ncdf.coop. Accessed Jan. 3, 2005.

82 CDFI Coalition, "What are CDFIs?" www.cdfi.org/whatare.asp. Kirsten Moy and Alan Okagaki, "Changing Capital Markets and their Implications for Community Development Finance." *Capital Xchange.* The Brookings Institution Center on Urban and Metropolitan Policy and Harvard University Joint Center for Housing Studies, July 2001. On the closing of bank branches, see James DeFilippis, "On Community, Economic Development and Credit Unions, paper presented on *COMM-ORG: The On-Line Conference on Community Organizing and Development.* http://wcomm-org.utoledo.edu/papers.html. See also Shore Bank, "Mission and History." www.sbk.com/livesite/aboutssb/ab_misshistory.asp. Accessed July 11, 2004.

83 Social Investment Forum, 2003 *Report on Socially Responsible Investing Trends in the United States.* Washington, D.C.: Social Investment Forum, Dec. 2003, p. 24. Pinsky, *op. cit.,* p. 25.

84 Julia Sass Rubin, *Community Development Venture Capital: A Report on the Industry.* New York: CDVCA, 2001, pp. 7-8. CDVCA, *Report on the Industry 2002.* New York: CDVCA, 2004, pp. 3-4.

85 The Aspen Institute, *1996 Directory of U.S. Microenterprise Programs,* Washington, D.C. Aspen Institute, 1997, p. xv-xvii, The Aspen Institute: *2002 Directory of U.S. Microenterprise Programs.* Washington, D.C.: Aspen Institute, 2002, pages xv-xix. List of growing microenterprise sectors comes from the sector's main trade association, Association for Enterprise Opportunity. http://www.microenterpriseworks.org/about/hotsectors.htm. Accessed September 3, 2004.

86 Chuck Matthei, "Faith and Finance." *Sojourners.* December 1993. Lynn Adler and Jim Mayer, "Interview of Sister Mary Lucie and Doris Gromley." *Faith Hope and Capital,* San Francisco and Portland: Tenth Street Media, Ideas in Motion and Oregon Public Broadcasting, 2000. http://www.pbs.org/capital/stories/sisters-print.html. Accessed Jan. 3, 2005. Also, Partners for the Common Good (profiled briefly later in this chapter) was founded by the Dominican order.

87 See Moy and Okagaki, *op. cit.,* p. 6. Jeanine Jacokes, Interview, June 22, 2004. Michael Swack, Personal Correspondence, Nov. 9, 2004.

88 CDFI Coalition. "CDFI Fund Awards." http://www.cdfi.org/cdfifunds.asp. Accessed April 24, 2004. The CDFI coalition contends that every dollar in equity provided by the CDFI Fund is matched 21:1 by private and non-federal dollars. See CDFI Coalition, "Recent Cuts to the CDFI Fund Result in Fewer Dollars for America's Distressed Communities," June 17, 2004. www.cdfi.org/policypr.asp and "CDFI Fund Appropriations History,"http://www.cdfi.org/approp.asp. On CRA, see Woodstock Institute, "CRA and CDFIs Revisited: The Importance of

Bank Investments for the Community Development Financial Institutions Industry and Implications for CRA Regulatory Review," *Reinvestment Alert,* no. 20, April 2003, see especially p. 3. Chart data is from Social Investment Forum (SIF). 2003 Report on Socially Responsible Investing Trends in the United States; Washington, D.C.: SIF Dec. 2003. *2001 Report on Socially Responsible Investing Trends in the United States.* Washington, D.C.: SIF Nov. 2001; and SIF. *1999 Report on Social Investing Trends in the United States.* Washington, D.C.: SIF, Nov. 1999.

89 Pinsky, *op. cit.,* page 1.

90 At press time, reduced oversight rules for the Community Reinvestment Act for banks with assets between $250 million and $1 billion had already been approved by the Office of Thrift Supervision (OTS) and were under consideration by the Federal Deposit Insurance Corporation. Additionally, in December 2004, OTS proposed further reductions in CRA regulations for thrifts with assets of over $1 billion. Clearly, these regulatory changes could compound the effects of the CDFI Fund cuts, particularly in rural areas where most banks and thrifts with assets in the $250 million-$1 billion range are located. See National Community Reinvestment Coalition (NCRC), *OTS' Proposed Changes to CRA Amounts to a Lump of Coal for Communities,* December 8, 2004 and Center for Rural Strategies, *Debunking the Myths put forth by the FDIC's proposed changes to the Community Reinvestment Act,* http://www.rural-strategies.org/cra/release2.html. Accessed January 3, 2005.

91 See Social Investment Forum, *op. cit.,* p. 24. For job and housing figures, see CDP Data Project 2002, calculations by author. See CDFI Coalition, *op. cit.* for CDFI Fund allocation numbers. Jeannine Jacokes, Executive Director, Partners for the Common Good, Interview, June 22, 2004. Mark Pinsky, CEO, National Community Capital Association, Interview, July 21, 2004.

92 See Citigroup. "Citigroup Financial Summary," Financial Supplement Spreadsheet, January 20, 2004. Figure refers to assets under Citigroup control as valued on December 31, 2003. Accessed at www.citigroup.com/citigroup/press/2004/040120a.htm. Quote is from Margaret Lund, Interview, July 2, 2004.

93 National Community Reinvestment Coalition, *CRA Commitments,* Washington, D.C., mimeo, no date, pp. 2-3.

94 Margaret Lund, Interview, July 2, 2004.

95 Benjamin, Rubin, and Zeilenbach, *op. cit.,* pp. 16-25. Quote on page 45.

96 Related market segments include high-cost mortgages (known as "sub-prime" lenders) and tax refund anticipation loans, the latter with interest rates ranging from 67 percent to 773 percent. H&R Block has been sued regarding this practice. See Rebecca Byrne, "H&R Block Sued Over Refund Loans." *The Street.* Nov. 1, 2002. www.thestreet.com/;markets/rebeccabyrne/10051929.html. Regarding sub-prime lenders, the Center for Responsible Lending (CRL) claims consumers pay $9.1 billion in "unnecessary fees and risk-rate disparities." See CRL, "Fact Sheet." Durham, NC and Washington, D.C.: www.responsiblelending.org/pdfs/2b001-CRL.pdf. Cite of Katy Jacobs, Center for Financial Services Innovation, from presentation at *Bootstrap Capitalism* conference, Washington, D.C., Sept. 17, 2004. Quote from David Stoesz, Policy America, presentation of paper by Howard Karger, University of Houston. *Bootstrap Capitalism* conference, Washington, D.C., Sept. 17, 2004. Center for Responsible Lending, "Payday Lending: How the Debt Trap Catches Borrowers," www.responsiblelending.org/payday/debttrap.cfm. Web sites accessed Sept. 20, 2004.

97 CRL, "Fact Sheet." Durham, NC and Washington, D.C.: www.responsiblelending.org/pdfs/ 2b001-CRL.pdf. Stoesz and Karger, *loc. cit.* Dave Bucholz, Corporation for Enterprise Development (CFED). *Bootstrap Capitalism* conference, Washington, D.C., Sept. 17, 2004. North Side Community Federal Credit Union, http://collaboratory.nunet.net/itrc/ncfcu/ index.htm. Dolores N. Sense, "Hot Funds/Cold Cash alternative to payday loans." Inside. Jan. 16-22, 2002 www.epagecity.com/site/epage/3857_162.htm. Web sites accessed Sept. 20, 2004.

98 Moy and Okagaki, *op. cit.,* pp. 10-16. Pinsky, *op. cit.*: quote on page 10. See also National Community Capital Association, *Aligning Capital with Social, Economic & Political Justice: National Community Capital Association's Strategic Plan 2004-2010.* Philadelphia: NCCA, 2004. Accessed on line at www.commuintycapital.org.

99 Charles Tansey, Interview, August 4, 2004.

100 Charles Tansey, Interview, August 4, 2004. Mark Pinsky, Interview, July 21, 2004. Margaret Lund, Personal Correspondence, November 22, 2004. Gregory A. Ratliff and Kirsten S. Moy with Laura Casoni, Steve Davidson, Cathie Mahon, and Fred Mendez, "New Pathways to Scale for Community Development Finance," *Profitwise News and Views.* Chicago: U.S. Federal Reserve, December 2004, quote on page 21.

101 Pinsky, *op. cit.,* p. 9.

102 Self-Help. "Impact." www.self-help.org/PDFs/impact sheet aug03.pdf. August 2003. Quote from Martin Eakes is from Lynn Adler and Jim Mayer, "Interview: Martin Eakes." *Faith, Hope and Capital.* Produced by Tenth Street Media, Ideas in Action, and Oregon Public Broadcasting. 2000. www.pbs.org/capital/stories/martin-eakes-print.html

103 Self-Help. "Impact." *loc. cit.*

104 Self Help, Ford Foundation, and Fannie Mae. "News Release: Self-Help, Ford Foundation, Bank of America, Chevy Chase Bank, and Fannie Mae Announce Successful Completion of $2 Billion Homeownership Initiative." Washington, D.C.: Oct. 28, 2003. www.self-help.org/PDFs/final press release.pdf. Web site accessed April 23, 2004.

105 Self-Help. "Mission Performance." *Annual Report 2003.* www.shorebankcorp.com/shore-bankcorp/main/2003AnnualReport/mission.html. After-tax income in 2003 was just over $7 million. www.shorebankcorp.com/ashorebnkcorp/main2003AnnualReport/charts/financial/ perf.html. Web sites accessed July 13, 2004.

106 Quotations from Richard Taub are from Lynn Adler and Jim Mayer, "Interview: Richard Taub." *Faith, Hope and Capital.* Produced by Tenth Street Media, Ideas in Action, and Oregon Public Broadcasting. 2000. www.pbs.org/capital/storeis/richard-taub-print.html. Regarding how to increase community capacity, see John Kretzmann and John McKnight, *Building Communities from the Inside Out.* Chicago: ACTA Publications, 1993.

107 For loan fund amounts, see Social Investment Forum, *loc. cit.* For venture capital figures, Kerwin Tesdell, Executive Director of the Community Development Venture Capital Association, writes that by the end of June 2003, the industry had $548 million under management vs. Social Investment Forum's estimate of $500 million. See Kerwin Tesdell and Charity Shumway, "Investing for Social Good: Community Development Venture Capital," *Community Investments Online.* http://www.frbsf.org/publications/community/invest-ments/0311/article1f.html.

108 On Northcountry's portfolio, see Northcountry, *2002 Annual Report.* www.ncdf.coop/pdfs/ ncdf_annual_02.pdf. On Partners for the Common Good's work with social enterprises, see www.pcg21.org/main.cfm?page=40, www.pcg21.org/main.cfm?page=41, and www.pcg21.org/ main.cfm?page=42.

109 Stephen Gasteyer and Randolph Adams, Rural Community Assistance Partnership, Jan. 25, 2005. RCAC, "Loan Fund," Visalia, CA: RCAC, www.rc ac.org/programs/serv-financial.html. Accessed Feb. 1, 2005.

110 Regarding Acción USA, see www.accionusa.org/wherewework.asp and www.accionus.org/ impact.asp. It should be cautioned that micro-enterprise strategies work best when combined with existing family or friend-based support networks coupled with a single-minded determination. With these traits, "The combination of additional business training and access to capital, which microenterprise provide," makes a significant difference. Absent these traits, success is much less common (Lisa Servon and Timothy Bates, "Microenterprise as an Exit Route from Poverty," *Journal of Urban Affairs,* Vol. 28, no. 4, pp. 419-441, quote on page 427).

111 Regarding the City of San Diego's effort, see CDVCA, *City of San Diego EmTek (Emerging Technologies) Revolving Loan Fund.* March 2004. www.cdvca.org/fund_emtek.html. Regarding SJF Ventures, see www.sjfund.com/cms. See also Julia Sass Rubin, Community Development Venture Capital: A Double-Bottom Line Approach to Poverty Alleviation." Paper presented at *Changing Financial Markets and Community Development* conference, Washington, D.C.: Federal Reserve April 4-6, 2001, pp. 121-154, see especially, pp. 130-131.

112 Rubin, *op. cit.,* pp. 139-140 and p. 151. Quote on page 140. Rubin notes that data was missing for the fourth fund, the Massachusetts Community Finance Corporation.

113 Margaret Lund, Interview, July 2, 2004.

114 The ESOP Association, "The Policy of Broadened Ownership." *#12 Issue Brief,* Washington, D.C.: The ESOP Association, 2002.

115 Estimates are based on IRS forms that most ESOPs are required to file on an annual basis (smaller ESOPs only have to file these every three years). There are two key difficulties with the estimates: 1) the most recent statistics published by the government (Department of Labor) date from 1998; 2) studies at the state level reveal that many companies known to have ESOPs do not "check the right box" (such as by failing to indicate that a 401(k) plan is also an ESOP) and thus are excluded from the count. Sources for the data on the below table are from NCEO, "A Statistical Profile of Employee Ownership." NCEO: Oakland, CA, 2003. www.nceo.org/library/eo_stat.html. Joseph Blasi and Douglas Kruse, "The Political Economy of Employee Ownership in the United Sates: From Economic Democracy to Industrial Democracy?" Paper presented at the *Industrial Relations Research Association* conference, San Diego, California. January 2-5, 2004, Appendix 1. Revised draft: January 16, 2004. Jacquelyn Yates, *State-by-state compilations: total and percents of ESOPs, leverage ESOPs and stock bonus plans, from IRS Form 5500 data reported for plan years ending 1999-2001.* Distributed by Larkspur Data Resources, CD data 2003. Jacquelyn Yates, Personal Correspondence, June 24, 2004. Jacqueline Yates and John Logue, "Democratic Employee Ownership and Economic Performance: Preliminary Results of a New Study." Prepared for the *American Political Science Association* (APSA) conference. Chicago: APSA, Sept. 2-4, 2004. IRS/Department of Labor, Form 5500 database, Washington, DC: 1998, provided to authors by Douglas Kruse. Peter A. Kardas, Adria L. Scharf, and Jim Keogh, *Wealth and Income Consequences of Employee Ownership: A Comparative Study of Washington State.* NCEO: Oakland, CA, 1998. See especially pages 6-12, 20-28.

116 The $297 billion figure is the lowest of the available estimates and is taken from Joseph Blasi and Douglas Kruse, "The Political Economy of Employee Ownership: From Economic Democracy to Industrial Democracy," *Industrial Relations Research Association* conference, San Diego, CA, January 2-5, 2004, Appendix 1. Yates and Logue (2004) estimate the size of ESOP holdings at $400 billion. NCEO gives an even higher estimate of $500 billion. See National Center for Employee Ownership (NCEO). "A Comprehensive Overview of Employee Ownership," Oakland, CA: NCEO, 2002, http://www.nceo.org/library/overview.html. Web site accessed on Sept. 12, 2004.

117 One obvious potential problem with ESOPs is their lack of diversification. However, ESOP pensions are usually supplemented by a 401(k) or other plan for this reason. For instance, a study of 60 ESOPs in Massachusetts found that 55 of them (92 percent) had a second retirement plan in addition to the ESOP. See Adria Scharf, "Show Them The Money," *ESOP Report.* Washington D.C.: The ESOP Association, Nov.-Dec. 2001. Furthermore, Blasi and Kruse found that ESOP companies are substantially more likely to offer additional retirement plans than comparable non-ESOP companies are to offer any kind of plan. NCEO, "Largest Study Yet Shows ESOPS Improve Performance and Employee Benefits." NCEO: Oakland, CA, 2001. http://www.nceo.org/library/esop_perf.html. Accessed Jan. 3, 2005.

118 The ESOP Association, "ESOP Facts and Figures #20 *Issue Brief,* The ESOP Association, Washington, DC, 2002 John Logue and Jacquelyn Yates, *The Real World of Employee Ownership.* Ithaca, NY: Cornell, 2001, pp. 12-14.

119 NCEO, "A Statistical Profile of Employee Ownership." Oakland, CA: NCEO, 2003. www.nceo.org/library/eo_stat.html. Joseph Blasi and Douglas Kruse, "The Political Economy of Employee Ownership in the United Sates: From Economic Democracy to Industrial Democracy?" Paper presented at the 56th Annual Meeting of the Industrial Relations Research Association, San Diego, California. January 2-5, 2004. Revised draft: January 16, 2004. Jacquelyn Yates, "State-by-state compilations: total and percents of ESOPs, leverage ESOPs and stock bonus plans, from IRS Form 5500 data reported for plan years ending 1999-2001." Distributed by Larkspur Data Resources, CD data 2003. Jacquelyn Yates, Personal Correspondence, June 24, 2004.

120 NCEO, "A Statistical Profile of Employee Ownership." Oakland, CA: NCEO, 2003. www.nceo.org/library/eo_stat.html. Joseph Blasi and Douglas Kruse, "Participation in Shared Capitalism Programs, from Survey of Individuals. Based on analysis of 2002 General Social Survey." June 16, 2004. Mimeo. Joseph Blasi and Douglas Kruse, "Participation in Shared Capitalism, from Survey of Firms: Based on analysis of 2003 National Organizations Survey." June 16, 2004, mimeo.

121 Logue and Yates, *op. cit.,* pp. 32-34, 72-109, 132-157. See page 32 for discussion of the 1985 GAO study's findings on productivity. The GAO study is still seen as a benchmark study for the ESOP field.

122 Joseph Blasi, Douglas Kruse, and Aaron Bernstein, *In the Company of Owners.* New York: Basic Books, 2003. See pp. 153-182, especially pages 153-157, on productivity issues. See pp. 82-84 for calculations on worker stock option exercise; quote is on page 223.

123 As NCEO President Corey Rosen summarizes the requirements, "All employees over age 21 who work for more than 1,000 hours in a plan year must be included in the plan, unless they are covered by a collective bargaining unit, are in a separate line of business with at least 50 employees not covered by the ESOP, or fall into one of several anti-discrimination exemptions not commonly used by leveraged ESOPs." Corey Rosen, *A Comprehensive Overview of Employee Ownership.* Oakland: NCEO. www.nceo.org/library/overview.html. Accessed on Jan. 24, 2005.

124 Adria Scharf, Personal Correspondence, Sept. 12, 2004. Blasi, Kruse, and Bernstein, *op. cit.*, p. 190. Blasi and Kruse, "Participation in Shared Capitalism Programs, from Survey of Individuals. Based on analysis of 2002 General Social Survey." June 16, 2004. Mimeo.

125 According to a 2004 article, the ten largest ESOPs (in terms of employee-participants) are Proctor and Gamble, Lifetouch, Inc., Anheuser-Busch Companies, Amsted Industries, Parsons Corporation, Brookshire Brothers JELD-WEN, Ruddick Corporation, Ferrell Companies, and W.L. Gore Associates. Most of these are large public companies, although W. L. Gore, the maker of Gore-Tex, is majority owned by employees. See ESOPs Popular, *Corporate Governance*, May-June 2004. http://www.corpgov.net/news/archives%202004/May-June.html. Accessed Jan. 31, 2005.

126 Corey Rosen, "A Comprehensive Overview of Employee Ownership," http://www.nceo.org/library/overview.html. Oakland: NCEO. 2002. Web site accessed on Sept. 12, 2004.

127 IRS/Department of Labor, Form 5500 database, Washington, DC: 1998. Provided to authors by Douglas Kruse.   Peter A. Kardas, Adria L. Scharf, and Jim Keogh, *Wealth and Income Consequences of Employee Ownership: A Comparative Study of Washington State*. Oakland, CA: NCEO, 1998. See especially pages 6-12, 20-28.

128 Vesting for ESOPs occurs in one of two ways. With "cliff" vesting, there need be no vesting at all for five years, but there must be 100 percent vesting after five years. The other, more common, structure is "graded" vesting. With "graded" vesting, there is a minimum of 20 percent vesting after three years, 40 percent after four, 60 percent after five, 80 percent after six, and 100 percent after seven years. In this case, an employee who left after three or more years would receive a partial payment upon leaving. A company may also elect to vest their employees earlier than the law requires. Adria Scharf, Personal Correspondence, Sept. 10, 2004. National Center for Employee Ownership. *ESOP Diversification and Distribution Rules.* http://www.nceo.org/library/distribution.html. Accessed Sept. 11, 2004. Corey Rosen, Personal Correspondence, Oct. 18, 2004.

129 A classic text on this issue is Albert O. Hirschman, *Exit, Voice, and Loyalty.* Harvard: Cambridge, MA, 1970. The basic argument is that where exit is precluded, it is more likely that people will choose to actively participate in order to be able to improve their conditions.

130 The ESOP Association alone lists 1,260 members in its 2003 Directory. See The ESOP Association, *2003 Membership Directory*, Washington D.C., 2003. On the relationship between ESOPs, participation, and productivity, see Blasi, Kruse, and Bernstein, *op. cit.*, pp. 171-182.

131 As noted below, companies in which a worker-owned ESOP owns a substantial share of the company contribute greatly to community economic stability, partly as a result of this legal requirement. Regarding the early 1980s' repeal effort, the ESOP Association wrote, "The Senate voted 94-3 to repeal this provision in 1981, but the House did not agree. Senator Alan Dixon (D-Illinois) sponsored a bill early in 1983 to accomplish this purpose, for which the Association has lobbied extensively." The ESOP Association, *1983 Survey*, Washington, D.C., p. 34.

132 The ESOP Association, "1982 Survey," pp. 28-29. The ESOP Association, "2000 Survey," page 1. Washington, D.C. J. Michael Keeling, Interview, April 7, 2004. Quote from Blasi and Kruse, "The Political Economy of Employee Ownership In the United States," page 14.

133 J. Michael Keeling, Interview, April 7, 2004. William Greider, *The Soul of Capitalism.* New York: Simon & Schuster, 2003, pp. 80-83.

134 The ESOP Association, "1987 Survey," p. 16. The ESOP Association, "2000 Survey," page 34. Washington, D.C. Blasi and Kruse, "The Political Economy of Employee Ownership In the United States," pp. 14-15. Map based on authors' calculation from The ESOP Association, *2003 Directory,* Washington, D.C.

135 The median size of member ESOP companies in The ESOP Association is lower than the mean and has stayed relatively constant, most likely between 200 and 250, but the survey does not provide exact data on this question. In 1982, 127 of 213 surveyed companies indicated that they had fewer than 250 plan participants (59.6 percent). By 2000, this had only changed slightly, as 54 percent of respondents indicated that they had fewer than 250 plan participants. The ESOP Association, *1982 Survey,* Washington, D.C.: The ESOP Association, p. 16. See also The ESOP Association, *2000 Survey,* Washington, D.C.: The ESOP Association, p. 4.

136 The ESOP Association, *1982 Survey,* Washington, D.C.: The ESOP Association, pp. 9,12-13. See also The ESOP Association. *2000 Survey,* Washington, D.C.: The ESOP Association, pp. 1, 4, and 32.

137 Corey Rosen, Personal Correspondence, July 16, 2004. NCEO. *Majority ESOP-Owned Companies,* Oakland, CA: NCEO, 2003.

138 See Corey Rosen, *Update for December 15, 2004,* Oakland, CA: NCEO. www.nceo.org/columns /cr172.html. Accessed Jan. 3, 2005. It should be cautioned that the NCEO categories may not correspond precisely with The ESOP Association's categories.

139 NCEO. *Majority ESOP-Owned Companies,* Oakland, CA: NCEO, 2003.

140 Douglas Kruse, "Research Evidence on Prevalence and Effects of Employee Ownership." *Testimony before the Subcommittee on Employer-Employee Relations—Committee on Education and the Workforce,* Washington, DC: US House of Representatives, February 13, 2002.

141 Northland Institute. *Employee Stock Ownership Plans as a Community Asset-Building Strategy.* http://www.northlandinst.org/EconDev_ESOP.cfm. Accessed Sept. 16, 2004.

142 A trustee, whether directed by management or employees, may act independently if s/he judges the instructions to be financially imprudent.

143 Preliminary results, presented in a September 2004 conference paper, indicate that the percentage of majority-owned companies has continued to rise to 40 percent, while the percentage of companies that pass through full voting rights to plan members may have fallen to 20 percent. However, the sample size (only 30 companies surveyed in 2004 versus 167 in 1992-93) is too small to draw definitive conclusions. See Jacquelyn Yates and John Logue, "Democratic Employee Ownership and Economic Performance: Preliminary Results of a New Study." Paper prepared for the *2004 Annual Meeting of the American Political Science Association* (APSA). Chicago: APSA, 2004, page 19 (table 7).

144 Logue and Yates, *op. cit.,* pp. 17-18. The ESOP Association: *2000 Survey,* Washington, D.C., pp. 34, 36. Logue and Yates, *op. cit.,* p. 32.

145 Jeff Ottum. Presentation at conference session, "Case Studies: Communicating in Large Employee Owned Companies." *Annual Conference: New Visions in Employee Ownership.* Chicago: NCEO and Beyster Institute, April 29, 2004. David Binns, Interview, May 12, 2004. It should be noted that managers are not always the main source of resistance to information sharing. According to Loren Rodgers of Ownership Associates, workers also often are hesitant (Loren Rodgers, Personal Correspondence, Nov. 2004).

146 Bill McIntyre. "Addressing Management Change in Companies with an Active Ownership Culture." *NCEO/Beyster Institute Joint Annual Conference,* Chicago, April 30, 2004. Regarding stock market performance, decline of the NASDAQ Composite Index during that period exceeded 50 percent. The Dow Jones index declined a more modest 8 percent during that same period. Spreadsheets downloaded from www.nasdaq.com and Dow Jones & Company, http://averages.dowjones.com/jsp/industrialAverages.jsp?sideMenu=true.html. Accessed September 3, 2004.

147 On Carris, see Cecile G. Betit, "Carris Companies' Practice of Employee Governance." *The Journal of Corporate Citizenship,* Issue 6, summer 2002, pp. 87-109; see especially pp. 88-91. See also Williamson, Imbroscio and Alperovitz, *op. cit.,* page 198-206 for additional examples and Alperovitz, *op. cit.,* pp. 81-89. Mary Landry, Board Member, Maryland Brush, Interview, June 30, 2004.

148 Data provided by Loren Rodgers of Ownership Associates. It should be noted that the surveyed companies are looking to increase participation. Companies satisfied with their level of participation, whether high or low, are thus self-selected out. One company was surveyed twice—we only used the more recent (2001) data for that company.

149 Kardas, Scharf, and Keogh, op. cit., pp. 6-12. Sarah Carleton and Michael Garland, *Employee Ownership: State Policy and Regional Economic Development.* MIT, May 17, 1993, mimeo, pp. 1-3, 5-8, 13-14, 36-37. Jacquelyn Yates, "Ohio's Employee-Owned Network: Helping Employee-Owned Companies to Help Themselves?" Paper presented at *Europe et Société Colloque.* Paris, April 28-29, 2004, pp. 1, 7. Williamson, Imbroscio and Alperovitz, *op. cit.,* p. 209.

150 Yates and Logue (2004), *op. cit.,* page 25.

151 John Emmeus Davis and Amy Demetrowitz. *Permanently Affordable Homeownership: Does the Community Land Trust Deliver on Its Promises?—A Performance Evaluation of the CLT Model Using Resale Data from the Burlington Community Land Trust.* Burlington Community Land Trust: Burlington, VT, May 2003, page 20.

152 Julie Orvis, *CLT Data Survey Overview Information,* Springfield, MA; ICE, April 19, 2004. Institute for Community Economics (ICE), *FY2001 Annual Data Report to the CLTs.* Springfield, MA: ICE, 2001. ICE. *Community Land Trust (CLT) Activity in the United States.* Springfield, MA: ICE, 2002. ICE estimates that at least 300 new housing units were built in 2000. From a base of 5,792, this works out to a minimum growth rate of 5.2 percent.

153 Land Trust Alliance, "Private Land Conservation in U.S. Soars." November 18, 2004. www.lta.org/newsroom/pr_111804.htm. Accessed January 3, 2005.

154 On the origins of the community land trust movement, see Susan Witt and Robert Swann, *Land: The Challenge and Opportunity.* Great Barrington, MA: E.F. Schumacher Society, 1992. www.schumachersociety.org/landpiece.html. Accessed January 3, 2005.

155 Cathy Cross, Stephanie Geller, Monica Logan, Kathleen Seipel and Melissa Zeman, *Community Land Trusts: Resource Manual.* College Park, MD: University of Maryland (School of Social Work) 1999, pp. 2-5. Susan Witt and Robert Swann, *Land: The Challenge and Opportunity,* Great Barrington, MA: E. F. Schumacher Society, pp. 2-3. www.schumachersociety.org/landpiece.html. Accessed Sept. 20, 2004.

156 For this example, this assumes that the housing trust fund forgives $25,000 of downpayment assistance on a house that sells for $125,000. In 2002, the median home price in the United

States was $150,900. See Julie G. Brady, "Home price changes in major U.S. markets."
www.bankrate.com/brm/news/mtg/20020715a.asp. North Palm Beach, FL: Bank Rate, Inc.,
July 15, 2002. Accessed on July 25, 2004.

157 Davis and Demetrowitz, *op. cit.*, pp. 14-23.

158 Julie Orvis, *op. cit.* ICE, *FY2001 Annual Data Report to the CLTs.* Springfield, MA: ICE, 2001.

159 James DeFilippis, *op. cit.*, pp. 90, 94. Pam Jones, New Columbia Land Trust, Interview, July 1, 2004.
Douglas M. Kleine, *Cooperative Housing in the United States.* National Association of Housing
Cooperatives: Washington, D.C., 2004. Policy Link, Community Land Trusts: Tools for Action."
www.policylink.org/EDTK/CLT/action.html. City of Boston, "Ribbon Cut for Woodward Park
III." *Mayor's Office.* www.cityofboston.gov/news/pr.asp?ID=1081. Accessed Sept. 20, 2004.

160 Coalition for Nonprofit Housing & Economic Development (CNHED), *A Study of Limited-
equity Cooperatives in the District of Columbia,* Washington, D.C.: CNHED, Spring 2004. Cathy
Cross et al., *op. cit.*, pp. 14-15. Pam Jones, Interview, July 1, 2004.

161 DeFilippis, *op. cit.*, pp. 89-91.

162 North Camden Land Trust, "What is a Land Trust?" Camden, NJ. http://www.nclandtrust.org/
whatis.html. Accessed September 2, 2004. Wayne Nelson, "Growing Land Trust nonprofit uses
unique development style." *BusinessNorth.com.* June 2, 2004. National Housing Partnership,
"Northeast Regional Report." *The Bullet.* Summer 2004. www.nhponline.org/Bullet/north-
east_page.htm. Policy Link, Community Land Trusts: Tools for Action." www.policylink.org/
EDTK/CLT/action.html. Accessed Sept. 20, 2004. ICE, *FY2001 Annual Data Report to the CLTs.*
Springfield, MA: ICE, 2001.

163 Julie Orvis quoted in Stephanie Lessans Geller, "Land Trust Trajectory." NCESA: Washington,
DC, 1997, p. 13. A community land trust, provided it goes through the appropriate applica-
tion procedures, can qualify for federal technical assistance dollars as a Community Housing
Development Organization (CHDO) under Section 233 (f) of the Cranston-Gonzalez
National Affordable Housing Act of 1990, which sets aside a minimum of 15 percent of feder-
al affordable housing development allocations for such organizations. See U.S. Department of
Housing and Urban Development (HUD). CHDO *Set-Aside.* Washington, D.C.: HUD, January
28, 2002, http://www.huyd.gov/offices/cpd/affordablehousingtraining/chdo/setaside.cfm, and
HUD, *HOMEfires,* vol. 3, no. 9, October 2001, http://www.hud.gov/offices/cpd/affordable-
housing/library/homefires/volume/vol3no9.cfm.

164 Catherine Toups, "Boston's Dudley Triangle." *Building Blocks,* winter 2000, volume 1, issue 2.
www.knowledgeplex.org/kp/text_document_summary/article/relfiles/bb_0102_toups.html. City
of Boston, "Ribbon Cut for Woodward Park III." *Mayor's Office.* www.cityofboston.gov/
news/pr.asp?ID=1081. Policy Link, Community Land Trusts: Tools for Action."
www.policylink.org/EDTK/CLT/action.html. Web sites accessed Sept. 20, 2004. Land trust resident
numbers are from ICE, FY2001 *Annual Data Report to the CLTs.* Springfield, MA: ICE, 2001.

165 Frank Adams. Panel Presentation. "The Historical Perspective on Co-ops and Worker
Ownership." *Eastern Conference on Workplace Democracy—Sharing the Promise: Economic
Democracy at Work.* Tripton, NC: Aurora Productions, 2002, CD #2-01.

166 A word of caution: the top 100 cooperatives in 2003 are not all the same cooperatives that were
on the list in 1992. As in the corporate sector, there have been mergers between some co-ops,

as well as a few spectacular failures. By and large, though, the economic performance of the cooperative sector has been solid during this period.

167 Credit Union National Assn. (CUNA), "United States Credit Union Statistics." Madison, WI, 2004. www.cuna.org/download/us_totals.pdf. Accessed January 3, 2005.

168 National Cooperative Bank (NCB), NCB's *Co-op 100*. Washington, D.C.: NCB, 2003 http://www.co-op100.coop/coop100/indextop100.htm. Accessed January 5, 2005. Bureau of Labor Statistics (BLS), Consumer Price Index–All Urban Consumers," Series ID CUUR0000SA0. Washington DC: BLS, 2004. http://data.bls.gov/servlet/SurveyOutputServlet. Accessed July 20, 2004. "Co-op Month 2003: Messages with Talking Points." National Cooperative Business Assn. (NCBA), Washington, D.C.: NCBA, 2003. www.co-opmonth.org/resources/talking_points.html. Accessed July 20, 2004.

169 NCB, *A Day in the Life of Cooperative America*, pp. 12-13, 18-19. Washington, D.C.: NCB, 1998. NCBA, "About Cooperatives: Co-op Statistics," Washington, D.C.: NCBA, 2002. www.ncba.coop/abcoop_stats.cfm. Accessed July 20, 2004. Founding of US Federation of Democratic Workplaces attended by Jessica Gordon Nembhard. Food co-op numbers are from Peg Nolan, Walden Swanson, Kate Sumberg, and Dave Gutknecht, "Retail Operations Survey 2001," *The Cooperative Grocer. July-August 2002.* Paul Hazen. "Statement of Paul Hazen, President, NCBA, Before the Senate Subcommittee on Antitrust, Competition, and Consumer Rights," hearing on *Hospital Group Purchasing: Lowering Costs at the Expense of Patient Health and Medical Innovation?* Apr. 30, 2002. American Public Power Association, *2004-05 Annual Directory and Statistical Report,* Washington, D.C.: APPA, 2004, page 20. Charles A. Kraenzle, "Co-ops' share of farm marketings up slightly in '98." *Rural Cooperatives.* Washington, D.C.: USDA, January 2000. www.rurdev.usda.gov/rbs/pbu/jan00/market.htm.

170 NCB, *op. cit.,* p. 7. Ronald Kumon, *History of the Rochdale Cooperative.* Austin, TX: Laurel House Co-op & Laurel Net Cooperative: 1999. http://uts.cc.utexas.edu/~laurel/cooproots/history.html. International Co-operative Information Centre. "The Massive Movement that Grew from Rochdale's Tiny Store." Madison, WI: University of Wisconsin Center for Cooperatives, 1994. http://www.wisc.edu/ uwcc/icic/orgs/ica/pubs/review/vol-88/movement.html. Accessed July 20, 2004.

171 NCB, *op. cit.,* pp. 12-13 and 18-19. NCBA, "About Cooperatives: Co-op Statistics," Washington, D.C.: NCBA. www.ncba.coop/abcoop_stats.cfm. Accessed July 20, 2004. Peg Nolan, Walden Swanson, Kate Sumberg, and Dave Gutknecht, "Retail Operations Survey 2001," *The Cooperative Grocer,* July-August 2002.

172 Definition for producer co-ops taken from People's Food Co-op (PFC), "How Co-ops Work." PFC: Ann Arbor, MI. www.peoplesfood.coop/whatscoop.html. Accessed April 2, 2005.

173 Patrick Duffy, ed., "The 1990s." *Rural Cooperatives.* Washington, D.C.: USDA, Jan./Feb. 1999, page 61. Celestine C. Adams, Katherine C. DeVille, Jacqueline E. Penn and E. Eldon Eversull, Service Report 62, *Farmer Cooperative Statistics, 2002.* Washington, D.C.: USDA, 2003, Charles A. Kraenzle, "Co-ops' share of farm marketings up slightly in '98." Rural Cooperatives. Washington, D.C.: USDA, January 2000. www.rurdev.usda.gov/rbs/pbu/jan00/market.htm. NCB: *op. cit.,* pp. 16-17 and 22-23.

174 NCBA, "About Cooperatives: Healthcare Cooperatives." Washington, D.C.: NCBA. www.ncba.coop/abcoop_health.cfm. Accessed July 20, 2004. NCB. "2003 Top Purchasing Co-ops in the United States." Washington, D.C.: NCB, 2004. http://www.co-op100.coop/coop100/index-purchase.htm. See also VHA, "Fact Sheet," Irving, TX: VHA, www.vha.com/news/public/fact-

sheet.asp, accessed Sept. 22, 2004; is.group, "Overview," Indianapolis, IN, is.group: http://www.isgroup.org, accessed April 2, 2005;and AMAROK Drywall Cooperative, "About Us." Phoenix, AZ: AMAROK, http://www.amarok.coop/aboutus.asp. Accessed Jan. 22, 2005.

175 John Curl, *History of Work Cooperation in America.* Berkeley, CA: Homeward Press, 1980. Accessed at http://red-coral.net/WorkCoops.html. Mondragón Corporación Cooperativa. (MCC) Frequently-Asked Questions: "How many employees are co-operative members and how many are not, and in which areas do non-members mainly work?" www.mcc.coop/ing/contacto/fas6.html. Mondragón Corporación Cooperativa, *Memoria: Annual Report 2003*, p. 5. www.mcc.coop. For a list of worker enterprises, see GEO, *An Economy of Hope.* Stillwater, PA: GEO, 2000. Regarding the new federation, see U.S. Federation of Worker Cooperatives and Democratic Workplaces, "Welcome," Minneapolis, MN: May 2004. http://www.usworkercoop.org.

176 NCB. "Co-op 100." Washington, D.C.: NCB, 2004. http://www.co-op100.coop/coop100/indexwelcome.htm. Accessed Jan. 7, 2005. Joe Folsom, *Measuring the Economic Impact of Cooperatives in Minnesota.* USDA: Rural Business-Cooperative Service, RBS Research Report 200. Washington, D.C. Dec. 2003.

177 Map is based on EIA figures as reported by Constance Newman. See Constance Newman, "Electric Market Restructuring: Issues for Rural America." *Rural America.* Vol. 17, no 1, spring 2002, pp. 2-10; see especially table on page 4.

178 Dan Campbell, "When the Lights Came On," and Pamela J. Kerg, "Iowa RECs reach 15-year milestone for rural development." Washington, D.C.: USDA, August 2000. www.rurdev.usda.gov /rbs/pub/aug00/light.htm. Hamilton Brown, NRECA, Interview, January 25, 2004. Nor is the Iowa example unique. Similar associations exist in North Carolina, Oregon, and South Carolina. A 2003 study of electric cooperatives, for instance, found that 60 percent of South Dakota's cooperatives operated revolving loan funds to support community economic development. See South Dakota Rural Electric Association (SDREA) and National Rural Electric Cooperative Association (NRECA), *South Dakota Electric Cooperatives' Contribution to the State's Economy,* March 2003. For an overview of electric co-op community development nationally, see NRECA, *The Cooperative Promise.* NRECA: Arlington, VA: 2002. See also NCBA, "About Cooperatives: Utilities." www.ncba.coop/abcoop_util.cfm. Accessed July 20, 2004.

179 Jessica Gordon Nembhard. "Non-Traditional Analyses of Cooperative Economic Impacts: Preliminary Indicators and a Case Study. Presented at the Conference: *Mapping Co-operative Studies in the New Millennium.* Conference sponsored by The Research Committee of the International Co-operative Alliance and the Canadian Association for the Study of Co-operation. Victoria, BC: University of Victoria, May 30, 2003. Jessica Gordon Nembhard, "Entering the New City as Men and Women, Not Mules." March 2003; forthcoming in Lewis Randolph and Gayle Tate, eds., *The Urban Black Community.* USDA. *Pigford v. Veneman: Consent Decree in Class Action Suit by African American Farmers: Background and Current Status,* Washington, DC, 2003. www.usda.gov/da/consenstsum.htm. Accessed July 21, 2004.

180 Donald H. Cooper and Paul O. Mohn, *The Greenbelt Cooperative: Success and Decline.* Davis, CA: University of California Center for Cooperatives 1992, p. 250. George Yasukochi, "The Berkeley Co-op—Anatomy of a Noble Experiment," *What Happened to the Berkeley Co-op?* Michael Fullerton, ed., Davis, CA: University of California Center for Cooperatives 1992, pp. 23-32. See especially pp. 26-27. Karen Zimbelman, "Berkeley: Lessons for Co-op Leaders." *Cooperative Grocer,* Issue 38, January-February 1992. Robert Grott, Jesse Singerman, Dave Gutknecht, and Pat Rogers. "Why Co-ops Die: An exchange on the fate of food co-ops." *Cooperative Grocer,* Issue 9, February-March 1987.

181 For information on CoCoFiSt, see www.cocofist.coop. Cooperative Grocer Information Network website is www.cgin.coop. Helena Enconomo. "Weaver Street Finds Success in Recruiting and Retaining Latino Staff." *Cooperative Grocer:* Issue 112. May/June 2004.

182 See *Cooperative Grocer,* various issues. http://cooperativegrocer.coop/articles/index.php? view_all=topics.

183 Peg Nolan, Walden Swanson, Kate Sumberg, and Dave Gutknecht, "Retail Operations Survey 2001: Strong Results, Debatable Future." *Cooperative Grocer,* Issue 101, July-August 2002. Dave Gutknecht, "The Editor Notes." *Cooperative Grocer,* Issue 107, July-August 2003. NCGA, "Ninety-four Independent Natural Food Co-ops Form One National Organization." Iowa City, IA: NCGA, April 26, 2004. www.ncga.coop/news_announce.html. Dave Gutknecht. "Local Co-ops Build National Presence." *Cooperative Grocer,* Issue 112, May-June 2004.

184 Conversions of non-profit hospitals to for-profit hospitals have stemmed considerable from their mid-1990s peak. In 1995, there were 347 such conversions. By contrast, between July 2001 and March 2002, there were a total of only 20 such conversions. See Representative Pete Stark, "The Pursuit of Profit: Non-Profit Hospitals Become the Big Public Giveaway of the Nineties." January 9, 1997. http://www.house.gov/stark/documents/coversion.html. Accessed Sept. 2, 2004, and Center for Medicare and Medicaid Services (CMS), *Health Care Industry Market Update: Acute Care Hospitals.* Baltimore, MD: CMS, April 29, 2002). Quote is from Paul Hazen. "Statement of Paul Hazen, President, NCBA, Before the Senate Subcommittee on Antitrust, Competition, and Consumer Rights," hearing on *Hospital Group Purchasing: Lowering Costs at the Expense of Patient Health and Medical Innovation?* Apr. 30, 2002. Industry statistics from Susan Greco, "The Declaration of Independents." *Inc.* Sept. 2001. Richard Dines, National Cooperative Business Association, Interview, November 18, 2004.

185 NCB. *NCB Co-op 100.* Washington, DC: 2003. Stacy Mitchell, *The Home Town Advantage.* Minneapolis: Institute for Local Self-Reliance, pp. 81-84. Susan Greco, "The Declaration of Independents." Inc. September 2001. www.inc.com/magazine/20010901/23348.html. Accessed April 2, 2005.

186 Mitchell, *loc. cit.* Greco, loc. cit.Business Wire. "Office Products Dealers Co-op Moves up the Supply Chain in Bid to Compete with 'Big Box' Competition." Indianapolis, January 27, 2004. Quote from Paul Hazen, *loc. cit.*

187 Christina Clamp, Interview, June 16, 2004. Quote of Greenberg from Greco, *loc. cit.*

188 Christina Clamp, "Cooperatives at the Start of the 21st Century: An Overview of the Cooperative Movement in the USA. Southern New Hampshire University: 2002, pp. 8-12. Mimeo. Greg Lawless and Anne Reynolds, *Worker Cooperatives: Case Studies, Key Criteria & Best Practices.* Madison, WI: Univ. of Wisconsin Center for Cooperatives, 2004, p. 1. GEO, *An Economy of Hope,* Stillwater, PA: GEO 2000.

189 Lawless and Reynolds, *op. cit.,* pp. 2-3. Erin Rice and Stu Schneider. Presentations at "Building and Replicating the Models." *Eastern Conference on Workplace Democracy—Sharing the Promise: Economic Democracy at Work.* Tripton, NC: Aurora Productions 2002, CD #2-09. Tim Huet, Presentation at "Providing for Success." *Eastern Conference on Workplace Democracy—Sharing the Promise: Economic Democracy at Work.* Tripton, NC: Aurora Productions, 2002, CD #2-02. Regarding the New York City cooperative, see Jamie Pietras, "News and Columns," *New York Press.* Nov. 25, 2003, volume 16, issue 48, www.nypress.com/print.cfm?content_id=9213. Accessed July 26, 2004. Richard Dines, Interview, November 18, 2004.

190 Another technical impediment faced by some successful worker co-ops was that the value of members' shares would become cost prohibitive to new members seeking to join. This problem was resolved by the Mondragón cooperative in Spain (discussed in the section on international initiatives of this report), by setting up a system of internal accounts, which effectively force co-op members to "reinvest heavily for expansion and defer profit distribution" until retirement. These accounts function much like a pension fund, and new members do not need to "buy in" to the cooperative. This model is now widely used by worker cooperatives in the United States. Tim Huet, "News from Mondragón." http://www.geo.coop/huet.htm. Accessed Sept. 11, 2004. Adria Scharf, Personal Correspondence, Sept. 10, 2004.

191 Tim Huet, Presentation at "Providing for Success." *Eastern Conference on Workplace Democracy— Sharing the Promise: Economic Democracy at Work.* Tripton, NC: Aurora Productions, 2002, CD #2-02. Bob Stone. Report back from "Learning as We Go." *Sharing the Promise: Economic Democracy at Work.* Tripton, NC, CD #2-13. Aurora Productions: Tim Huet. Comment at workshop led by Gar Alperovitz on "Movement Building and the Future of Democracy." *Sharing the Promise: Economic Democracy at Work.* Tripton, NC: Aurora Productions, 2002, CD #2-11.

192 Ray Daffner, Interview, June 25, 2004.

193 Regarding this point, see also Susan E. Clarke and Gary L. Gaile, *The Work of Cities.* Minneapolis: University of Minnesota, 1998, p. 7, who note that American cities "work under the constraints imposed by the political logic of federalism and the economic imperatives of global capitalism."

194 For instance, Robert Shively, who has practiced economic development for the past 40 years, writes that, "There are indications that incentives are losing some of their allure." Robert Shively, *Economic Development for Small Communities.* Washington, D.C.: National Center for Small Communities, 2004. Quote on page 73. It should be noted, however, that the new strategies outlined here do not so much *replace* traditional incentive program efforts, as *supplement* them. Greg Leroy of the activist group Good Jobs First contends that little or no reduction in the use of economic incentives has occurred (Greg Leroy, Interview, Jan. 27, 2005). Jeff McElravy of the Government Finance Officers Association confirms that traditional incentive programs remain the norm. But even within this traditional approach, McElravy says state and local officials have sought to alter these to "make investments in assets that are immobile to spur development" such as infrastructure improvements, "rather than writing a check" to private companies. (Jeff McElravy, Interview, July 1, 2004).

195 Tony Sutton, *Special Study: Municipal Enterprise Activities.* St. Paul, MN: Government Information Division, (Office of the State Auditor, State of Minnesota) March 18, 2004. Christopher Hoene and Michael Pagano, "'Enterprising' Cities: An Exploratory Analysis of Municipal Enterprise Revenues, User Fees and Charges, and Service Delivery." *Association for Budgeting and Financial Management* conference: Washington, D.C., January 17-19, 2002, www.abfm.org/pdf_2001_conf/hoene.pdf. Accessed Feb. 13, 2005. Kent Lassman and Randolph J. May. "A Survey of Government-Provided Telecommunications: Disturbing Growth Trend Continues Unabated." *Progress on Point: Periodic Commentaries on the Policy Debate.* Release 10. 17. Washington, D.C.: The Progress and Freedom Foundation, October 2003., pp 2-3. APPA, *Payments and Contributions by Public Power Distribution Systems to State and Local Governments, 2002 Data.* Washington, D.C., APPA, June 2004. APPA, *2004-05 Annual Directory & Statistical Report,* Washington, D.C.: APPA, 2004, pp. 21, 41. City of San Diego, *Annual Budget, Fiscal Year 2004,* page 83. Accessed on September 22, 2004 at http://www.sandiego.gov/budget/annual/volume1/pdf/v1genfundrev.pdf. Elisa Hill, Interview, August 6, 2004. Regarding hotels, see text below.

196 Adria Scharf, with Thad Williamson, Alex Campbell and Jeff Pope. *Municipal Enterprise: A Strategy for Job Creation and Stabilization.* Sondra Myers, ed. The Democracy Collaborative at the University of Maryland and The National Center for Economic and Security Alternatives, November 2003, page 4. See also David L. Imbroscio, *Restructuring Cities: Alternative Economic Development and Urban Regimes.* Thousand Oaks, CA: SAGE, 1997, pp. 139-158. According to a paper written by Christopher Hoene of the National League of Cities and Michael Pagano of the University of Illinois at Chicago, even before the most recent recession, municipal general fund revenues had barely kept pace with per capita income; between 1988 and 2000, city general revenue growth outpaced income growth by only 2 percent and grew 27 percent slower than GDP, during a period when state and federal revenues both outpaced GDP growth. See Hoene and Pagano, *op. cit,* page 9.

197 The case of a municipal hotel that lost money in the Atlanta suburb of Murrieta, Georgia— profiled below—provides one example where such political control was exercised.

198 See Williamson, Imbroscio, and Alperovitz, *op. cit.,* page 164.

199 Beverly S. Bunch, "Changes in the Usage of Enterprise Funds by Large City Governments." *Public Budgeting and Finance.* Summer 2000, pp. 15-19. Hoene and Pagano, *op. cit.*

200 Tony Sutton, *op. cit.,* pp. 1-3, 10-20. Although the study says it found 2,087 enterprises, this appears to involve an arithmetic error. Regarding the Minnesota League of Cities' estimate, see Dan Wascoe. "Welcome to Hutchinson, city of business," *Minneapolis Star Tribune,* July 27, 2003, p. 1B.

201 Sutton, *op. cit.,* pp. 14, 18-20; average calculated by authors based on chart on page 14. While Minnesota is unusual in allowing small cities to own liquor stores (the city must have fewer than 10,000 people when the store opens), many states earn revenue from liquor stores. For instance, in Pennsylvania, the state Liquor Control Board reported record sales of $1.25 billion in 2003. *Knight Ridder Tribune Business News,* "Liquor Sales Are Up in Pennsylvania." Washington, DC. February 13, 2004, page 1.

202 Wascoe, *loc. cit.*

203 Saxton, *op. cit.,* pp. 20, 52, 61, 66.

204 If the median and the mean were equal, then the net contribution (5.8 percent of $39.5 billion) would be just shy of $2.3 billion. In the survey, APPA asked respondents to identify a sales range; they then derived medians for each sales range. Medians in the high sales categories were a *greater* percentage of income than for the whole, so $2.3 billion is likely an *underestimate.* See APPA, *Payments and Contributions by Public Power Distribution Systems to State and Local Governments, 2002 Data.* Washington, DC: APPA, June 2004. Ron Lunt, APPA, Interview, October 26, 2004. Sales figures are based on EIA (Energy Information Administration) data as reported in APPA, *2004-05 Annual Directory & Statistical Report,* Washington, D.C.: APPA, 2004, pp. 21, 41. APPA, *Shining a Light on Public Service,* Washington, D.C.: APPA, 2004: www.appanet.org/about/publicpower/PPFactSheet.pdf.

205 APPA, *2004-05 Annual Directory & Statistical Report* Washington, D.C.: APPA, 2004, pp. 36, 62. On the DWP scandals of the early 1900s, see Tim Dirks, "Review of *Chinatown* (1974)." http://www.filmsite.org/chin.html, as well as the film Chinatown. See also Catherine Mulholland, *William Mulholland and the Rise of Los Angeles.* Berkeley, CA: University of California Press, August 2000. On DWP's recent awards, see http://www.ladwp.com/ladwp/cms/ladwp001978.jsp. For a succinct study of the 2001 California electricity crisis, including analysis of municipal utilities, see Sam Weinstein and David Hall, *The California Electricity Crisis—*

overview and international lessons. Greenwich, UK: University of Greenwich, February 2001. http://www.eldis.org/static/DOC8861.htm. Web sites accessed January 7, 2005.

206 Kent Lassman and Randolph J. May. "A Survey of Government-Provided Telecommunications: Disturbing Growth Trend Continues Unabated." *Progress on Point: Periodic Commentaries on the Policy Debate*. Release 10. 17. Washington, D.C.: The Progress and Freedom Foundation, October 2003, pp 2-3, Map based on authors' calculations culled from the list and data provided by Lassman and May, pp. 10, 16-28. Ron Lutt, Interview, Oct. 26, 2004.

207 Glasgow Electric Plant Board, "Glasgow EPB Delivers $318,000 to Local Agencies in 2002." Glasgow EPB: Glasgow, KY, Dec. 27, 2002. www.glasgow-ky.com/releases/#Glasgow_EPB_ Delivers_122702. Williamson, Imbroscio, and Alperovitz, *op. cit.*, page 152.

208 Glasgow EPB. "2003 Annual Audit for the Glasgow Electric Plant Board, City of Glasgow," Glasgow EPB: Glasgow, KY, 2003. www.glasgow-ky.com/EPB/Audit19.htm and www.glasgow-ky.com/EPB/Audit20.htm. Accessed July 23, 2004. Thomas M. Leonard, "Government Entry into the Telecom Business: Are the Benefits Commensurate with the Costs?" *Progress on Point*. Release 11.3. Washington, D.C.: Progress and Freedom Foundation, February 2004, pp. 8, 30; quote on page 30.

209 According to APPA, public enterprises face at least some restrictions on entry in Arkansas, Florida, Missouri, Minnesota, Nebraska, Nevada, South Carolina, Tennessee, Texas, Utah, Virginia, Washington, and Wisconsin. www.appanet.org/legislativeregulatory/industry/ TelecomFactSheet050104.pdf. Washington, D.C.: APPA, May 2004.

210 Jim Baller quoted in Marguerite Reardon, "Broadband for the masses?" CNET News.com. April 14, 2004.http://nws.com/com/2008-1037-5190220.html. APPA, *Community Broadband: Separating Fact from Fiction*. Washington, D.C., APPA, January 2004. http://www.appanet.org/legislativeregulatory/broadband/fact/fact.cfm. Accessed July 23, 2004.

211 Doris Kelley, Telecommunications Coordinator, Iowa Association of Municipal Utilities, *Economic and Community Benefits of Cedar Fall, Iowa's Municipal Telecommunications Network*. October 2, 2003. Both quotes are on page 8.

212 Marguerite Reardon, "City-owned network moves forward." *CNET News.com*. July 16, 2004. http://news.com/2100-1034-5272638.html. Accessed July 23, 2004.

213 DTE Biomass. *Success stories*. www.dtebe.com/stories/stories.html, US Environmental Protection Agency: Landfill Methane Outreach Program, *City of Riverview*. www.epa.gov/lmop/res/ riverview.htm, Alperovitz, *op. cit.*, page 93. Web sites accessed Sept. 30, 2004.

214 Glendale Water & Power, *Road Map to Tomorrow: Annual Report 2002-2003*, page 15. For a list of 362 landfill energy projects, see U.S. Environmental Protection Agency (EPA), *Energy Projects and Candidate Landfills*. Washington, D.C.: EPA, July 19, 2004. www.epa.gov/lmop/proj/index.htm. Web site accessed Sept. 30, 2004. Sutton, *loc. cit.*, Energy Information Administration (EIA): *Voluntary Reporting of Greenhouse Gases, 2002*. Report No. #DOE/EIA-0608/2002. Washington, D.C.: EIA, January 2004.

215 Conor Dougherty. "San Marcos, Inc.: Going into the development business pays off for charter city." *The San Diego Union-Tribune*. October 5, 2003, page N-4. City of San Diego, *Annual Budget, Fiscal Year 2004*, page 83. Accessed at http://www.sandiego.gov/budget/annual/volume1/pdf/v1genfundrev.pdf on Sept. 22, 2004. Williamson, Imbroscio, and Alperovitz, *op. cit.*, pp. 156-158.

216 Karina Ricks, Washington D. C. Office of Planning, Interview, August 9, 2004. Fred Selden, Fairfax County Planning, Interview, August 3, 2004. Elisa Hill, Washington Metropolitan Area Transit Association (WMATA), Interview, August 6, 2004. Many TOD advocates prefer to reserve the term "transit oriented development" for fully integrated development and label less ambitious projects "transit-adjacent" or "transit-related." See Dena Belzer and Gerald Autler, *Transit Oriented Development: Moving from Rhetoric to Reality.* Washington, D.C.: Brookings, June 2002. While we sympathize with these goals, in this study we use TOD broadly to refer to any and all efforts to capture real estate value and ridership revenue through development of real estate in the immediate vicinity of mass transit stations.

217 Elisa Hill, Interview, August 6, 2004.

218 Al Dobbins: Prince George County. Mayoral Task Force on Transit-Oriented Development. "Report to Mayor Anthony A. Williams." Washington, D.C.: Government of the District of Columbia Office of Planning and Department of Transportation, June 20, 2002. D.C. Office of Planning, *Trans-Formation: Recreating Transit-Oriented Neighborhood Centers in Washington D.C.* Washington DC: September 2002. Interview, August 3, 2004. Elisa Hill, Interview, August 6, 2004. Robert Grow, Interview, June 21, 2004. Robert Brosnan, Interview, August 16, 2004.

219 Williams, Imbroscio, and Alperovitz, *op. cit.,* page 157. District of Columbia, Office of Planning, "Neighborhoods," Section 5, page 1. *The AWI Framework Plan,* Washington, D.C., http://planning.dc.gov/planning/cwp/view,a,1285,q,582200,planningNav_GID,1708.asp. WMATA, Joint Development Solicitation." Washington, D.C.: WMATA, Issued July 28, 2004.

220 Thomas Hazinski and Mark Laubacher, "Tax-Exempt Hotel Financing: A Primer for Finance Officers," *Government Finance Review,* February 2002, pp.32-35. Allan Brettman, "Break Lets Cities into Hotel Business, *The Oregonian,* Dec. 29, 2003, p. B-1. Barbara De Lollis, "Debate rages over convention hotels," *USA Today.* March 15, 2004, p. 1-B. Charles Belfoure, "A Resort Replaces a Mental Hospital in Maryland." *New York Times,* January 6, 2002, Section 11, page 4. Laura Ingram, "City-owned hotel posts $162K losses in Oct.," November 22, 2003. *Marietta Daily Journal,* Lola Sherman, "How Suite It Is: Much work needed, but city-owned oceanfront hotel is a moneymaker." *San Diego Union-Tribune,* March 17, 2004, p. NC-1. Chris Bender, DC Deputy Mayor's Office, Interview, May 13, 2004. Richard Williamson, "Phoenix Council to Pick New Hotel Site." *Bond Buyer.* June 16, 2004, page 3. Carlos Guerra, "City must study convention data behind rosy forecast for hotel." *San Antonio Express-News,* June 20, 2004, p. 1B.

221 Heywood Sanders, "Risk and Reality in Public Headquarters Hotel Development." *Government Finance Review,* June 2004, pp. 21-24, "preliminary" quote on page 21. In January 2005, a study by Sanders on the related convention industry showed a sharp drop nationally in convention center business since the late 1990s. See Heywood Sanders, *Space Available: The Realities of Convention Centers as Economic Development Strategy.* Brookings: Washington, D.C.: Jan. 2005. Kirsten Mack, "Rise in convention business reported," *The Houston Chronicle,* July 15, 2004, p. B-4.

222 Ginger D. Richardson and Jennifer Autrey. "City-owned hotels have seen mixed results so far." *Fort Worth Star-Telegram,* December 8, 2002. Ingram, *loc. cit;* Sherman, *loc. cit.* An interesting point about the Murrieta example is that voters were able to monitor the situation and held officials accountable for their failure by electing in 2000 Mayor Bill Dunaway on a platform to change management of the city-owned hotel, which he did. See, for instance, Philip Taylor, "Marietta: Hotel Debt Still $265,000." *Atlanta Journal-Constitution.* January 8, 2003, page 3-B.

223 Doug Hoffer, *A Survey of Economically Targeted Investments: Opportunities for Public Pension Funds: A report for the Vermont State Treasurer and the State Retirement Boards.* Montpelier, VT: February 16, 2004.

224 Susan E. Clarke and Gary L. Gaile, *The Work of Cities.* Minneapolis: University of Minnesota, 1998, page 84. Robert G. Heard and John Sibert, *Growing New Business with Seed and Venture Capital: State Experiences and Options.* Washington, D.C.: National Governors' Association, 2000, page 48. Study by Vineeta Armand cited in Jayne Elizabeth Zanglein, "Overcoming Institutional Barriers on the ETI Superhighway." *The Second National Heartland Labor Capital Conference,* Washington, D.C.: Heartland Labor Capital Research Project. Apr. 1999, p. 2. Richard H. Moore, "State Treasurer Richard Moore Announces Landmark Public Pension Fund Investment Initiative." Raleigh: North Carolina Department of State Treasurer, July 1, 2002. George F. Pappas, *Report of the Governor's Commission on the Development of Advanced Technology,* Annapolis: MD, Jan. 12, 2004. www.gov.state.md.us/pdfs/pappas.pdf. Accessed Feb. 7, 2005.

225 Peter K. Eisinger, *The Rise of the Entrepreneurial State: State and Local Economic Development Policy in the United States.* Madison: University of Wisconsin, 1988, pp. 333-334, quote on page 333. Clarke and Gaile, *op. cit.,* pp. 72, 79-86. Quote on page 72. To reiterate a point made above, this does not mean that traditional strategies to lure business from one city to another have disappeared. Better put, the "toolbox" of economic development policies has been expanded to include new options, such as the asset-based policies reviewed here. For more on the continuation of traditional incentive policies, see Martin Saiz, "Politics and Economic Development: Why Governments Adopt Different Strategies to Induce Economic Development," *Policy Studies Journal,* volume 29 (2), 2001.

226 Locally focused economic development efforts have become even more common in the wake of the popularity of the "creative economy" thesis promoted by Richard Florida of George Washington University. According to Florida, communities gain competitive advantage in the new economy not by providing business incentives, but rather by promoting cultural spaces that attract professional workers. See Richard Florida, *The Rise of the Creative Class.* New York: Basic Books, 2002. For further information on Florida's work, see www.creativeclass.org.

227 Pennsylvania Industrial Development Authority (PIDA) Loan Program. http://www.pidc-pa.org/svc-fina-loanprog-h.asp?itemid=1. Accessed August 14, 2004. PIDA, *Annual Report.* Philadelphia: PIDA, 2002, page 2.

228 William Amt, "Menu of Loan Programs an Advantage for Regions." *Economic Development Digest,* vol. 12, no. 4, February-March 2001. See also the EDC's website at www.tricountyedc.org. Accessed Jan. 24, 2005.

229 Faye Kenn, National Center for Small Communities, Interview, Jan. 27, 2004. Faye Kenn, Personal Correspondence, Jan. 28, 2004. Group's website is at http://abe.midco.net/necog/index.html. Accessed Feb. 4, 2005.

230 Development Corporation of Austin (DCA). "Economic Development for Austin and Mower County." Austin, MN: DCA, Nov. 7, 2002. http://www.spamtownusa.com/dca. Accessed Aug. 14, 2004.

231 Queens County Overall Economic Development Corporation. "Services." http://www.queensny.org/serv/qc_qais.html, and "Who We Are," http://www.queensny.org/who/index.html. Accessed August 14, 2004.

232 Dan Loague, "Enterprising Capital: Bringing the Knowledge-Based Economy Home." *Economic Development America*, Spring 2004, pp. 16-18.

233 Edward Siedle quoted in Mary Williams Walsh, "Concerns Raised Over Consultants to Pension Funds." *New York Times*, March 21, 2004. Heard and Sibert, *op. cit.*, p. 48. "Profiles of Top 200 Pension Funds. The P&I 1,000." *Pensions & Investments*, Jan. 20, 2003. Data as of Sept. 30, 2002. Mike Francis, "Oregon Venture Capital Fund of Funds Excites Investors." *Oregonian*. February 6, 2004. Gov. Jeb Bush quoted in Stephen Pounds, Jeff Ostrowski, and Stacey Singer. "Florida to Put $1 Billion from Pension into Venture for Biotech." *Palm Beach Post*, April 17, 2004.

234 Robert Elder Jr., "End of the line for Texas Growth Fund? State investment pool may have run its course." *Austin American-Statesman*, March 14, 2004. Colorado Venture Capital Association, "CVM Equity Partners," www.coloradovca.org/members/19.html. Accessed on July 25, 2004. Heard and Sibert, *op. cit.*, pp. 25-37, quote on page 33.

235 Hoffer, *op. cit.*, pp. 2-3.

236 Study of Armand cited by Zanglein, *op. cit.*, page 2.

237 Public funds estimate from Richard H. Moore, "State Treasurer Richard Moore Announces Landmark Public Pension Fund Investment Initiative." Raleigh, NC: North Carolina Department of State Treasurer, July 1, 2002, www.treasurer.state.nc.us/NR/rdonlyres/AA243C7D-D01B-474A-9BBA95672BAC2DB2/0/InvestmentProtection.pdf. Accessed April 4, 2005.

238 CalPERS, "Sean Harrigan." Sacramento, CalPERS, Accessed Aug. 15, 2004. http://www.calpers.ca.gov/index.jsp?bc=/about/organization/board/members/sean-harrigan.xml. Other states where union members serve as pension trustees include Ohio, Maryland, and New Mexico. According to a February 2005 article by William Greider, nation-wide there are 50 members of the American Federation of State, County, and Municipal Employees (AFSCME) who serve as trustees on public pension boards. See William Greider, "The New Colossus," *The Nation*. February 28, 2005.

239 There are some exceptions. For instance, the AFL-CIO Mortgage Investment Trust Fund, a forerunner of the AFL-CIO Housing Investment Trust, which invests in real estate built by union members, was formed in 1965. See AFL-CIO History Investment Trust, "History," http://aflcio-hit.com/company/history.html. Accessed Jan. 4, 2005.

240 Quote from Robert Pleasure; Interview, May 13, 2004. Mike Garland, AFL-CIO Office of Investment, Interview, June 24, 2004, also mentioned the traditional union reticence to get involved with pension fund management issues.

241 U.S. Department of Labor (DOL), *29 CFR 2509.94-1 – Interpretive bulletin relating to the fiduciary standard under ERISA in considering economically targeted investments*. Washington, D.C.: DOL, 1994. Accessed at www.dol.ogv/dol/allcfr/Title_29/Part_2509/29CFR2509.94-1.htm. Accessed January 4, 2005.

242 Michael Calabrese, "Building on Past Success: Labor-Friendly Investment Vehicles and the Power of Private Equity," *The Second National Heartland Labor Capital Conference*, Washington, DC: Heartland Labor Capital Research Project. April 1999, page 7.

243 The Maryland study compiled their figures based on Sept. 2002 figures as published in Jan. 2003 by *Pensions & Investments*. See Pappas, *loc. cit.* The same study also indicates that state

pension funds as of 2002 had invested a total of $69.4 billion in real estate, another area used by many pension funds to invest in local economic development.

244 CalPERS, "Asset Allocation," www.calpers.ca.gov/print.jsp?bc=/investments/assets/assetalloca-tion.xml. Accessed Feb. 3, 2005. Phil Angelides, "A California Investment Policy for the 21st Century." *California Policy Issues Annual,* Nov. 2001, pp. 3-10. Tom Croft and Teesa Hebb, "Collaboration Between Labor, Academics and Community Activists to Advance Labor/Capital Strategies: The Origins of Heartland Network." April 14, 2002. Presented at the *Using Pensions for Social Control of Capitalist Investment* conference. Madison: The Havens Center-University of Wisconsin, June 2004, page 29. John E. Peterson, "Guide to Municipal Finance: Find Me the Money." *Governing* June 2004, page 54. Wisconsin targets 5 percent of assets for real estate and an additional 5 percent for private equity. See State of Wisconsin Investment Board, "Fixed Trust Fund," www.swib.state.wi.us/fixed.asp. Accessed Aug. 15, 2004

245 U.S. General Accounting Office (GAO), *Public Pension Plans: Evaluation of Economically Targeted Investment Programs.* Report GAO/PEMD-95-13. Washington, D.C.: GAO, 1995. Estimate for 2004 is from Chris Gabrieli, "Economically Targeted Investments: Key Factors for Success." Boston: Northeast State Treasurers and the National Association of Unclaimed Property Administrators Conference, Aug. 22-25, 2004. Accessed on Feb. 2, 2005 at http://www.nast.net/2004.neast.naupa/program.htm. Gabrieli's estimate is conservative because the figure assumes that the amount invested is only 2 percent of total assets, compared with the 2.4 percent the GAO estimated a decade before. Hoffer's estimate for 2004, based on 2.4 percent of assets, is $55 billion. Because many state pension funds have added economically targeted investments to their portfolios in recent years, the actual total may be even higher. In 2003, for instance, both the states of Massachusetts and Washington instituted new economically target-ed investment programs. See, Luke Timmerman, "Investment Board May Put More Cash in State Start-Ups." *Seattle Times,* March 13, 2003, p. D-1; Stephen Dunphy, "The Newsletter," *Seattle Times,* January 23, 2004, p. C-1; and Andrew Caffrey, "Pension Board Eyes Investing, Treasurer Cahill Says Goal is Economic, Social Gains," *Boston Globe,* August 14, 2003, p. E-1.

246 Aziza Agia, *Innovative Significant Scale Models of Community Asset-Building: Learning from International Experience.* College Park, MD and Washington, DC: The Democracy Collaborative and the National Center for Economic and Security Alternatives, 2004, page 2.

247 *Ibid.*

248 *Ibid.* See pp. 51-68, 81-83, and 85-89. See also Mondragón Corporación Cooperativa. *Memoria. Annual Report 2003,* page 5, www.mcc.coop.

249 As of 1993, there were 760 million members of cooperatives worldwide, of whom roughly 15 per-cent (114 million) were members of consumer cooperatives. As of 2004, it is estimated that over-all cooperative membership worldwide has increased to over 800 million. See J. M. Rana, *ICA Membership from Developing Countries.* Geneva, Switzerland and Madison, Wisconsin: International Co-operative Information Centre (International Co-operative Alliance and the University of Wisconsin Center for Cooperatives), 1995. www.wisc.edu/uwcc/icic/orgs/ica/pubs/review/vol-88/member.html. For 2004 figure, see ICA, "Co-operatives for Fair Globalisation: Creating Opportunities for All." July 3, 2004. www.ica.coop/ica/ica/coopday/enmessage2004.html. Web sites accessed Sept. 30, 2004.

250 Agia, *op. cit.,* pp. 58-62.

251 *Ibid.,* pp. 62-65.

252 *Ibid.*, pp. 65-70.

253 Agia, *op. cit.*, pp. 45-46. Regarding co-ops in the United States, see the section on cooperatives above.

254 *Ibid.*, pp. 51-54. See also Gregory Macleod, *From Mondragón to America.* Halifax, NS: UCCB Press, 1997.

255 Agia, *op. cit.*, pp. 55-58.

256 *Ibid.*, pp. 51-58.

257 *Ibid.*, pp. 17, 51-54.

258 *Ibid.*, pp. 86-87.

259 *Ibid.*, pp. 87-90. Key scholarly studies of town and village enterprises include Enrico Perotti et al., "State-Owned versus Township and Village Enterprises in China," *Contemporary Economic Studies,* 1999, vol. 41 (2/3): 151-179; and Jeffrey Sachs and Wing Thye Wood. "Understanding China's Economic Performance." *NBER Working Paper,* number 5935, Cambridge, MA: NBER, 1997; and Liaxiang Sun, "Anticipatory Ownership Reform Driven by Competition: China's Township-Village and Private Enterprises in the 1990s," *Comparative Economic Studies* (2000), volume 42 (3): 49-75.

260 *Ibid.* See pp. 75-79 and the section of this report on CDFIs, above.

261 *Ibid.*, pages 81-83. While microenterprise is not as extensive in the United States, over 40,000 business start-ups had resulted from microenterprise loan activity up to 1998. U.S. microenterprise loan funds vary in terms of their exact operating practices, but maintain a similar focus, as Lisa Servon notes, of serving as "lenders of last resort, providing credit to people who want to be self-employed but who cannot obtain credit through ordinary channels. See Lisa Servon, *Bootstrap Capital: Microenterprise and the American Poor.* Washington, D.C.: The Brookings Institution, 1999, quote on page 3; quoted in Williamson, Imbroscio, and Alperovitz, *op. cit.*, p. 226.

262 Regarding current federal policy, our estimate of the ESOP tax credit value is from Williamson, Imbroscio, and Alperovitz, *op. cit.*, page 131. The FY2005 estimate of the Low Income Housing Tax Credit program is from Office of Management and Budget (OMB), www.whitehouse.gov/omb/budget/fy2002/bud22_4.html.

263 The $1.5 trillion figure for combined assets was calculated by adding up the separate figures cited in the chapters of this text: 1) The top 100 co-ops, excluding the three credit unions on the list, had assets of $247 billion; 2) Credit union sector assets are $629 billion; 3) ESOP sector assets are $297 billion; 4) Other employee stock assets, including stock employees own in the companies they work for through 401(k) plans and employee stock purchase plans, are estimated at $258 billion; 5) CDFI assets are $14 billion; 6) Economically targeted pension investments are estimated at $43.6 billion); and 7) Municipal utility assets are $39.5 billion. All told, these figures add up to $1.528 trillion. The $37.8 trillion in total U.S. assets is for 2002. See CUNA & Affiliates and Michigan Credit Union League, "Bank Attacks: Credit Unions Fight Back!" Presentation to Taxation Lawmakers, Aug. 2004. http://mcul.cusiteonline.com/governmental_affairs/leg_affairs/taxation_lawmaker_presentation.ppt.

264 The spillover effect of ShoreBank's community lending in Chicago was highlighted by a panel of private Chicago lenders at the Orientation to the Capital Market conference, held by Wall

Street Without Walls and Federal Reserve Bank of Chicago in Chicago on November 3, 2004.

265 Regarding cross-sectoral efforts cited in this paragraph and below, information comes from a number of sources. Mark Pinsky, head of the National Community Capital Association, cited The Reinvestment Fund and Coastal Enterprises as two groups that performed the roles of both CDCs and CDFIs at an address to the NCCED 34th Annual Conference, Los Angeles, October 8, 2004. Regarding New York City's affordable housing pension investments, see William C. Thompson Jr., "Pension Funds to Make First Investment in Community Preservation Corporation's Loan Syndicate for $25 Million." www.comptroller.nyc.gov/press/2003_releases/pr03-12-105.shtm. Other sources regarding cross-sectoral efforts are: National Cooperative Bank Development Corporation (NCBDC), *2000 Annual Report, 2001 Annual Report,* and *2003 Annual Report,* pp. 4, 22 — all available at www.ncbdc.org; Northland Institute, "About the Northland Institute," www.northland.org/About.cfm; and New Hampshire Community Loan Fund, "Micro Credit-New Hampshire." www.nhclf.org/MNCH01.html.

266 Sources for the policy paragraphs are as follows: regarding the Canadian worker co-op fund, see Hazel Corcoran, Executive Director, Canadian Worker Co-op Federation, "Building and Replicating Models" *Eastern Conference on Workplace Democracy — Sharing the Promise: Economic Democracy at Work.* Tripton, NC: Aurora Productions, 2002, CD #2-09. Regarding the national housing trust fund proposal, see National Low Income Housing Coalition (NLIHC), "National Housing Trust Fund." Washington D.C.: NLIHC, 2004, www.nhtf.org. Information about inclusionary zoning comes from Noreen Beatley, The Enterprise Foundation, Interview, Dec. 15, 2004. Regarding the community development implications of transit-oriented development, see Scott Bernstein, "The New Transit Town: Great Places and Great Nodes That Work for Everyone." In *The New Transit Town: Best Practices in Transit-Oriented Development.* Hank Ditttmar and Gloria Ohland, editors. Washington, D.C.: Island Press, 2004, pp. 232-248.

267 Regarding community foundations, Janet Tapolsky of The Aspen Institute, (Interview, July 13, 2004) called our attention to these efforts. See also Rhode Island Foundation, "RI Foundation awards $1 million in grants; focuses on economic/community development." Aug. 30, 2002. www.rifoundation.org/matriarch/DisplayLinksPage.asp_Q_PageID_E_223_A_PageName_E_AboutPressReleasesIntro_A_LinksPageID_E_53; Center for Venture Philanthropy, "Assets for All Alliance," www.pcf.org/venture_philanthropy/afaa.html; and East Bay Community Foundation, "Living Communities Initiative: LCI in Action." http://www.lcinitiative.org/cgi-bin/lci/action/where/index.html?id=jDsnJkdA.

268 Regarding the role of universities, see Anne Habiby, "Revving Up: Universities and Colleges as Urban Revitalization Engines." Economic Development America, winter 2004, pp. 6-8; Yale's Partnership on Nonprofit Ventures web site is at http://ventures.yale.edu.

269 Quote of CEO Cicero Wilson is from an Interview conducted on Dec. 9, 2004.

APPENDICES

Appendix A: Future Research Agenda

This report has provided a preliminary attempt to map and examine a range of socially important asset-based strategies across the board. Key research needs are outlined below.

Individual development accounts have received considerable attention, a result no doubt of the origins of the movement in academia, as well as the fact that the idea has been tested in numerous pilot projects. A critical—but unanswered—question is this: What happens if the IDA idea becomes general social policy, rather than being restricted to a small (and, at least in part, self-selecting) minority of the low-income population? In 2005, Great Britain is slated to be the first large country to give an IDA program universal application. The United States may soon follow. Watching this social policy experiment unfold and assessing its performance will be an important priority.

Social enterprise may be one of the most intriguing areas for further study. Jed Emerson in 2003 led an effort that resulted in a "blended value map" of organizations that mix economic and social goals. Our study approaches the growth of social enterprise from a somewhat different asset-based direction, but we believe that these approaches are broadly complementary. One major research need is simply to conduct a national census of the sector, which would let us know the scope of the sector, help define areas of concentration, provide a more concrete sense of how it differs from traditional non-profit enterprise, and so on. A second priority is a comprehensive attempt to examine the effectiveness of social enterprise as a strategy that integrates diverse functions across sectors. Circumstantial evidence from our study, Emerson's, and others suggests that social enterprise can be highly effective, but this remains, at this point, only a working hypothesis.

The community development corporation (CDC), like IDAs and unlike social enterprise, has been the subject of considerable research and analysis. One problem, however, is the increasingly dated nature of the available studies. The last industry census took place in 1998 and was published in 1999. The only recent published data source is Christopher Walker's study of the first ten years of the National Community Development Initiative, published in 2002, but this only focused on 23 cities. At press time, a new census was scheduled to take place in 2005. Two specific questions we would like to investigate are the effects of supermarket center development on CDC economic sustainability and assessments of the overall community impact of CDC wealth-building activities.

The sector of community development financial institutions (CDFIs) has matured more recently than CDCs. Perhaps for this reason it has not been the subject of as much research as CDCs, although the number of studies is steadily increasing. In part because the sector is newer, industry data available through the CDFI Data Project is more current as well. The first census of the sector occurred in 2001 and the second in 2002. A major question facing the sector is how to reach a balance between expansion in scale (achieved by gaining greater access to capital markets) and maintaining a broad scope of activities that includes riskier (and hence "non-conforming") types of community development financing. Further research on how CDFIs are striking this balance is important.

Employee stock ownership plan (ESOP) companies, like CDCs, have been widely studied. One important difficulty, however, stems from the fact that ESOPs are established under pension law. As a result, unlike CDCs or CDFIs, there are many companies with ESOPs that don't self-identify as ESOPs. Not surprisingly, getting precise estimates of the number of ESOPs or ESOP members is difficult—and government statistics are only of moderate usefulness in sorting this out. For ESOPs that do self-identify as ESOPs, there is a substantial body of evidence that strongly suggests that ESOPs coupled with worker participation lead to productivity gains, as well as strong evidence that ESOP members tend to earn more and have much greater retirement benefits than employees of non-ESOP companies. Two gaps in the ESOP data concern the effect of majority ownership and the impact of ESOPs on capital mobility. We believe a census of majority ESOPs could provide a way to confirm existing studies that strongly suggest that ESOPs lead to greater community economic stability.

The Institute for Community Economics regularly surveys its membership, which roughly coincides with the extent of the community land trust sector itself. The survey data provides basic information about membership, staffing, and budget, but deeper qualitative data would be helpful and a more detailed questionnaire would be the obvious, albeit time consuming, way to get it. A major question facing the sector is how to reach significant scale. Answering this question requires more detailed analysis of data from Vermont, where the community land trust sector has achieved significant scale, as well as analysis of the constraints to capacity building that are holding back community land trusts in many other parts of the country.

The body of past research on cooperatives is extensive, but there is limited current research outside the agricultural sector. Nonetheless, the empirical evidence strongly suggests a resurgence of the cooperative form in some key sectors, such as food co-ops, purchasing co-ops, and worker co-ops. A priority would be to examine these areas of growth. It would also be important to investigate whether the democratic nature of worker cooperatives has any positive "social capital" benefits in terms of civic values and participation in the greater society.

Municipal enterprise is perhaps the least studied sector of all. A report from the National League of Cities on this issue is expected to come out in 2005. This report will likely provide us with the most complete census of enterprise funds compiled nationally to date. But many types of municipal activity do not fall under enterprise funds, such as real estate development, which, in addition to basic lease income, includes the hotel development and transit-oriented development trends examined in this study. There are many research needs in this sector, two of which are a comprehensive survey of municipal enterprise activity (more broadly defined, as we have done here) and assessment of the community impact of municipal enterprise on local economies.

Research on municipal and state venture fund and pension fund activity is somewhat more extensive than with municipal enterprise. Data on the pension fund sector is stronger than with venture funds, however. A comprehensive listing of local and state venture funds that evaluated performance over time would be a major contribution to our understanding of this new economic development tool. As with municipal enterprise, assessments of community impact should be an important part of this overall research project.

Internationally, this report summarizes a preliminary survey done by The National Center for Economic and Security Alternatives and The Democracy Collaborative. The survey suggests that international experience offers important lessons for the United States—especially in terms of how large-scale efforts can be achieved. However, this survey—

like the preliminary work on U.S. municipal enterprise—only opens the door on what is clearly a much more extensive arena of activity. No census of any kind exists which allows us to map the field internationally to assess impact, learn lessons, etc.

Finally, there is need for work on linkages across and between sectors. We have noted some cases, for instance, a CDC that has helped create social enterprises and a community land trust that helped create housing cooperatives. Much more systematic analysis of cross-sectoral possibilities is clearly warranted.

Appendix B: Resource Guide

Section One: Individual Development Accounts

Section Two: Social Enterprise

Section Three: Community Development Corporations and
                Community Organizing

Section Four: Community Development Finance and
                Microenterprise

Section Five: Employee Ownership

Section Six: Community Land Trusts

Section Seven: Cooperatives

Section Eight: Municipal Enterprise and Transit-Oriented
                Development

Section Nine: Pension Funds and Targeted Investments

Section Ten: International

Section 1: Individual Development Accounts

ASSET-BASED COMMUNITY DEVELOPMENT INSTITUTE
Institute for Policy Research
Northwestern University
2040 Sheridan Rd.
Evanston, IL 60208
T   847-491-8711
F   847-467-4140
abcd@northwestern.edu
www.northwestern.edu/ipr/abcd.html
   The Asset-Based Community Development Institute (ABCD Institute) provides
   research, training videos, workshops, publications, and consultation services for
   those interested in capacity-building community development and neighborhood asset mobilization. The Institute's work is based on the premise that
   through mobilizing their own assets, neighborhoods can substitute for imports
   and become more self-sufficient.

ASSETS FOR INDEPENDENCE DEMONSTRATION PROGRAM
Office of Community Services, Dept. of Health & Human Services
901 D Street, SW, Suite 500 West
Washington, DC 20447
T   202-401-4626
AFIProgram@acf.hhs.gov
www.acf.hhs.gov/assetbuilding
   The Assets for Independent Act Demonstration Program is the office that manages the federal pilot IDA program, the Assets for Independence Act (AFIA) and
   maintains information on federal programs that assist low-income families to
   accumulate assets and rise out of poverty.

CENTER FOR SOCIAL DEVELOPMENT (CSD)
George Warren Brown School of Social Work
Washington University, Campus Box 1196
One Brookings Drive
St. Louis, MO 63130
T   314-935-7433
F   314-935-8661
csd@gwbmail.wustl.edu
http://gwbweb.wustl.edu/csd

Founded by Michael Sherraden in 1994, the Center for Social Development is widely credited with developing and popularizing the idea of individual development accounts as a method for promoting greater asset accumulation by low-income individuals. The Center regularly provides a directory of state-level IDA programs as well as publishing research papers.

CORPORATION FOR ENTERPRISE DEVELOPMENT (CFED)

777 North Capitol St, NE, Ste. 800
Washington, DC 20002
T   202-408-9788
info@cfed.org
www.cfed.org

The Corporation for Enterprise Development works to promote asset-building strategies for both distressed individuals and communities as a way to ensure a sustainable economy accessible to all segments of the community. CFED maintains the IDA network, which links IDA programs across the nation. CFED provides economic policy design, research and analysis services as well.

INSTITUTE ON ASSETS AND SOCIAL POLICY

The Heller School for Social Policy and Management
Brandeis University, Mailstop 077
Walthma, MA 02524
T   781-736-8885
F   781-736-3925
assetinstitute@brandeis.edu
www.assetinstitute.org

Formerly known as the Asset Development Institute, the Institute on Assets & Social Policy aims to promote and advance individual asset-building policy choices that promise to reduce hunger and poverty in the nation by addressing their root causes. Its mission is to broaden and redefine the asset development concept and familiarize the public, media, and policy leaders with the asset development approach.

NEW AMERICA FOUNDATION

1630 Connecticut Ave., NW, 7th Fl.
Washington, DC 20009
T   202-986-2700
F   202-986-3696
www.assetbuilding.org

Founded in 2002, the New America Foundation is dedicated to do research, media promotion, and policy advocacy for the expansion of individual development accounts and other inclusive asset-building strategies.

NORTHLAND INSTITUTE
13911 Ridgedale Dr., Ste. 260
Minneapolis, MN 55305
T   952-541-9674
F   952-541-9684
www.northlandinst.org
Founded as a nonprofit organization in 1996, Northland's mission is to develop innovative asset-building strategies for local-income individuals, entrepreneurial non-profits, and community economic development organizations. The Institute is an active participant in national IDA coalitions, promotes social enterprise, and advocates ESOPs as a way to build assets among asset-poor workers and root businesses more firmly in their communities.

Section Two: Social Enterprise

BLENDEDVALUE.ORG
2121 Sand Hill Road
Menlo Park, CA 94025
JEmerson@hewlett.org
www.blendedvalue.org
Blended Value.Org is a web site that contains a research report that looks at a variety of different enterprises, including social enterprises, that seek to "blend," in one form or another social, financial (and sometimes also environmental) benefits in their work.

CENTER FOR CIVIL SOCIETY STUDIES
Institute for Policy Studies
The Johns Hopkins University
3400 North Charles Street
Baltimore, MD 21218
T   410-516-5463
F   410-516-7818
ccss@jhu.edu
www.jhu.edu/~ccss
The Center for Civil Society Studies of the Johns Hopkins Institute for

Policy Studies conducts research on the role that nonprofit organizations
play in modern society as well as providing training and capacity-building
activities designed to strengthen non-profit organizations.

COMMUNITY WEALTH VENTURES
1730 M Street, NW, Ste. 700
Washington, DC 20036
T   202-478-6570
F   202-347-5868
www.communitywealth.com
Community Wealth Ventures is a for-profit subsidiary of Share Our
Strength dedicated to expanding the resources generated by profitable enter-
prise for the purpose of promoting social change, especially by assisting and
documenting the efforts of nonprofit organizations to create businesses.
Community Wealth Ventures maintains with the Social Enterprise Alliance a
database of hundreds of social enterprises throughout the United States.

INDEPENDENT SECTOR
1200 Eighteenth St., NW, Ste. 200
Washington, DC 20036
T   202-467-6100
F   202-467-6101
info@independentsector.org
www.independentsector.org
The Independent Sector is an association of national nonprofit organizations, foundations, and corporate philanthropy programs. It acts as an advocate for the non-profit sector, as well as publishing research on nonprofit
sector activities.

INSTITUTE FOR SOCIAL ENTREPRENEURS
9560 Dogwood Circle
Eden Prairie, MN 55347
T   952-942-7715
F   952-942-8059
institute@orbis.net
www.socialent.org
The Institute for Social Entrepreneurs is a nonprofit organization that seeks
to encourage entrepreneurship throughout the non-profit sector through
education and consulting services.

NATIONAL CENTER FOR CHARITABLE STATISTICS
Center on Nonprofits and Philanthropy – The Urban Institute
2100 M Street, NW
Washington, DC 20037
T   202-833-7200
http://nccsdataweb.urban.org
   The National Center for Charitable Statistics, a program of the Urban
   Institute's Center on Nonprofits and Philanthropy, is the national clearing-
   house of data on the nonprofit sector in the United States.

NATIONAL CENTER FOR NONPROFIT ASSOCIATIONS
1030 15th Street NW Suite 870
Washington, DC 20005-1525
T   202-962-0322
F   202-963-0321
www.ncna.org
   Established in 1989, the National Center for Nonprofit Associations has
   grown to become a network of 39 state associations of nonprofits representing 22,000 nonprofits in 35 states and DC. It seeks to strengthen state associations through linking them with national groups as well as through research,
   publication dissemination, education, and leadership development training.

NONPROFIT SECTOR RESEARCH FUND
The Aspen Institute
One Dupont Circle, NW, Ste. 700
Washington, DC 20036
T   202-736-5800
F   202-293-0525
nsrf@aspeninstitute.org
www.nonprofitresearch.org
   The Nonprofit Sector Research Fund awards research grants, convenes sec-
   tor leaders, and disseminates research findings to expand knowledge of the
   nonprofit sector, improve practices, and inform public policy.

ORIGO
153 Kearny Street, Suite 401
San Francisco, CA 94108
T   415-296-1280
F   415-296-9819
info@origoinc.com
www.origoinc.com

Origo does consulting work with business, foundations, government agencies, and others to assist clients to develop social-enterprise strategies and cross-sector partnerships. Since 2000, Origo has published Fourth Sector News, a biweekly on-line newsletter on social enterprise.

PARTNERSHIP ON NONPROFIT VENTURES
Yale School of Management - The Goldman Sachs Foundation
560 Sylvan Avenue
Englewood Cliffs, NJ 07632
T   201-894-8950
F   201-894-8610
venturesinfo@yale.edu
http://ventures.yale.edu

Since 2002, the Partnership on Nonprofit Ventures has operated an annual National Business Plan Competition for Nonprofit Organizations, the first of its kind in the United States. In the first three years of the competition, there have been over 1,000 entrants. The partnership provides winners with both cash awards and hundreds of hours of technical assistance to implement their plans. The group also publishes research and case studies.

REDF (formerly ROBERTS ENTERPRISE DEVELOPMENT FUND)
P.O. Box 29566
San Francisco, CA 94129
T   415-561-6677
F   415-561-6685
www.redf.org

The Roberts Enterprise Development Fund provides technical assistance and philanthropic investments to help nonprofit organizations in the San Francisco area attain marketplace sustainability in their enterprise ventures. REDF also works with organizations across the U.S. that use nonprofit enterprise strategies.

SOCIAL EDGE
c/o Skoll Foundation
250 University Ave, #200
Palo Alto, CA 94301
T   650-331-1031
F   650-331-1033
socialedge@skollfoundation.org
http://skoll.socialedge.org
  Social Edge is a project of the Skoll Foundation that aims to connect social
  entrepreneurs and allies to discuss issues shaping the field. Social Edge's web
  site has a number of articles on social enterprise, publishes a monthly electronic newsletter, and hosts issue-based web discussion groups.

SOCIAL ENTERPRISE ALLIANCE
43 South Cassady Avenue
Columbus, OH 43209
T   614-235-0230
www.se-alliance.org
  The Social Enterprise Alliance is a leading trade association in the United
  States of non-profits engaged in mission-oriented business. It has hosted a
  number of "national gathering" conferences and maintains a listserv of over
  1,000 non-profit social enterprise practitioners.

SOCIAL VENTURE NETWORK
P.O. Box 29221
San Francisco, CA 94129-0221
T   415-561-6501
F   415-561-6435
svn@svn.org
www.svn.org
  Founded in 1987, Social Venture Network is a nonprofit network committed
  to building a just and sustainable world through business. Social Venture
  Network advocates for a "triple bottom line" of economic, social, and envi-
  ronmental returns and maintains a number of resource links on its web site.

Section Three: Community Development Corporations and Community Organizing

ACORN
88 3rd Avenue
Brooklyn, NY 11217
T   718-246-7900
F   718-246-7939
natexdirect@acorn.org
www.acorn.org
ACORN is a national grassroots organization that seeks to empower low-income communities and individuals by working toward economic and social justice on the local and national levels through community organizing.

CENTER FOR COMMUNITY CHANGE
1000 Wisconsin Ave., NW
Washington, DC 20007
T   202-342-0519
info@communitychange.org
www.communitychange.org
The Center for Community Change (CCC) provides research, technical assistance, networking, and coalition building in an effort to support grass-roots organizations that foster community development.

COMMITTEE FOR ECONOMIC DEVELOPMENT
2000 L St., NW, Suite 700
Washington, DC 20036
T   202-296-5860
F   202-223-0776
info@ced.org
www.ced.org
The Committee for Economic Development (CED) is a nonpartisan organization that provides business and education leaders with research and policy recommendations on economic and social issues such as budget reform, school reform, and global markets.

COMMUNITY AND ECONOMIC DEVELOPMENT PROGRAM
Center for Urban Affairs
Michigan State University
1801 West Main St.
Lansing, MI 48915-1097
T   517-353-9555
F   517-484-0068
www.msu.edu/~cua

The Community and Economic Development Program at Michigan State University provides research, training, and technical assistance to community-based organizations throughout Michigan. Among other activities, CEDP has developed the Community Income and Expenditure Model, which allows communities to track income and expenditure flows.

COMMUNITY DEVELOPMENT RESEARCH CENTER
Graduate School of Management and Urban Policy
New School for Social Research
72 Fifth Avenue, 7th Floor
New York, NY 10011
T   212-229-5311 x1609
F   212-229-5904
www.newschool.edu/milano/cdrc
oliverom@newschool.edu

The Community Development Research Center provides research, analysis, evaluation, and publications about community revitalizing practices and policies and their effect on urban neighborhoods. Topics evaluated include local and federal policies, as well as a number of studies on community development corporations.

ENTERPRISE FOUNDATION
10227 Wincopin Circle, Suite 500
Columbia, MD 21044
T   410-964-1230
F   410-964-1918
www.enterprisefoundation.org

The Enterprise Foundation is a nonprofit community development and housing organization that works through a national network of more than 1,200 organizations to provide community development in areas such as employment and housing for low income individuals and neighborhoods.

THE FANNIE MAE FOUNDATION
4000 Wisconsin Ave., NW
North Tower, Suite One
Washington, DC 20016
T   202-274-8000
F   202-274-8100
www.fanniemaefoundation.org
   The Fannie Mae Foundation publishes numerous journals and periodicals
   on the subjects of affordable housing and community development.

GREAT CITIES INSTITUTE
University of Illinois at Chicago
412 South Peoria Street, Suite 400
Chicago, IL 60607
T   312-996-8700
F   312-996-8933
gcities@uic.edu
www.uic.edu/cuppa/gci
   The Great Cities Institute is a program of the University of Illinois at
   Chicago. GCI is an interdisciplinary research program designed to dissemi-
   nate information on urban development. Areas of research focus include
   metropolitan sustainability and community/human development.

HIGHLANDER CENTER
1959 Highlander Way
New Market, TN 37820
T   865-933-3443
F   865-933-3424
hrec@highlandercenter.org
www.thehighlandercenter.org
   The Highlander Center provides resources and assistance, including research,
   education, and workshops to community organizations struggling with a variety of problems, economic and social, throughout Appalachia and the South.

HOUSING AND URBAN DEVELOPMENT (HUD), US DEPARTMENT OF
P.O. Box 23268
Washington, DC 20026
T   800-245-2691

www.huduser.org
The U.S. Department of Housing and Urban Development (HUD)'s Office of Policy Development and Research (PD&R) sponsors HUD USER, an information service that provides data, research reports, and policy analysis relating to issues of housing and community development.

INDUSTRIAL AREAS FOUNDATION
220 West Kinzie St., 5th Floor
Chicago, IL 60610
T   312-245-9211
F   312-245-9744
www.industrialareasfoundation.org
The Industrial Areas Foundation was built on the principles and practices of legendary community activist Saul Alinsky. The IAF provides progressive leadership training in organizing and coalition building with faith-based, private, public, and non-profit institutions.

INITIATIVE FOR A COMPETITIVE INNER CITY (ICIC)
727 Atlantic Avenue, Suite 600
Boston, MA 02111
T   617-292-2363
F   617-292-2380
initiative@icic.org
www.icic.org
Founded in 1994 by Harvard Business School Professor Michael Porter, Initiative for a Competitive Inner City works to promote sustainable inner city economic development, focused on encouraging capital reinvestment by private investors.

LOCAL INITIATIVES SUPPORT CORPORATION
773 3rd Ave, 8th Floor
New York, NY 10017
T   212-455-9800
F   212-682-5929
www.lisc.org
The Local Initiatives Support Coalition works to foster the growth and development of Community Development Corporations (CDCs) with public, private, and non-profit organizations by helping to channel grants and technical support to some of the nation's most distressed areas.

LIVING CITIES
95 West 125th Street
New York, NY 10027
T   646-442-2200
www.livingcities.org
  Living Cities provides financial and technical support to nonprofit CDCs
  engaged in improving economically distressed inner city neighborhoods. It
  creates a mechanism through which major corporations, foundations and
  federal government can invest in the revitalization of urban neighborhoods.

NATIONAL CONGRESS FOR COMMUNITY ECONOMIC DEVELOPMENT (NCCED)
1030 15th St, NW, Suite 325
Washington, DC 20005
T   202-289-9020
F   202-289-7051
www.ncced.org
  The National Congress for Community Economic Development is the trade association for the Community Development Corporation sector, representing more
  than 3,600 CDCs nationally through research, policy analysis, and advocacy.

NATIONAL COUNCIL OF LA RAZA
1111 19th Street, Ste. 1000
Washington, DC 20036
T   202-785-1670
www.nclr.org
  The National Council of La Raza, a leading U.S. civil rights organization
  working with the United States' growing Latino/a community, has become an
  increasingly important participant in community economic development,
  helping over 3,000 families become homeowners a year.

NATIONAL DEVELOPMENT COUNCIL
51 East 42nd St.
New York, NY 10017
T   212-682-1106
F   212-573-6118
www.ndc-online.org
  The National Development Council is a nonprofit organization that provides
  training and development services to the public, private, and nonprofit sec-

tors to design economic development and affordable housing programs throughout the country.

NATIONAL ECONOMIC DEVELOPMENT AND LAW CENTER
2201 Broadway, Suite 815
Oakland, CA 94612
T   510-251-2600
F   510-251-0600
www.nedlc.org
The National Economic Development and Law Center (NEDLC) is a resource organization dedicated to addressing the needs of low-income persons. NEDLC's three branches focus on the needs of children and families, jobs and income, and community infrastructure. Through collaborations with outside organizations, NEDLC provides both legal and economic research and resources for those local groups working for the economic and social advancement of their respective communities.

NATIONAL HOUSING INSTITUTE
460 Bloomfield Avenue, Ste. 211
Montclair, NJ 07042-3552
T   973-509-2888
F   973-509-8005
www.nhi.org
The National Housing Institute is a nonprofit organization that examines the issues affecting affordable housing and community development practitioners. The Institute publishes the magazine Shelterforce, a leading community development journal.

NATIONAL LOW INCOME HOUSING COALITION
1012 14th Street, NW, Ste. 610
Washington, DC 20005
T   202-662-1530
F   202-393-1973
www.nlihc.org
The National Low Income Housing Coalition is a coalition of affordable housing advocates that is leading the campaign for the creation of a National Income Housing Trust Fund. In addition, the coalition does considerable public education, research, and policy advocacy on fair housing, homelessness, and rural housing issues.

NATIONAL NEIGHBORHOOD COALITION

1221 Connecticut Avenue, NW, 2nd Floor
Washington, DC 20036
T   202-429-0790
www.neighborhoodcoalition.org
  The National Neighborhood Coalition seeks to improve communication
  between national and local community leaders to develop solutions that better
  address low-income human and neighborhood needs.

NEIGHBORHOOD REINVESTMENT CORPORATION (NRC)

1325 G St., NW, Suite 800
Washington, DC 20005
T   202-220-2300
F   202-376-2600
www.nw.org
  The Neighborhood Reinvestment Corporation is a government supported non-
  profit organization that builds and supports networks of residents and public,
  private, and nonprofit sector organizations to revitalize declining neighborhoods.

PRATT INSTITUTE CENTER FOR COMMUNITY AND ECONOMIC DEVELOPMENT

379 DeKalb Ave.
Brooklyn, NY 11205
T   718-636-3486
www.picced.org
  The Pratt Institute works with professionals, academics, and students interested in achieving ecological sustainability and economic and social justice
  through responsible rural and urban planning policies. Its web site also
  hosts the CDC Oral History Project, which provides capsule summaries of
  over a dozen exemplary community development corporations.

POLICYLINK.ORG

101 Broadway
Oakland, CA 94607
T   510-663-2233
F   510-663-9684
info@policylink.org
www.policylink.org
  PolicyLink is an online resource promoting innovative community-based

efforts to promote more equitable regional economic development. PolicyLink provides resources and information organized around the four core themes of regions, the economy, technology and democracy, with the aim of fostering strengthened relationships among nonprofits, activist groups, and others engaged in regional development issues.

RURAL LISC

1825 K Street, N.W.
Suite 1100
Washington, DC 20006
T   202-739-9283
F   202-785-8030
info@ruralisc.org
www.ruralisc.org

Rural LISC seeks to build the capacity of resident-led rural community development corporations, increase their production and impact, demonstrate the value of investing in and through rural community development corporations, and make the resource and policy environment more supportive of their work.

RURAL POLICY RESEARCH INSTITUTE

214 Middlebush Hall
University of Missouri
Columbia, MO 65211
T   573-882-0316
lchristopher@rupri.org
www.rupri.org

The Rural Policy Research Institute (RUPRI) conducts research and facilitates public dialogue with a focus on the effects of policy on rural areas. RUPRI involves researchers, practitioners, and analysts from numerous other universities, research institutes, governmental units, and other organizations.

THE URBAN INSTITUTE

2100 M Street, NW
Washington, DC 20037
T   202-833-7200
www.urban.org

The Urban Institute is a nonpartisan economic and social policy research organization that has produced many studies on community development, including evaluations of the Living Cities program and surveys of the CDC industry.

Section Four: Community Development Finance and Microenterprise

ACCION USA
56 Roland Street, Suite 300
Boston, MA 02129
T   617-625-7080
F   617-625-7020
info@accionusa.org
www.accionusa.org
Acción USA is a nonprofit micro-lending organization that provides direct aid in the form of loans, as well as business and technical support for micro-enterprise development.

ASSOCIATION FOR ENTERPRISE OPPORTUNTIY (AEO)
1601 N. Kent St., Ste. 1101
Arlington, VA 22209
T   703-841-7760
F   703-841-7748
aeo@assoceo.org
www.microenterpriseworks.org
The Association for Enterprise Opportunity is a trade association of microenterprise loan funds and supporters. It provides members with a forum, information, and a voice to promote enterprise opportunity for people and communities with limited access to economic resources.

CATHOLIC CAMPAIGN FOR HUMAN DEVELOPMENT
3211 Fourth St., NE
Washington, DC 20017
T   202-541-3000
www.nccbuscc.org/cchd/index2.htm
The Catholic Campaign for Human Development, the social justice program of the U.S. Catholic Bishops, is a loan organization designed to fund low-income groups working for institutional change, providing assistance to worker-ownership enterprises, as well as other economic development projects within low-income communities.

CDFI FUND

601 13th Street, NW, Suite 200

Washington, DC 20005

T   202-622-8662

F   202-622-7754

www.cdfifund.gov

The CDFI Fund is the section of the U.S. Department of Treasury that administers the CDFI Fund and the New Markets Tax Credit, and other community finance programs. Its web site has information on how to apply for awards, as well as listing previous awardees.

COALITION OF COMMUNITY DEVELOPMENT FINANCIAL INSTITUTIONS

1601 N. Kent St., Ste. 803

Arlington, VA 22209

T   703-894-0475

F   703-841-7748

info@cdfi.org

www.cdfi.org

The Coalition of Community Development Financial Institutions represents more than 350 CDFIs throughout the U.S., providing networking and information to the CDFI industry. The Coalition also serves as an advocate for community development financial institutions by providing information and resources to lawmakers, media, and the general public in order to increase financial and public support of CDFIs.

COMMUNITY DEVELOPMENT VENTURE CAPITAL ALLIANCE

330 7th Avenue, 19th Floor

New York, NY 10001

T   212-594-6747

F   212-594-6717

www.cdvca.org

The CDVCA is a membership organization that works to provide members with technical assistance, information, and resources to maximize the implementation of community development venture capital funds in distressed communities throughout the world.

FIELD – MICROENTERPRISE FUND FOR INNOVATION, EFFECTIVENESS, LEARNING AND DISSEMINATION

The Aspen Institute
One Dupont Circle, NW Suite 700
Washington, DC 20036
T   202-736-1071
F   202-467-0790
fieldus@aspeninstitute.org
http://fieldus.org

Through its FIELD program, the Aspen Institute facilitates through the development of microenterprise in order to generate income and employment in disadvantaged communities.

FINANCIAL MARKETS CENTER

PO Box 334
Philmont, VA 20131
T   540-338-7754
F   540-338-7757
www.fmcenter.org

The Financial Markets Center is a non-profit organization that provides research, information, and analysis on the financial markets, the Federal Reserve System, and the impact of their policies. Information provided by the Financial Markets Center is available for use by the public, private, and non-profit sectors alike in an effort to increase the Federal Reserve System's level of accountability to the public.

GRAMEEN FOUNDATION, USA

1029 Vermont Avenue, NW, Ste. 400
Washington, DC 20005
T   202-628-3560
F   202-628-3880
www.grameenfoundation.org

The Grameen Foundation, USA is a non-profit organization taking its name from the micro-credit movement started in the village of Grameen, Bangladesh. It aims to eliminate poverty in the United States through the creation of micro-credit related institutions and programs.

INSTITUTE FOR SOCIAL AND ECONOMIC DEVELOPMENT
910 23rd Avenue

Coralville, IA 52241

T   319-338-2331

F   319-338-5824

www.ised.org

The Institute for Social and Economic Development is a non-profit organization that seeks to alleviate poverty by providing research, consulting, and
technical assistance in the development of microenterprise.

NATIONAL COMMUNITY CAPITAL ASSOCIATION
620 Chestnut Street, Suite 572

Philadelphia, PA 19106

T   215-923-4754

F   215-923-4755

ncca@communitycapital.org

www.communitycapital.org

The National Community Capital Association is a membership organization
comprised of CDFIs, CDCs, community development loan funds, microenterprise funds, and community development venture capital funds from
across the U.S. NCCA provides members with a variety of resources including networking services, workshops, training, and publications.

NATIONAL COMMUNITY REINVESTMENT COALITION
733 15th St., NW, Ste. 540

Washington, DC 20005

T   202-628-8866

F   202-628-9800

www.ncrc.org

The National Community Reinvestment Coalition is a membership organization that promotes community reinvestment and the necessary public and
financial support to increase capital flow to under-served areas. Members
participate in workshops, lectures, conferences, and a variety of outreach
activities designed to realize these objectives.

NATIONAL COOPERATIVE BANK

1725 Eye St., NW Suite 600

Washington, DC 20006

T   800-955-9622

F   202-336-7800

www.ncb.coop

The National Cooperative Bank provides financial services to cooperative organizations, CDCs, and other community development agencies, particularly through its subsidiary organization, the National Cooperative Bank Development Corporation (NCBDC). Services offered include real estate, small business, and commercial lending programs as well as a variety of community development services.

NATIONAL FEDERATION OF COMMUNITY DEVELOPMENT CREDIT UNIONS

120 Wall St., 10th Floor

New York, NY 10005

T   212-809-1850

F   212-809-3274

info@natfed.org

www.natfed.org

The National Federation of Community Development Credit Unions serves as an advocacy organization on behalf of CDCUs. Through outreach and training, NFCDCU actively promotes the advancement of community development credit unions throughout the nation.

NORTHCOUNTRY COOPERATIVE DEVELOPMENT FUND

219 Main Street, SE, Suite 500

Minneapolis, MN 55414

T   612-331-9103

F   612-331-9145

info@ncdf.coop

www.ncdf.coop

The Northcountry Cooperative Development Fund is a community loan fund that focuses its lending, technical assistance, and education activity on supporting producer, worker, consumer, and housing cooperatives.

SELF-HELP

301 Main St., POB 3619
Durham, NC 27702
T   919-956-4400
www.self-help.org

Self-Help is the parent of the nation's largest community development credit union, providing direct lending to low income communities and individuals, particularly women, minorities, and rural residents throughout North Carolina. With Fannie Mae and others, Self-Help has also provided assistance on a national scale, through a $2 billion national homeownership initiative program.

SHOREBANK CORPORATION

7054 S. Jeffrey Blvd.
Chicago, IL 60649
T   800-669-7725
F   773-493-6609
information@shorebankcorp.com
www.shorebankcorp.com

The Shorebank Corporation is the nation's largest community development banking corporation. It is the parent corporation of South Shore Bank, the flagship community development bank in Chicago, and it also operates banks in Cleveland, Detroit, the Upper Peninsula of Michigan, and the Pacific Northwest.

WOODSTOCK INSTITUTE

407 S. Dearborn St., Suite 550
Chicago, IL 60605
T   312-427-8070
F   312-427-4007
woodstck@woodstockinst.org
www.woodstockinst.org

The Chicago-based Woodstock Institute works at both the grassroots and national levels to promote community reinvestment and economic sustainability through technical assistance, education, and research in areas such as CRA, Fair Lending Policies, financial and insurance services, CDFIs, and small business lending.

Section Five: Employee Ownership

BEYSTER INSTITUTE
PO Box 2149
La Jolla, CA 9203
T   858-826-6000
F   858-826-6001
www.beysterinstitute.org
   The Beyster Institute is a non-profit organization that provides and pro-
   motes strategies for employee ownership and equity compensation through
   research, education, and consulting programs.

CAPITAL OWNERSHIP GROUP
c/o Ohio Employee Ownership Center
309 Franklin Hall
Kent State University
Kent, OH 44242
T   330-672-3028
F   330-672-4063
cog@kent.edu
http://cog.kent.edu
   The Capital Ownership Group (COG) is an on-line think-tank that works
   to promote the advancement of broad-ownership systems, specifically
   employee ownership, and the raising of social and wage standards on an
   international level through policy proposals and advocacy.

CENTER FOR ECONOMIC AND SOCIAL JUSTICE
P.O. Box 40711
Washington, DC 20016
T   703-243-5155
F   703-243-5935
thirdway@cesj.org
www.cesj.org
   The Center for Economic and Social Justice is a non-profit, non-partisan edu-
   cation and research organization dedicated to promoting economic justice on
   a global scale by expanding capital ownership to a broader segment of society.

EMPLOYEE STOCK OWNERSHIP PLANS ASSOCIATION

1726 M St. N.W., Suite 501
Washington, D.C. 20036
T   202-293-2971
F   202-293-7568
esop@esopassociation.org
www.esopassociation.org

The ESOP Association is a membership organization composed of companies with employee ownership and those transitioning to employee ownership status. This non-profit organization provides educational materials and training seminars necessary for the successful management of employee-owned companies.

INDUSTRIAL COOPERATIVE ASSOCIATION (ICA GROUP)

One Harvard St., Suite 200
Brookline, MA 02445
T   617-232-8765
F   617-232-9545
www.ica-group.org

The Industrial Cooperative Association (ICA Group) is a non-profit organization that promotes worker ownership by providing education and technical assistance to those organizations seeking to start a community-based or worker-owned business.

NATIONAL CENTER FOR EMPLOYEE OWNERSHIP (NCEO)

1736 Franklin St., 8th Floor
Oakland, CA 94612
T   510-208-1300
F   510-272-9510
nceo@nceo.org
www.nceo.org

NCEO is a research organization dedicated to advancing worker ownership by providing information, publications, and research on Employee Stock Ownership Plans (ESOPs) and other forms of employee-ownership.

OHIO EMPLOYEE OWNERSHIP CENTER

Kent State University

309 Franklin Hall

Kent, Ohio 44242

T   330-672-3028

F   330-672-4063

oeoc@kent.edu

www.kent.edu/oeoc

The Ohio Employee Ownership Center is a non-profit organization that provides research and technical assistance to those interested in employee-ownership, as well as ownership training to established employee-owned businesses.

OWNERSHIP ASSOCIATES

122 Mt. Auburn Street, Harvard Square

Cambridge, MA 02138

T   617- 868-4600

F   617-868-7969

oa@ownershipassociates.com

www.ownershipassociates.com

Ownership Associates is a consulting firm providing a range of services to corporations interested in broadening ownership and workplace participation opportunities for employees, specializing in the design and implementation of employee surveys and education and training programs.

THE SHARED CAPITALISM INSTITUTE

570 Cress

Laguna Beach, CA 92651

T   949-494-4437

F   617-868-7969

jeffgates@mindspring.com

www.sharedcapitalism.org

The Shared Capitalism Institute prepares policy papers and educational materials to inform public debates about the role of economic inclusion in addressing key social issues, with a heavy focus on promoting employee ownership.

VERMONT EMPLOYEE OWNERSHIP CENTER (VEOC)
33 Main Street
P.O. Box 546
Burlington, VT 05402
T   802-861-6611
F   802-861-6613
info@veoc.org
www.veoc.org
> The Vermont Employee Ownership Center is a non-profit organization whose mission is to promote and foster employee ownership in Vermont in order to broaden capital ownership, deepen employee participation, retain jobs, increase living standards for working families, and stabilize communities.

WORKER OWNERSHIP INSTITUTE
Five Gateway Center, 7th Floor
Pittsburgh, PA 15522
T   412-562-2254/55
F   412-562-6978
webmaster@workerownership.org
www.workerownership.org
> The Worker Ownership Institute provides a forum for both management and labor from worker-owned firms to educate and interact with one another, as well as training programs in areas such as collective bargaining, financial training, and labor-management committees.

Section Six: Community Land Trusts

E.F. SCHUMACHER SOCIETY
140 Jug End Rd.
Great Barrington, MA 01230
T   413-528-1737
efssociety@smallisbeautiful.org
www.schumachersociety.org
> The E.F. Schumacher Society is dedicated to achieving the goals of economic and ecological sustainability through the principle of decentralism. In support of these aims, the Schumacher Society offers lectures, educational programs, and extensive research resources.

INSTITUTE FOR COMMUNITY ECONOMICS

57 School St.
Springfield, MA 01105-1331
T   413-746-8660
F   413-746-8862
info@iceclt.org
www.iceclt.org
The Institute for Community Economics is a nonprofit organization that promotes community land trusts as a tool to support sustainable economic development through its Revolving Loan Fund.

NEW RULES PROJECT

Institute for Local Self Reliance
1313 5th Street, SE
Minneapolis, MN 55414
T   612-379-3815
F   612-379-3920
info@islr.org
www.newrules.org
The New Rules Project, a program of the Institute for Local Self Reliance, provides research, analysis, and education about those factors and policies that support economically sustainable communities, local ownership, and local control in order to promote pro-community policies that reverse the dislocating effects of global capital mobility.

Section Seven: Cooperatives

(Note: Cooperative banks and credit unions are in section 4 above).

ASSOCIATION OF COOPERATIVE EDUCATORS (ACE)

c/o The Cooperative Foundation
PO Box 64047
St. Paul, MN 55164
T   651-451-5481
F   651-451-5073
www.wisc.edu/uwcc/ace/ace.html
The Association of Cooperative Educators is an association of co-op educators, based primarily in the United States, Canada, and Puerto Rico. The association holds an annual conference of cooperative practitioners who teach cooperative educators and trainers.

CENTER FOR COOPERATIVES
University of Wisconsin
230 Taylor Hall, 427 Lorch St.
Madison, WI 53706
T   608-262-3981
F   608-262-3251
www.wisc.edu/~uwcc
The Center for Cooperatives at the University of Wisconsin conducts research, training, and education on cooperatives. Its web site includes an extensive clearinghouse of information on nearly all sectors of the cooperative movement.

COOPERATIVE DEVELOPMENT SERVICES
131 West Wilson St., Suite 400
Madison, Wisconsin 53703
T   608-258-4396
F   608-258-4394
CDS@co-opdevelopmentservices.com
www.cdsus.coop
A non-profit organization founded in 1985, Cooperative Development Services has provided consulting services for over 500 cooperatives in a number of sectors, including food co-ops, senior housing co-ops, forestry co-ops, and value-added agriculture.

COOPERATIVE GROCERS' INFORMATION NETWORK (CGIN)
PO Box 399
Arcata, CA 95518
info@cgin.coop
www.cgin.coop
The Cooperative Grocers' Information Network is a web-based clearinghouse of information on retail food cooperatives. Annually, the network organizes the Consumer Cooperative Management Conference.

COOPERATION WORKS!
P.O. Box 527
213 South Fork
Dayton, WY 82836
T   307-655-9162
F   307-655-3785
cw@vcn.com

www.cooperationworks.coop

A national organization of 17 rural-based cooperative development centers, CooperationWorks! helps its members work together to revitalize communities through effective cooperative enterprise development. Members provide expertise across all aspects of cooperative development, including feasibility analysis, business plan development, training, and education.

CREDIT UNION NATIONAL ASSOCIATION (CUNA)

601 Pennsylvania Ave.

Washington, DC 20004

T   202-638-5777

F   202-638-7734

www.cuna.coop

Credit Union National Association is the national trade association of credit unions. In cooperation with state credit union leagues, CUNA provides research, advocacy, education, and business development services to member credit unions.

FEDERATION OF SOUTHERN COOPERATIVES-LAND ASSISTANCE FUND (FSC-LAF)

2769 Church Street

East Point, GA 30344

T   404-765-0991

F   404-765-9178

www.federation.coop

Founded in 1967, the Federation of Southern Cooperatives has provided self-help economic opportunities for many low-income communities across the South. A primary objective of the Federation is the retention of black-owned land and the use of cooperatives for land-based economic development.

NATIONAL ASSOCIATION OF HOUSING COOPERATIVES

1707 H Street, NW, Ste. 201

Washington, DC 20006

T   202-737-0797

F   202-783-7869

www.coophousing.org

The National Association of Housing Cooperatives is a nonprofit national federation of housing cooperatives, mutual housing associations, member associations, other resident-owned or controlled housing, professionals, organizations, and individuals interested in promoting the interests of cooperative housing communities.

NATIONAL COOPERATIVE BUSINESS ASSOCIATION (NCBA)
Suite 1100
1401 New York Ave., NW
Washington, DC 20005
T   202-638-6222
F   202-638-1374
ncba@ncba.coop
www.ncba.coop
The National Cooperative Business Association is a trade association that represents cooperatives in a wide variety of fields, including agricultural cooperatives, credit unions, food co-ops, purchasing co-ops, worker co-ops, and others.

NATIONAL COOPERATIVE GROCERS ASSOCIATION (NCGA)
361 East College St.
Iowa City, IA 52240
T   319-499-9029
F   866-600-4588
www.ncga.coop
The National Cooperative Grocers' Association is the largest trade association of retail food cooperatives with 94 member co-ops with 400,000 member-owners in 31 states. Founded in 1999, the association aims to develop joint purchasing, marketing, and other mutual support activities.

NATIONAL COUNCIL OF FARMER COOPERATIVES
50 F Street, NW, Ste. 900
Washington, DC 20001
T   202-626-8700
F   202-626-8899
www.ncfc.org
Founded in 1929, NCFC is a trade association of nearly two million farmers and ranchers. NCFC members include nearly 50 national, regional, and federated farmer cooperatives, which, in turn, are comprised of some 3,000 local cooperatives, and 27 state and regional councils.

NATIONAL RURAL ELECTRIC COOPERATIVE ASSOCIATION

4301 Wilson Blvd.

Arlington, VA 22203

T   703-907-5500

nreca@nreca.coop

www.nreca.coop

The National Rural Electric Cooperative Association is a national trade association of 900 member cooperatives that serve 37 million people in 47 states. The association represents members in regulatory hearings, as well as providing research, training, education, and advocacy services.

NATIONAL RURAL TELECOMMUNICATIONS COOPERATIVE

2121 Cooperative Way

Herndon, VA 20171

T   866-672-6782

www.nrtc.coop

The National Rural Telecommunications Cooperative (NRTC) represents the advanced telecommunications and information technology interests of more than 1,200 rural utilities and affiliates in 47 states, reducing internet supply costs through negotiating joint purchasing deals. NRTC is leading distributor of satellite television service to rural America.

NATIONAL TELECOMMUNICATIONS COOPERATIVE ASSOCIA- TION (NTCA)

4121 Wilson Blvd., Ste. 1000

Arlington, VA 22203

T   703-351-2000

F   703-351-2001

www.ntca.org

The National Telecommunications Cooperative Association is a national trade association representing more than 550 local telecommunications companies throughout rural America, including both cooperatives and small, independently owned companies.

NORTH AMERICAN STUDENTS OF COOPERATION

PO Box 7715
Ann Arbor, MI 48107
T   734-663-0889
F   734-663-5072
info@nasco.coop
www.nasco.coop

Founded in 1968, the North American Students of Cooperation is a trade association of U.S. and Canadian-based campus and community cooperatives, providing education, training, and technical assistance to member cooperatives.

U.S. FEDERATION OF DEMOCRATIC WORKPLACES

2129 Franklin Avenue East
Minneapolis, MN 55404
T   415-775-0124
info@usworker.coop
www.usworker.coop

The U.S. Federation of Democratic Workplaces is a newly formed (May 2004) national trade association of worker cooperatives and other employee-owned, democratically run workplaces. The federation aims to provide education, training, and technical assistance to its members.

Section Eight: Municipal Enterprise and Transit-Oriented Development

AMERICAN PUBLIC POWER ASSOCIATION

2301 M St., NW
Washington, DC 20037
T   202-467-2900
F   202-467-2910
www.appanet.org

The American Public Power Association is the trade association for publicly owned electric utilities. APPA serves to help keep publicly owned utilities competitive in today's market through a variety publications, networking, and information services.

THE BROOKINGS INSTITUTION

Metropolitan Policy
1775 Massachusetts Ave., NW
Washington, DC 20036
T   202-797-6139
F   202-797-2964
urbancenter@brookings.org
www.brookings.edu/metro
  The Metropolitan Policy Program at The Brookings Institution publishes a
  wide variety of studies on community development issues including land
  use and transportation issues.

CENTER FOR URBAN AND REGIONAL POLICY

343 Holmes Hall, Northeastern University
Boston, MA 02115
www.curp.neu.edu
  Founded in 1999, the center focuses on a wide range of issues dealing with
  cities, including research and advocacy work relating to transit-oriented
  development.

GLASGOW ELECTRIC PLANT BOARD

P.O. Box 1809
Glasgow, KY 42142
T   270-651-8341
F   270-651-7572
wray@glasgow-ky.com
www.glasgow-ky.com/epb
  The Glasgow Electric Plant Board governs the municipally owned power
  company in Glasgow, Kentucky. The service division provides consulting
  services and viability studies to those communities interested in starting a
  municipally owned utility, the acquisition of a privately operated facility, or
  the diversification of existing services.

GOVERNMENT FINANCE OFFICERS ASSOCIATION

203 N. LaSalle St., Ste. 2700
Chicago, IL 60601
T   312-977-9700
Inquiry@gfoa.org
www.gfoa.org

The Government Finance Officers Association is a trade association of government finance officers in Canada and the United States. The association has published articles both in favor and against city ownership of hotels in its trade publication, Government Finance Review.

INTERNATIONAL CITY/COUNTY MANAGEMENT ASSOCIATION
777 North Capitol St., NE, Suite 500
Washington, DC 20002
T   202-289-4262
F   202-962-3500
www.icma.org
The International City/County Management Association is a professional and educational organization that represents local government administrators throughout the U.S. and the world. Membership services include policy research and analysis, networking, workshops and symposiums, as well as online research services.

INTERNATIONAL ECONOMIC DEVELOPMENT COUNCIL
734 15th Street NW, Suite 900
Washington, DC 20005
T   202-223-7800
F   202-223-4745
www.iedconline.org
Established via a merger of the Council of Urban Economic Development (CUED) and the American Economic Development Association (AEDC), the International Economic Development Council (IEDC) is a large membership organization for economic and community development professionals. It provides resources such as information, research, and technical assistance to local development specialists in both the public and private sectors.

LINCOLN INSTITUTE OF LAND POLICY
113 Brattle St.
Cambridge, MA 02138
T   617-661-3016
F   617-661-7235
help@lincolninst.edu
www.lincolninst.edu
The Lincoln Institute of Land Policy is a nonprofit educational organization that provides research, analysis, and education in the areas of land taxation, land markets, and land as common property.

NATIONAL LEAGUE OF CITIES

1301 Pennsylvania Ave., NW, Ste. 550

Washington, DC 20004

T   202-626-3000

F   202-626-3043

www.nlc.org

The National League of Cities was founded in 1924 as a representative organization for America's cities. The NLC has since expanded to include over 18,000 municipal members. Through a variety of programs NLC works to educate and assist both government officials and public servants in their capacity as policymakers.

SURFACE TRANSPORTATION POLICY PROJECT

1100 17th Street, NW, 10th Floor

Washington, DC 20036

T   202-466-2636

F   202-466-2247

stpp@transact.org

www.transact.org

The Surface Transportation Policy Project is a nonprofit organization that leads a diverse, nationwide coalition working to ensure safer communities and smarter transportation choices that enhance the economy, improve public health, promote social equity, and protect the environment.

U.S. CONFERENCE OF MAYORS

1620 I Street, NW

Washington, DC 20006

T   202-293-7330

F   202-293-2352

info@usmayors.org

www.usmayors.org

As the official organization of cities with over 30,000 members, The Conference of U.S. Mayors contributes to the development of national urban policy. At U.S. Mayors' conferences, the respective mayors represent each of the more than 1,000 member-municipalities. In adopting policy positions, the Conference helps make federal officials aware of the concerns and needs of urban areas.

WASHINGTON METROPOLITAN AREA TRANSIT AUTHORITY (WMATA)
Joint Development Program
600 Fifth Street, NW
Washington, DC 20001
T   202-962-1593
F   202-962-2396
www.wmata.com
Washington Metropolitan Area Transit Authority, which runs the Washington DC bus and rail transit system, has been the nation's leading practitioner of transit-oriented development.

Section Nine: Pension Funds and Targeted Investments

ACEnet
94 Columbus Rd.
Athens, OH 45701
T   740-592-3854
F   740-593-5451
info@acenetworks.org
www.acenetworks.org
ACEnet promotes local economic sustainability by assisting those local businesses seeking to manufacture complex goods on a regional level through the creation of informal networks with other local businesses.

AFL-CIO HOUSING INVESTMENT TRUST
1717 K St., NW, Suite 707
Washington, DC 20036
T   202-331-8055
F   202-331-8190
info@aflcio-hit.com
www.aflcio-hit.com
The AFL-CIO Housing Investment Trust (HIT) is one of the nation's largest pension investment programs specializing in housing investment.

AFL-CIO OFFICE OF INVESTMENT

815 16th St., NW
Washington, DC 20006
T   202-508-6969
F   202-508-6992
www.aflcio.org/corporateamerica/capital
The AFL-CIO Office of Investment works with union trustees on active government for corporate sector and promotes investment that generates benefits for workers, without sacrificing pension returns, including the development of worker-friendly investment products.

APPALACHIAN REGIONAL COMMISSION

1666 Connecticut Ave., NW, Ste. 700
Washington, DC 20009
T   202-884-7799
www.arc.gov
The Appalachian Regional Commission is a U.S. government agency responsible for promoting economic development in the Appalachian region. Agency activities include the publishing of research reports, as well as grants and loans to promote small business development.

CALIFORNIA PUBLIC EMPLOYEES RETIREMENT SYSTEM (CALPERS)

Lincoln Plaza
400 P Street
Sacramento, CA 95814
T   916-795-3829
www.calpers.ca.gov
The California Public Employees' Retirement System pension fund, the largest public pension fund in the United States, is noted for its active engagement in targeted investment and serves as a resource for information on the policy issues surrounding this practice.

CENTER FOR WORKING CAPITAL

c/o AFL-CIO
888 16th St., NW
Washington, DC 20006
T   202-974-8020
F   202-974-8029

CWC@centerforworkingcapital.org
www.centerforworkingcapital.org
The Center for Working Capital is an independent, nonprofit organization
formed by the AFL-CIO. The Center provides training and education of
pension trustees who are union members to promote capital stewardship
practices.

CENTER ON WISCONSIN STRATEGY
University of Wisconsin-Madison
1180 Observatory Dr., Rm. 7122
Madison, WI 53706
T   608-263-3889
F   608-262-9046
cows-info@cows.org
www.cows.org
The Center on Wisconsin Strategy (COWS) is a research and policy analysis
program at the University of Wisconsin-Madison. COWS provides research,
policy analysis, feasibility studies, and technical assistance in the area of
high-road economic alternatives that foster worker-friendly, high-wage jobs
in the state of Wisconsin.

CO-OP AMERICA
1612 K St., NW, Suite 600
Washington, DC 20006
T   1-800-58-GREEN
info@coopamerica.org
www.coopamerica.org
Co-op America is a non-profit organization dedicated to addressing social
and environmental problems through a variety of programs, research, and
education. Co-op America hosts the Social Investment Forum, which reports
on and promotes the targeting investments to benefit local communities.

HEARTLAND LABOR CAPITAL NETWORK
One Library Place, Suite 201
Duquesne, PA 15110
T   412-460-0488
F   412-460-0487
heartland.sva@att.net
www.heartlandnetwork.org

The Heartland Labor Capital Network works to implement jobs, creating economic development investment strategies that utilize the capital held by labor in pension funds and other institutions in order to create high road workplaces and build sustainable regional economies.

INSTITUTE FOR FIDUCIARY EDUCATION

350 University Ave., Suite 250

Sacramento, CA 95825

T   916-922-1100

F   916-922-9688

www.ifecorp.com

The Institute for Fiduciary Education (IFE) is an educational organization that provides workshops and seminars for private, public, and nonprofit executives in the area of economically targeted investments (ETIs.)

MOUNTAIN ASSOCIATION FOR COMMUNITY ECONOMIC DEVELOPMENT

433 Chestnut St.

Berea, KY 40403

T   859-986-2373

F   859-986-1299

info@maced.org

www.maced.org

MACED is a regional organization serving communities in Kentucky and the Central Appalachian region. Services offered include the Business Development Program, which helps to finance job-creating enterprises, particularly for those of lower income levels. Other programs are designed to promote entrepreneurial activity and sustainable development throughout the region.

NATIONAL ASSOCIATION OF COUNTIES

440 First St., NW, Suite 800

Washington, DC 20001

T   202-393-6226

F   202-393-2630

www.naco.org

The National Association of Counties is a national organization that represents county governments. Services for participating counties include legislative analysis and research, technical and public affairs assistance, and advocacy.

NATIONAL ASSOCIATION OF DEVELOPMENT ORGANIZATIONS

400 North Capitol St., NW, Suite 390

Washington, DC 20001

T   202-624-7806

F   202-624-8813

info@nado.org

www.nado.org

The National Association of Development Organizations is a public interest group that provides a variety of services for regional development organizations across the U.S., including training, advocacy, and research in support of a regional approach to economic development.

NATIONAL ASSOCIATION OF REGIONAL COUNCILS

1666 Connecticut Ave., NW, Ste. 300

Washington, DC 20009

T   202-986-1032

F   202-986-1038

www.narc.org

The National Association of Regional Councils is a nonprofit membership organization that serves the interest of regional councils and metropolitan planning organizations nationwide, conducts research, and promotes regional economic development strategies among its members.

NATIONAL ASSOCIATION OF STATE DEVELOPMENT AGENCIES (NASDA)

12884 Harbor Drive

Woodbridge, VA 22192

T   703-490-6777

F   703-492-4404

mfriedman@nasda.com

www.nasda.com

The National Association of State Development Agencies (NASDA) is a national, nonprofit, trade association that provides members with a wide variety of training services, workshops, technical assistance, and data analysis in the area of economic development. Members come from economic development agencies across the country as well as from public, private, and nonprofit enterprises.

NATIONAL ASSOCIATION OF STATE AND LOCAL EQUITY FUNDS (NASLEF)

c/o Merritt Community Capital Corp.

1736 Franklin St., Suite 600

Oakland, CA 94612

T   510-986-1350

F   510-986-1353

info@naslef.org

www.naslef.org

The National Association of State and Local Equity Funds (NASLEF) is a professional, nonprofit association formed in 1994 to promote the efficient management of state and local equity funds. Collectively, member funds have created or rehabilitated more than 45,000 units of affordable housing and have raised $2.1 billion in equity capital for rental housing developments throughout the United States.

NATIONAL BUSINESS INCUBATORS ASSOCIATION

20 East Circle Dr. #37198

Athens, OH 45701

T   740-593-4331

F   740-593-1996

info@nbia.org

www.nbia.org

The National Business Incubators Association is a nonprofit membership organization that provides technical assistance, hands on management assistance, and access to financing opportunities to help ensure the long-term viability of participating member-businesses in incubators.

RETIREMENT SYSTEMS OF ALABAMA

135 South Union Street

Montgomery, AL 36104

T   1-800-214-2158

F   334-240-3032

rsainfo@rsa.state.al.us

www.rsa.state.al.us

Retirement Systems of Alabama (RSA) manages the state's pension funds. It has been a leader and innovator among state pension funds in the area of economically targeted investments (ETIs).

UNION LABOR LIFE INSURANCE COMPANY
111 Massachusetts Ave., NW
Washington, DC 20001
T   202-682-0900
www.ullico.com/b

One of the nation's leading union-friendly investors, the Union Labor Life Insurance Company (ULLICO) is working to support sustainable development through labor-based pension activism such as the "J for Jobs" program, a tax-exempt pension plan that invests in income-producing properties that are exclusively union built.

Section Ten: International

ACCION INTERNATIONAL
56 Roland Street, Suite 300
Boston, MA 02129
T   617-625-7080
F   617-625-7020
info@accion.org
www.accion.org

Acción International is the non-profit umbrella organization for microfinance institutions across the U.S. and Latin America, providing technical assistance, planning, policy research and analysis, and publications to their international network of microfinance affiliates.

COOPERATIVE LEAGUE OF THE USA (CLUSA)
Suite 1100
1401 New York Ave., NW
Washington, DC 20005
T   202-638-6222
F   202-638-1374
ncba@ncba.coop
www.clusa.coop/clusa.cfm

The Cooperative League of the USA (CLUSA) is the international arm of the National Cooperative Business Association, which provides technical assistance to develop cooperatives internationally. Since 1953, CLUSA has managed over 200 projects in 53 countries and has performed over 1,000 short-term consultancies in 79 countries.

FOUNDATION FOR INTERNATIONAL COMMUNITY ASSISTANCE

1101 14th St., NW
11th Floor
Washington, DC 20005
T   202-682-1510
F   202-682-1535
www.villagebanking.org
   The Foundation for International Community Assistance (FINCA) is an
organization dedicated to fighting poverty through the creation of micro-
credit programs known as "village banks," or peer groups of approximately
50 persons who receive capital loans for self-employment.

INTERNATIONAL COOPERATIVE ALLIANCE

15, route des Morillons
1218 Grand-Saconnex
Geneva, Switzerland
T   (+41) 022 929 88 88
F   (+41) 022 798 41 22
www.ica.coop
   The International Cooperative Alliance is the peak association that repre-
sents over 800 million members of cooperatives worldwide.

MONDRAGON CORPORACION COOPERATIVA

Pº José María Arizmendiarrieta,
nº 5 20500 Mondragón.
Guipúzcoa, España
T   34-943 779 300
F   34-943 796 632
wm@mcc.coop
www.mcc.coop/ing
   Mondragón, located in the Basque region of Spain, is the world's largest
worker cooperative with over 34,000 members as of 2004.

WORLD COUNCIL OF CREDIT UNIONS
5710 Mineral Point Road
Madison, WI 53705
T   608-231-7130
F   608-238-8020
mail@woccu.org
www.woccu.org

The World Council of Credit Unions is a representative organization for credit unions around the world. Through publications, meetings, and technical assistance, WCCU works to extend credit unions as viable tools of economic development.

Appendix C: Interview Subjects and Contributors

More than 100 people contributed to this project by participating in interviews. Over half were conducted in-person. The rest were by telephone. Telephone interviews are denoted with an asterisk. Specific contributions are acknowledged in footnotes in the text; other support was of a more general nature—sources, leads, and comments that are not tied to any specific piece of data, but nonetheless greatly added to the work. We wish to thank all who generously gave of their time and insights to this research effort.

April 2004

Michelle Levy-Benitez	Association for Enterprise Opportunity
Siobhan Sanders	Association for Enterprise Opportunity
Todd Larsen	Co-op America
Justin Conway	Co-op America
Dave Bucholz	Corporation for Enterprise Development
J. Michael Keeling	The ESOP Association
Jeffrey Barber	Integrated Strategies Forum*
Douglas Kleine	National Association of Housing Cooperatives
Kevin Kelly	National Congress for Community Economic Development
Chris Hoene	National League of Cities
Roger Eldridge	National Milk Producers Federation
Leah Kalinosky	National Neighborhood Coalition

May 2004

Robert Pleasure	AFL-CIO Center for Working Capital
David Binns	Beyster Institute
Jennifer Vasiloff	CDFI Coalition
Dushaw Hockett	Center for Community Change
Marcia Sigal	Council of State Community Development Agencies*
Dwain Brown	Local Initiatives Support Corporation*
Jacqueline Byers	National Association of County Officials

Laurie Thompson	National Association of Development Officers
Sherry Brady	National Center of Nonprofit Associations
Carol Weyman	National Congress for Community Economic Development
Esmail Baku	Neighborhood Reinvestment Corporation
Dave Parkinson	City of Tampa (FL): Dept. of Urban Development
Christopher Walker	The Urban Institute
Chris Bender	Washington, D.C., Office of the Deputy Mayor: Planning Dept.

June 2004

Mike Garland	AFL-CIO Office of Investment
Ray Daffner	Appalachian Regional Commission
Barbara Abell	Consultant*
Andy Robinson	Consultant*
Gerry Widdicombe	Downtown DC Business Improvement District
Robert Grow	Greater Washington Board of Trade
Dominic Moulden	Manna CDC
Loretta Tate	Marshall Heights CDC
Mary Landry	Maryland Brush*
Bev Nykwest	National Association of Regional Councils
Terry Barr	National Council of Farmer Cooperatives
Nilda Ruiz	National Council of La Raza
Bernadin Arnason	National Telephone Cooperative Association
Jeannine Jacokes	Partners for the Common Good
Christina Clamp	Southern New Hampshire University*
Michael Swack	Southern New Hampshire University*

July 2004

Janet Topolsky	The Aspen Institute, Community Strategies Group, *
David Soule	Center for Urban Regional Policy, Northeastern University*
Jeff McElrevy	Government Finance Officers Association*
Sandra Venner	Institute on Assets and Social Policy, Brandeis University*

Toby Rittner	International Economic Development Council*
Mark Pinsky	National Community Capital Association*
Pam Jones	New Columbia Community Land Trust*
Margaret Lund	Northcountry Cooperative Development Fund*

August 2004

Robert Brosnan	Arlington County, Virginia, Office of Planning*
Renee Bryce-LaPort	Corporation for Enterprise Development
Fred Selden	Fairfax County, Virginia, Office of Planning*
Sarah Dewees	First Nations Development Institute*
Charles Tansey	Neighborhood Reinvestment Corporation
Leslie Parrish	New America Foundation
Al Dobbins	Prince George's County, Maryland, Office of Planning*
Amy DeBenedetto	Time Dollars USA
Christine Gray-Cahn	Time Dollars USA
Edgar Cahn	Time Dollars USA
Karina Ricks	Washington D.C. Office of Planning
Elisa Hill	Washington Metropolitan Area Transit Agency

October 2004

Joel Solomon	AFL-CIO Center for Working Capital
Ron Lunt	American Public Power Association
Jim Baller	Baller Herbst Law Group*
Jennifer Meeropol	Campus Compact (Providence)*
Ken Reardon	Cornell University, Department of City and Regional Planning *
Richard Meister	DePaul University*
Robert Moore	Development Corporation of Columbia Heights
Stockton Williams	The Enterprise Foundation
Lisa Lopinski	Foundation for Rural Service
Rex LaMore	Michigan State, Community & Economic Development Program*
Sam Leiken	National Governors' Association
Penelope Cuff	Partners for Livable Communities

Connie Flanagan	Penn State University*
Brett Rosenberg	U.S. Conference of Mayors

November 2004

Liying Gu	Airports Council International-North America*
Allan Kotin	Allan D. Kotin & Associates (Los Angeles)*
June Holly	Appalachian Center for Economic Networks (Athens, OH)*
Jonathan Stern	Bay Area Economics (Berkeley, CA)*
Deborah Olson	Capital Ownership Group
Deb Markley	Center for Rural Entrepreneurship*
Brian Schmitt	Community Development Venture Capital Association
Pat Levine	Development Counsellors International (New York)*
Steven Landau	EDR Group (Boston)*
Eric Pages	Entreworks Consulting (Arlington)*
Robin Hunden	Johnson Consulting (Chicago)*
Jim Benedict	KMK Consulting (Cincinnati)*
Dan Logue	National Association of Seed and Venture Funds*
Richard Norment	National Center for Public-Private Partnerships (DC)*
Richard Dines	National Cooperative Business Association*
Gary Gorsching	Southwest Oklahoma Council of Governments*
Dave Muchnick	Sustainable Enterprise (New York)*

December 2004

Cliff Kellogg	City First Community Development Bank (DC)*
Jeremy Gunderson	Center for Transit Excellence
Michael Torrens	Corporation for Enterprise Development
William Schweke	Corporation for Enterprise Development*
Michael Stevens	DC Marketing Center
Marty Mallett	DC Support Collaborative
Noreen Beatley	The Enterprise Foundation

Nat Bottigheimer	Maryland Department of Transportation
Cicero Wilson	Mid Bronx Desperadoes (MBD) Development Corporation
Richard Brewster	National Center on Nonprofit Enterprise*
Steve Collier	National Rural Telecommunications Cooperative
Adam Schwartz	National Rural Telecommunications Cooperative
Dale Robinson Anglin	New Communities Corporation
Tom Pierson	U.S. Federation of Worker Cooperatives & Democratic Workplaces*
John Nelson	Wall Street Without Walls
Greg Stanton	Wall Street Without Walls
Otto Candon	Zimmer Gunsul Frasca*
Bart Guthrie	Zimmer Gunsul Frasca*
Rich Hubacher	Zimmer Gunsul Frasca*

January 2005

Greg LeRoy	Good Jobs First*
Faye Kenn	National Center for Small Communities
Matthew Achhammer	National Low Income Housing Coalition
Hamilton Brown	National Rural Electric Cooperative Association
Randolph Adams	Rural Community Action Partnership
Stephen Gasteyer	Rural Community Action Partnership
Jeff Mosley	Rural LISC

Contributors

The following individuals deserve special mention for their support, which included assistance with access to databases, private libraries, and other difficult-to-find or confidential information.

Laura Casoni	The Aspen Institute
Stephanie Lessans Geller	Center for Civil Society, Johns Hopkins University
Janelle Kerlin	Center on Nonprofits & Philanthropy, The Urban Institute

Dennis Livingston	Community Builders
Ed Barker	Community Wealth Ventures
Barbara Abell	Consultant
Alice Shabakoff	Consultant
Michael Shuman	Consultant
Robert Zdenek	Consultant
Amy Gwiazdowsky	The ESOP Association
Connie Matheson	The Enterprise Foundation
Diana Meyer	The Enterprise Foundation
Julie Orvis	Institute for Community Economics
Neil Seldman	Institute for Local Self-Reliance
Erin Kelley	Local Initiatives Support Corporation
Martha Rosoff	Local Initiatives Support Corporation
Annie Singh	Local Initiatives Support Corporation
Altoria Bell Ross	National Association of Housing Cooperatives
Corey Rosen	National Center for Employee Ownership
Kevin Kelley	National Congress for Community Economic Development
Mark Pinsky	National Community Capital Association
Noelle Melton	National Community Reinvestment Coalition
Annie Donovan	National Cooperative Bank Development Corporation
Terry Lewis	National Cooperative Bank Development Corporation
Adriane Aul	Neighborhood Reinvestment Corporation
Tom Austin	Neighborhood Reinvestment Corporation
Ken Wage	Neighborhood Reinvestment Corporation
Dan Bell	Ohio Employee Ownership Center
John Logue	Ohio Employee Ownership Center
Jacqueline Yates	Ohio Employee Ownership Center
Douglas Kruse	Rutgers University
Joseph Blasi	Rutgers University
Beth Bubis	Social Enterprise Alliance
Dan Bell	Ohio Center for Employee Ownership
John Logue	Ohio Center for Employee Ownership
Jacqueline Yates	Ohio Center for Employee Ownership
Loren Rodgers	Ownership Associates

Naomi Giszpenc   Ownership Associates
Christopher Walker   The Urban Institute

We would also like to thank the following individuals for their contributions through arranging meetings, helping us identify key people to contact, and providing other assistance.

Mary Rule   American Public Power Association
John Neff   American Public Transportation Association
Steve Wahlstrom   Applied Development Economics
                       (Berkeley, CA)
Kirsten Moy   The Aspen Institute
Bill Edwards   Association for Enterprise Opportunity
Haydee Orijalva   Association for Enterprise Opportunity
Jed Emerson   Blendedvalue.org
Robert Puentes   The Brookings Institute
Gillian Coulter   Campus Credit Union Council
Robert Brandwein   Consultant
Greg Dees   Fuqua School of Business, Duke University
Heidi Kaplan   CDFI Fund
Don Macke   Center for Rural Entrepreneurship
                       (Lincoln, NE)
Linda Lampkin   Center on Nonprofits and Philanthropy,
                       The Urban Institute
James DeFilippis   City University of New York
Len Foxwell   Greater Washington Board of Trade
Ellen Jones   Greater Washington Board of Trade
Jessica Bowen   ICMA Center for Performance Measurement
Ed Gilliland   International Economic Development Council
Gordon W. Green   The Independent Sector
Nadine Jalandoni   The Independent Sector
Jocabel Michel   The Independent Sector
Yashica Carrington   Mid Bronx Desperadoes (MBD)
                       Development Corporation
Sarah Nusser   National Assn. for County Community
                       & Economic Development
Peggy Tadej   National Association of Regional Councils
Greg Von Behren   National Association of State Budget Officers

Lisa Hasegawa	Nat'l Coalition for Asian-Pacific American Community Development
Sam Shah	National Center for Employee Ownership
Beth Lipson	National Community Capital Association
Jill Lukas	National Community Capital Association
Dave Oliver	National Rural Electric Cooperative Association
Jessie Georgieva	National Rural Electric Cooperative Association
Christine Sterling	National Academy of Public Administration
Andrew Brown	National Rural Telecommunications Cooperative
Jay Kayne	Page Center for Entrepreneurship, Miami University (Ohio)
Barry Feldman	City of West Hartford, Connecticut